somebody told me

somebody told me

THE NEWSPAPER STORIES OF

RICK BRAGG

The University of Alabama Press Tuscaloosa & London

1   2   3   4   5   6   7   8   9
08   07   06   05   04   03   02   01   00

Text design by Rich Hendel.

♾ The paper on which this book is printed meets the
minimum requirements of American National Standard
for Information Science-Permanence of Paper for
Printed Library Materials, ANSI z39.48-1984.

Library of Congress Cataloging-in-Publication Data
Bragg, Rick.
Somebody told me : the newspaper stories of Rick Bragg / Rick Bragg.
p. cm.
ISBN 0-8173-1027-4 (alk. paper)
1. United States—Social conditions—1980– I. Title.
HN59.2 .B72 2000
306'.0973—dc21
99-050494

British Library Cataloguing-in-Publication
Data available

Contents

Introduction

Thank God for talkers.

I grew up at the knee of front-porch talkers, of people who could tell a story and make you believe you had been there, right there, in the path of the bullet or the train, in the warm arms of a new mother, in the teeth of a mean dog. The men, sometimes dog drunk, sometimes flush with religion but always alight with the power of words, could make you feel the breath of the arching blade as it hisssssssed past their face on the beer joint floor, could make you taste the blood in your mouth from the fist that had smashed into their own, could make you hear the loose change in the deputy's pocket as he ran, reaching for them, just steps behind.

The women in my world, aunts and cousins and grandmas and a girlfriend or two, could telegraph straight to your brain the beauty of babies you never touched, songs you never heard, loves you never felt. They could make you cry about a funeral you never saw, make you mourn for a man you had never even met. They could make you give a damn about the world around you. They had a gift, one the rest of us who aspire to be storytellers can only borrow.

That tradition of storytelling was still strong when I was born in 1959. I notice, every time I go home to Alabama, that it still is. Television hasn't killed it. It might, yet. But it is nice to believe it will be there forever.

My people told stories for the fun of it, mainly, but also because it was the best way to get the word out on things you should know and things they just thought you should know. It was so much quicker and easier than waiting for the one distant relative who actually took the newspaper to bother passing it on to you, one week late, faded yellow and smelling strongly of Karo syrup and canned tomatoes.

I owe those storytellers, all of them, because without them I would have no skills, no foundation, no accent, no voice. Their blood had trickled down to Alabama from a lot of places, from Ireland and Germany and France, mixing along the way with that of the Cherokee and Creek, finally pooling here. A drop from that pool is in every story I have ever written for wages, and I believe that if there is anything good in the stories I have done for newspapers, even those for the *New York Times,* it can be traced back to Sunday afternoons under willow trees, to the words and sweat that mixed over hard, pick-and-shovel work, to the music of mountains.

I took that borrowed ability and did some things with it, even made a living from it. Since my first newspaper job in 1977, I have written about everything from bloody coups in Haiti to bloody courtyards in New Orleans, from soldiers in the Persian Gulf, waiting to risk their lives, to eighty-year-old prison inmates in Alabama, just waiting to die. I sat under a tree at the last leper colony in Louisiana, dodged rocks in Miami, fell out of a boat on Lake Okeechobee, and got shot at, a little bit, here and there. I know what the desert in Arizona looks like, whizzing past the rental car window, coming back from an interview with an ancient Navajo woman whose husband was poisoned to death in the uranium mines. I know what the snow in the air smells like in Arkansas, coming back from a triple execution. Storytelling, even if it is just a stolen skill, gave me a currency to trade for Times Square at midnight, for Mardi Gras, for Liberty City in flames, for the Los Angeles freeways and Brooklyn subways and skinny blacktop roads in the Deep South that led me nowhere, and everywhere.

I made my living in a thousand cheap hotel rooms, where I would sleep without even bothering to pull back the covers, and in a half-dozen expensive ones, where I stole the soap. I wrote through the night so many times that the hands of the clock barely registered, and would look up, with dismay, at the gray of dawn creeping through the curtains of my 123rd Ramada Inn. The only thing that made it worthwhile was the words, which sometimes made sense and sometimes, once in a happy while, even sounded as if a real storyteller had put them together on some metaphorical front porch.

And sometimes, the words read like some monkey had pounded them out on an old Underwood, and I would look at them on the page and ask myself, "Did I write that?" And then answer myself, "Musta did."

I was tickled to death when I heard that someone, anyone, was interested in gathering some of those newspaper stories in a book, something with hard covers. Newspaper stories are fleeting things. The thing that makes this business so remarkable, that every day we get a new canvas to paint on, is also what makes it so unsatisfying. The story, almost always, dies with the day, the pages of the day-old paper turning yellow in the sun.

Books, even if they are just newspaper stories bound tight, last a little bit longer.

This is not intended to be a history of any particular work, just some stories that I liked, that I thought were important, even if just for a sliver in time. Some of them are in here just because I thought they read pretty, or because I like the people I wrote about, or because I thought the story might actually have done some good. It's no more complicated than that.

There is a lot of sadness in this particular binding because the best stories in the newspaper are those of people in trouble, and those are the ones I care about writing. It is mostly about ordinary people who found themselves, for so many reasons, in the path of the train. They were gracious enough to share with me their lives before, during, and after the extraordinary events that made them, for a time, news. I thank them for that.

The ones I especially thank are those who helped me put a human face on those who cannot speak for themselves, those whose faces I never saw, voices I never heard. Often, in the grip of agony, survivors would tell me why a lost life mattered, if only to them.

Over the years, I did a lot of it. Thank you for reading it.

Survivors

At first I wanted to call this chapter "Victims," but that cheapened the people I wrote about. I decided on "Survivors" because so many of the people herein were seized by an outside force, terrified or damaged, and let loose to try and live again. I like these people because of their backbone. I do not mind that some of them became haters. Some of them had a right.

Tried by Deadly Tornado, An Anchor of Faith Holds

New York Times, April 3, 1994

DATELINE: Piedmont, Ala., April 2

This is a place where grandmothers hold babies on their laps under the stars and whisper in their ears that the lights in the sky are holes in the floor of heaven. This is a place where the song "Jesus Loves Me" has rocked generations to sleep, and heaven is not a concept, but a destination.

Yet in this place where many things, even storms, are viewed as God's will, people strong in their faith and their children have died in, of all places, a church.

"We are trained from birth not to question God," said 23-year-old Robyn Tucker King of Piedmont, where 20 people, including six children, were killed when a tornado tore through the Goshen United Methodist Church on Palm Sunday.

"But why?" she said. "Why a church? Why those little children? Why? Why? Why?"

The destruction of this little country church and the deaths, including the pastor's vivacious 4-year-old daughter, have shaken the faith of many people who live in this deeply religious corner of Alabama, about 80 miles northeast of Birmingham.

It is not that it has turned them against God. But it has hurt them in a place usually safe from hurt, like a bruise on the soul.

They saw friends and family crushed in what they believed to be the safest place on earth, then carried away on makeshift stretchers of splintered church pews. They saw two other nearby churches destroyed, those congregations somehow spared while funerals for Goshen went on all week and the obituaries filled an entire page in the local paper.

But more troubling than anything, said the people who lost friends and family in the Goshen church, were the tiny patent-leather children's shoes scattered in the ruin. They were new Easter shoes, bought especially for church.

"If that don't shake your faith," said Michael Spears, who works at Lively's Food Market in downtown Piedmont, "nothing will."

The minister of the Goshen church, the Rev. Kelly Clem, her face covered with bruises from the fallen roof, buried her daughter Hannah on Wednesday. Of all people, she understands how hurtful it is to have the walls of the church broken down.

"This might shake people's faith for a long time," said Mrs. Clem, who led a congregation of 140 on the day of the storm. "I think that is normal. But having your faith shaken is not the same as losing it."

Ministers here believe that the churches will be more crowded than usual on Easter Sunday. Some will come for blessings, but others expect an answer.

Mrs. Clem and her husband, Dale, who is also a minister, do not believe God sent the storm that killed their daughter and 40 other people across the Southeast in a few short hours that day. The Clems make a distinction between God's laws and the laws of nature, something theologians have debated for years: what does God control, and not control?

The people here know only that they have always trusted in the kindness and mercy of God and that their neighbors died in His house while praising His name. It only strengthens the faith in some people, who believe that those who die inside any church will find the gates of heaven open wide.

Others are confused. Beyond the sadness and pain is a feeling of something lost, maybe forever.

"It was church," said Jerri Kernes, delivering flowers to a funeral home where the dead and their families filled every room.

"It isn't supposed to happen in church."

The blooming dogwood trees stand out like lace in the dark pine barrens in the hills around Piedmont. The landscape is pastoral, mountain ridges and rolling hills divided by pastures of fat cows and red-clay fields that will soon be high cotton and sweet corn.

The people, the children of farmers, mill workers, carpenters and steelworkers, now make tires at the Goodyear plant in Gadsden, spin yarn at the cotton mill and process poultry for Tyson Foods Inc., which is known here as just the chicken plant.

Yet, Piedmont, population 5,200, depending on who is home, exists in the failed economic promise of the New South. The roof on the empty brickyard has rusted through, and the pretty little train station on the Selma, Rome & Dalton line is just for show. The cotton mill just had a new round of layoffs.

As economic uncertainty grows, the people go to the altar for hope, said Vera Stewart, Piedmont's 70-year-old Mayor. Piedmont, after all, has two doctors' offices but 20 churches.

"As long as we have our faith, we are as strong as our faith," Mrs. Stewart said. "Because no matter how dark it is, if I have faith, I have a song in the night."

But in the long days since last Sunday, when the sky opened, she, too, has felt that belief tremble. What all the troubles of the everyday failed to do, one sudden, violent moment did.

Tornadoes snapped 200-year-old trees and ruined houses and lives in five states. Goshen was the centerpiece of an agony shared by Spring Garden, Rock Run, Possum Trot, Bennefield's Gap, Knighten's Crossroad and Webster's Chapel. At Mount Gilead Church, about 10 miles from Goshen, the wind pulled tombstones from the earth and smashed them.

People here are accustomed to the damage that the winds do, but what happened at the Goshen church last Sunday was off the scale of their experience. Rescue workers found neighbors limp and broken on the ground, and strong men sobbed like babies in the arms of other men when the last of the living and dead had been dug from the rubble.

In a makeshift morgue in the National Guard Armory, one volunteer wiped the faces of the dead children before zipping up the body bags. The bags were too long, and had to be rolled up from the bottom.

But in the days after, the shock started to wear off, and the pride took hold again. So, when the truckloads of donated food and clothes arrived, some of the needy refused aid because they did not earn it with their own sweat.

Sam Goss runs a filling station, and believes in heaven the same way he believes that walking in the Coosa River will get him wet.

Mr. Goss, 49, stood in a line 50 yards long to pay respects to the dead at the town's largest funeral home. He smoked a cigarette, cried and talked of going to Glory.

He was a friend of Derek Watson, who died with his wife, Glenda Kay, and their 18-year-old daughter, Jessica. Mr. Goss said Derek, who worked at the Super Valu, had not planned to go to church that day but changed his mind.

"Maybe that's what people mean when they say God works in mysterious ways," Mr. Goss said. "I know the boy. He could not have lived if his wife and child were gone."

It is the same reason, he said, that God took both Ruth Peek, 64, and Cicero Peek, 72.

"It's hard not to question God in this," he said. "But they say there ain't no tears in heaven. We're the ones left to hurt. You see, God took them because he knew they were ready to go. He's just giving all the rest of us a second chance."

The first step toward healing might have been in a funeral processional for a child.

In life, 4-year-old Hannah Clem had been a dancer and painter and singer.

In death she has become a focus of the question why.

For three days Kelly and Dale Clem worked for their friends and parishioners and swallowed their own pain, gracious and strong. They did not shake their fist at heaven, but told Vice President Al Gore that a better storm warning system might have saved lives.

It was wind and not God, they said, that killed their daughter.

"My God is a God of hope," Mr. Clem said. "It is never his will for anyone to die."

It is a departure from the Christian mainstream belief that God controls all. But then so is Mrs. Clem herself, a female minister with a growing congregation in a small town in the Deep South.

On Wednesday, she followed Hannah's tiny white and pink casket up the aisle at the First United Methodist Church in Anniston, 20 miles from Goshen. Members of her congregation and old friends filled the church.

"People have asked, why did it happen in a church," said the Rev. Bobby Green, in his service. "There is no reason. Our faith is not determined by reason. Our faith is undergirded by belief, when there is no reason."

In the Bible, Palm Sunday is a day of destruction, not hope, he said. Hope comes later, on Easter Sunday.

The 400 mourners stood and said the Lord's Prayer. Then, Hannah's coffin was moved slowly back down the aisle to the hearse. The organist played "Jesus Loves Me."

On Walls, Memories of the Slain Are Kept

New York Times, January 28, 1994

Somewhere, between one more killing in the inner city and the obscurity of the grave, is a wall in Brooklyn.

Khem Hubbard recorded her brother's name there last week, in big silver letters. Now Kyle Rasheim Hubbard, 19, shot to death on Jan. 6, 1990, will be remembered in a New York neighborhood where the dead disappear in the crowd.

The memorial wall at the corner of Crown Street and Bedford Avenue in the Crown Heights section of Brooklyn is like the ones in Bedford-Stuyvesant, the ones in the South Bronx, the ones in Harlem. They hold the names of dead children, innocent bystanders, stone-cold killers, untrue lovers and fallen angels.

They are remembered with elaborate murals that plead for a stop to the senseless killing, or just a few thin lines scrawled by a friend with a felt-tip pen and a broken heart. They tell us that PAPA RESTS IN PEACE, and that Kiki has found God.

No one is sure how many walls there are in New York, or how many inner-city victims have taken their place on the lists of the dead that decorate the sides of dry cleaners, clinics and corner stores. People who live beside the walls guess that there are hundreds scattered around the city, embroidered with thousands of names. Around the nation are thousands more, from Atlanta to Los Angeles.

The dead have been carried off to cemeteries outside the inner city, but people here like to believe their spirit is still in the neighborhood and that is where the shrine should be. People leave flowers in Dr. Pepper cans. They touch the names and pray for souls. The murals, some with hundreds of names, are almost never desecrated. The respect Kiki and Papa, Rasheim and the others couldn't find in life is now theirs.

"I don't have the power to save their lives," said Richard Green, a community organizer in Crown Heights and a caretaker of the Brooklyn walls. "But I can keep their spirit close."

In Philadelphia, they make little shrines for the dead in the back windows of cars. In Miami, Haitians and Dominicans place plastic flowers and a cup of rum where the dead fall. Here in New York the sidewalks are decorated with spray-painted crosses or ankhs, the ancient Egyptian symbol for life, where a person was killed. On some corners it is difficult to step without walking on hallowed ground.

But the wall is the final benediction to urban violence. Without it, few people would know or care that 19-year-old Dion (Raisin) Maczyk died over a $1 bet in a dice game in June 1993, or remember how Darkeesha Foster's 16-year-old brother, Troy, was shot through the neck at a party on Classon Avenue last Halloween.

"I walk by and see the names and think about those people in life," said Ms. Hubbard, 29, who lives in Crown Heights. "I want people to do that, when they see my brother's name. And I want them to remember how he died, and care about it."

People have been painting the names and faces of the dead on walls in the city for decades, but in smaller, more personal murals. But the blackboard-type listings of the dead on murals began appearing in the mid-80's, said Joseph Sciorra, an urban folklorist who has just finished a book on the walls.

In the last few years, they have spread rapidly through the city, mostly in black and Hispanic neighborhoods.

"It is people being honored in a public way for a death that was in most cases also public," he said.

As the killing has become more obvious, more common, so have the memorial walls, said Mr. Green, who, as chief executive of the Crown Heights Youth Collective, works to save young people from violence.

"I had a friend who died in Vietnam. I couldn't go to his funeral," said Mr. Green, a former Marine. "Later, I went to the wall, the Vietnam War Memorial, and saw his name.

"That name, there was still power in it."

Some walls were commissioned by gangs and drug lords to honor fallen soldiers, and are used by police to track gang members, said Detective David Carbone of the New York Police Department. Police also watch for changes on neighborhood walls, to piece together a recent history. "We get lots of information there," he said.

Most neighborhood walls were started by friends, families, churches and business or civic groups, the names added over time to murals painted by a neighborhood artist. Angels fly across some walls, the names written between the wings.

There are no rules as to who can be added to most of these walls, or when. Sometimes, people dead for years appear in fresh paint.

"The Jews have their Wailing Wall," said Syl Williamson, a Brooklyn businessman who has commissioned work on several murals. "We have this."

Soon, Ali Abuwi will paint his son's name on the dark-green wall at the corner of Bedford Avenue and Crown Street, a bowling alley on the inside but a neighborhood icon outside. His son, Kyma Kenyatta, 16, was shot in June 1990.

Mr. Abuwi stood on the sidewalk and watched as Khem Hubbard finished her dedication to her brother, just as a small boy and his father walked hand-in-hand around the corner.

"Daddy, I want to put my name there," said the little boy. His father jerked his hand, almost swinging the boy off his feet, and walked a little faster.

Mr. Abuwi stared at the sidewalk until they were past.

"No," he said to the ground, "you don't."

THE CORNER: RESPECT IN DEATH IF NOT IN LIFE

Richard Green has an undertaker's voice, the sad, smooth kind that carries images of polished pine and satin pillows. He goes softly through a litany of the dead: "Raisin, Pappy, Kiki, Shah, Twin, Dion . . . there was James Willis, he died in my arms across from the school on Union Street. James had been shot, but it was cold, so he didn't bleed a lot. That was '86, I think."

If an outsider comes looking for the source that feeds these walls, Mr. Green can take them there.

It is a bitter-cold Saturday morning, and the 46-year-old Mr. Green is on his way to witness the signing of a name to the wall at Bedford Avenue and Crown Street. First, he has to stop off and paint an ankh on the sidewalk where another young man died. He said he does these things out of respect.

As he weaves through the ice and traffic he points to this corner or that corner, and tells who died, and when. He sees a young girl on the street. "Darkeesha — we call her Keesha. I buried her brother."

It continues until he pulls into a space at the corner of Franklin Avenue and Lincoln Place, one of those intersections where the danger is something you feel, like cold. Young men crowd the corners, faces partly hidden by hooded sweatshirts. Look in their eyes, and there is nothing there.

"I hate this corner," Mr. Green says.

This is where Raisin died. Mr. Green puts down a wooden stencil and sprays the ankh, which has a broken arm to symbolize the death. One of Raisin's friends, Charles Richards, watches from a few feet away. Five of his best friends were killed.

"Their names are on the wall because they stepped on someone's sneakers, or because they looked at somebody hard," Mr. Green said.

He said it is young men like them who make up most of the names on the walls. They are between 16 and 25, some in gangs and in the drug business, others just trapped in neighborhoods that consume them. If the walls were reserved for spotless souls, most of that space would be blank, Mr. Green believes.

"The life they lived when they still walked, that's wiped away now," he said. "These young people deserve the maximum respect we can give them, and these walls elevate them to that."

Mr. Hubbard's wings dragged in the dust a long time ago. He went to jail at 14 for robbery, then sold drugs — one of thousands who begin the day by sliding a semiautomatic in the waistband of their jeans.

He was trying to change, his sister said, and had taken a test for a job with the phone company days before he died. He was killed in an argument with a 16-year-old, who shot him seven times.

"Look at you now," his killer said, and walked off.

A letter came from the phone company a few days later. Mr. Hubbard had passed his test.

The Rev. Paul Chandler of the Fellowship Baptist Church in Crown Heights is troubled by all the dead children on the wall. But he said there is no denying the murals have woven themselves into the fabric of the neighborhoods, and the city.

"They have become a place to heal," he said, and that is the tragedy of it.

"Where are all the live heroes?" he said.

The white face on the wall at Bedford Avenue and Temple Boulevard in Crown Heights is out of place in this part of Brooklyn, where there is fierce pride in things African and the Jesus on the wall of a Baptist church is prone to be a black man.

The eyes of the mural are bright blue, and they are painted so that they seem to look right at you, no matter where you stand.

Even in death, Jeff Herman watches over Crown Heights.

Officer Herman, pride of the 71st Precinct and a hero here because he treated people with respect, was killed when he answered a call about a domestic dispute in June 1989. A man using a woman as a shield shot him.

He is buried in Pine Lawn National Cemetery in Long Island, about 45 minutes from here, but his mother, Bebe, and sister Jill don't visit him much there. They come to his wall.

"I Feel His Presence"

"I went to the grave site for the first few months, but I don't feel any connection to Jeff there," said Jill Herman. "This is the place he worked, where people knew and respected him. I feel his presence here."

Some days Bebe Herman just sits in her car and watches the people pass by. Now and then one will stop and read a poem on the mural that the neighborhood children wrote for him.

The mural has never been desecrated. Most walls in this part of Brooklyn have not been touched.

"That would be signing your death warrant," said Detective Carbone.

In a place where the taking of a life is quick and easy, there is profound respect for the dead, said Mr. Chandler.

"They do tell the legacy, they tell the history, of our community," he said. "And that is young people who did not live out their potential. Like tombstones."

Darkeesha Foster has her brother's name written in a secret place. She goes and sits with him, sometimes.

"I think about him, and it makes me feel good," she said.

Just off Fulton Street in Bedford-Stuyvesant is a massive wall intended to honor Yusuf Hawkins, the 16-year-old who was surrounded by a gang of 30 white youths in Bensonhurst on the evening of Aug. 23, 1989, then shot twice in the chest.

One old man who lives there, John Rashid, calls it "Our church."

Over time, countless names have been added to it. But it is hard to tell who is being memorialized and who is just signing their name to wish Mr. Hawkins and the other dead a peaceful rest. The living and the dead all run together.

"Well," said Mr. Rashid, "the ones alive are not far from being up there for real."

Mr. Green wants to take his respect for the dead young people one step further. He is planning an eternal flame in a park in the Fort Green section of Brooklyn.

"It would be lit for all the young people who have died in this holocaust," he said, in his undertaker's voice.

Someone has to sit up with the dead.

Still Haunted, Families See Justice in Shape of a Killer's Grave

New York Times, June 3, 1997

DATELINE: Oklahoma City, June 2

After the explosion, people learned to write left-handed, to tie just one shoe. They learned to endure the pieces of metal and glass embedded in their flesh, to smile with faces that made them want to cry, to cry with glass eyes. They learned, in homes where children had played, to stand the quiet. They learned to sleep with pills, to sleep alone.

Today, with the conviction of Timothy J. McVeigh in a Denver Federal court, with cheers and sobs of relief at the lot where a building once stood in downtown Oklahoma City, the survivors and families of the victims of the most deadly attack of domestic terrorism in United States history learned what they had suspected all along: That justice in a far-away courtroom is not satisfaction. That healing might come only at Mr. McVeigh's grave.

"I want the death penalty," said Aren Almon-Kok, whose daughter, Baylee, was killed by the bomb one day after her first birthday. Pictures of the baby, bleeding and limp in the arms of a firefighter, became a symbol of that crime, of its cruelty. "An eye for eye. You don't take lives and get to keep your own."

Mrs. Almon-Kok saw the announcement of the verdict on television at her mother's house, then went immediately to the site of her daughter's death, where she was joined by some people who had lost children in the bombing, by others who had just felt drawn there. She said how happy she was with the verdict, but her face was stricken, haunted.

"I cried, and I cheered," Mrs. Almon-Kok said. "I don't think there will ever be closure. I love her so much, and I miss her, still, a lot. Baylee meant the world to me."

In what some people here see as poetic justice, the powerful image of Baylee, taken by an amateur photographer, will be used by prosecutors in the penalty phase of the trial to try to send Mr. McVeigh to his death.

Throughout Oklahoma City and the little towns that surround it, the people who lost something in the explosion said the same thing, over and over: that the verdict is a victory on paper. It insures that Mr. McVeigh, a failed Green Beret and Persian Gulf War veteran who came to hate the Government, will pay for his crime somehow. The penalty phase of his trial, the battle for his life, is what counts here.

"Not until the day I die will I be over this," said Stan Mayer, who was shredded with shrapnel when a truck crammed with explosives went off at 9:02 A.M., April 19, 1995. More than 300 fragments of metal and glass bored into him as he walked along a sidewalk outside the Alfred P. Murrah Federal Building, gouging muscles and nerves. More than 100 pieces are still inside him.

The same Federal jury that took four days to convict Mr. McVeigh will now decide whether he will die by lethal injection or live in prison. Mr. Mayer, a 41-year-old civil servant who reviews grants for historical research, was not in favor of the death penalty before that morning. Now, he cannot rationalize any other punishment for Mr. McVeigh, or for his co-defendant, Terry L. Nichols, or for anyone who knew of the bomb and did nothing. "None of these people should be alive and eating and breathing," Mr. Mayer said.

As the days dragged by and no verdict came, some survivors and relatives began to fear the unthinkable. It had happened to the Goldman and Brown families in the O. J. Simpson murder trial, they warned one another. It could happen here. Instead, people talked about renewed faith in the justice system.

"It was beautiful," Jannie Coverdale said about the prosecution's case. Mrs. Coverdale lost two grandsons in the bombing, and became one of the most visible examples of its cost. Aaron, 5, and Elijah, 2, died in that avalanche of concrete as they played in the building's daycare center. Mrs. Coverdale went to the trial every day in Denver. "It was like they had a puzzle they were putting together," boxing Mr. McVeigh in, she said of the prosecutors in a telephone interview.

The survivors talked hopefully of another victory in the penalty phase. How, once the jury is privy to so much pain, can it deny them Mr. McVeigh's life?

Ronald L. Fields, who tends the newspaper printing press at The Daily Oklahoman, lost his wife, Chip, who worked in the Murrah Building.

"All she lived for was her family, her garden and her home," Mr. Fields said. "He took away my past, my present and my future."

It was the same with Tina Tomlin in nearby Piedmont, who lost her husband, Rick. Her entry in the phone book, two years after his funeral, still reads "Rick and Tina."

"I can take a step toward healing," Mrs. Tomlin said. But if the jury votes for his execution, "there will be joy. I only wish they would let me do it."

"He smiled during the trial," she said of Mr. McVeigh. "I want to see him squirm" as the executioner hovers over him. "Smile now."

Mr. McVeigh's act taught some people here how to hate. But the hatred he delivered in his rental truck is not the chaos he hoped for, the kind that he read about in anti-government fiction and pamphlets. People joined, across lines of color and money and religion, against him, against the militias, against conspiracy rhetoric that, before this, had been so much less menacing to them.

"He got the attention he wanted, but he did not win," Mrs. Tomlin said. "If anything, he brought us closer, people of all races. Our petty differences were blown away by this."

Their hatred is like a laser, glowing, steady, narrow. Even the ones who say they do not hate him said, in the next breath, that they want him to die for the damage he caused.

Jim Denny and his wife, Claudia, saw both of their children, Brandon, now 5, and Rebecca, now 4, badly injured in the explosion. Rebecca received 133 stitches above the neck. Brandon, who had a quarter-size hole blown in his head, spent 71 days in intensive care and endured four brain surgeries. "We take it a day at a time," Mr. Denny said, "a minute at a time."

"We've never had any anger," he said. "Our system will show that there will be accountability. The justice system works."

He will testify at the penalty phase. He thinks the death penalty is the only acceptable penalty, the only reasonable one.

His children were too young to understand what happened to them. One day, he said, they will ask, and Mr. Denny said he will tell them the truth.

Sometimes, he said, Rebecca talks about "the bad building — about the thunder and the lightning."

Later in the evening, survivors, victims' families and people who just wanted to be part of this news gathered at a tree near the bomb site. The tree, shredded by the blast, had appeared to be dead, little more than a tall stump. But it now seems to be thriving. Here in Oklahoma City, people see it as a symbol, a sign that in the middle of so much destruction, life can begin again.

Bud Welch, 57, lost his daughter, 23-year-old Julie Marie, who, he said with pride, spoke five languages. He is one of the few people who do not want Mr. McVeigh to die. "My little girl was killed 40 feet from where we are now standing," he said. "I don't need another death." He would rather that Mr. McVeigh spend his life in prison, in hope that someday, he will tell them why.

The Valley of Broken Hearts

St. Petersburg Times, August 1, 1993

DATELINE: Pitted Rock, N.M.

If heartaches were matches, her little house would have burned down a long time ago. Most days now the old woman just sits in the yard and dreams of a dead husband, in a valley crowded with ghosts of men who died too soon.

The passing years have worn most of the rough edges from Little Joe, so all that is left for his wife is smooth and perfect memory. Mary Ann Joe remembers a sweet man who took a job down the dark hole so he could buy things for her. She remembers his joy on that first big payday, and her fear the first time he coughed blood.

She remembers how he would leave his work clothes at the end of a red-sand road and walk naked to the house, so he wouldn't bring the poison dust inside to the children. She remembers that the government men never told him digging uranium would kill him, even though they knew the radiation would destroy his lungs.

She remembers, before any of this ever happened, how he made her feel safe and warm.

"I miss being warm," she said.

Little Joe died from lung cancer 13 years ago. It is the Navajo custom to mourn four days and get on with life, but it is impossible to put aside death in a place where there is so much of it. In some parts of this reservation, a generation of men have been all but exterminated by a lingering legacy of the mines.

About 1,500 Navajo worked in government-supervised mines between 1947 and 1971, in tunnels the miners nicknamed dog holes. Now almost 200 men are dead from cancer and other respiratory disease and hundreds are sick because the government — in its rush to wage a Cold War — saw them as expendable.

"The government knew," Mary Ann said. "They knew that what they were doing was killing him."

The mines, abandoned in peace, are lost in a red, brown and purple maze of mesa and ancient valleys in Arizona, New Mexico, Utah and Colorado. The landscape is specked every 20 miles or so with clusters of tiny homes, filled with young men and women who swing babies on their hips and old women who sit alone.

There are almost no old men here.

In places like Cove, Red Valley and Pitted Rock on the New Mexico–Arizona border, the people tell hauntingly similar stories of one fleeting period of prosperity that vanished into the ground with their fathers, husbands and brothers.

Mary Ann softly lists the dead who lived in her valley.

"Ray Benally, Clyde Begay, Charlie Begay, Fred Charlie, Fred Jim, Phillip Harrison . . . Little Joe . . . some more."

Fred Charlie was her brother. Fred Jim was her brother-in-law.

In 1990, after years of legal battle, the U.S. government issued a formal apology to the Navajo and promised to compensate families of miners who died from exposure to radiation in government-run mines. It has been an empty promise. Of hundreds of Navajo who filed for compensation, 54 have been paid.

The checks, when they come, often bring only more anguish. The Navajo, with a profound fear and reverence for death, think the money is mortgaged with the breath of dead men. Some are ashamed to cash the $100,000 check while neighbors still suffer. Their money — a fortune here — waits untouched in banks and coffee cans.

Mary Ann got a letter the other day telling her the United States of America is giving her $100,000 for Little Joe.

She is 68 years old. She has been cold for 13 years.

The money brings no more joy than digging a nickel from the dust.

THE FAMILY

Down the hill from her house, past miles of sand and tumble-down houses where the only ornament is a plastic Jesus on the living room wall, there is a house tied with ribbons and covered with red and blue balloons. From a distance, it looks like a tree in bloom in a dead orchard.

A child in Paul Belin's extended family is celebrating her birthday, and people have come from all over the valley. Everyone is dressed in new Stetsons and old silver, hammered out by master silversmiths 100 years ago. It is their chance to show off babies and, for one day, forget their common pain.

Six or seven families are here. Every one of them has lost at least one man to the poison in the mine. Even when it looks as though a family has been spared, it shows up, as if they were carrying it around in a pocket all these years and just forgot to look.

Belin worked 11 years in the mines. He eased gracefully into old age with good health. At 67, he had beaten it.

Three months ago, doctors found a spot on his lungs.

"I'm infected," he said.

The young people stand in a circle around him, respectful, waiting long moments after he is through talking to make sure they don't interrupt. The Navajo revere their old people.

"Who looks out for us now?" said Irma Livingston, whose father, Phillip Harrison, died of cancer in 1970. "My father would have cared for us. They took him away from us. They have taken almost all the fathers away from us."

THE 20-YEAR SILENCE

The Navajo are not tall people. They were perfect for the dog holes.

World War II had just ended when geologists, surveyors and engineers came into their valley looking for laborers for top-secret work. They said they would pay more money than the Navajo men would ever earn herding cattle or making silver and turquoise jewelry to sell to lost tourists.

Little Joe was a wizard with silver. He could turn a fistful of Liberty head dimes and turquoise pebbles into a family heirloom.

"They came to the house, in '51 I think, and told him he could be a driller," said Mary Ann. "We were very happy. He had a job."

The pay stubs piled up. Little Joe bought a GMC pickup and sent their children to boarding schools.

The federal men were racing the Russians to make more bombs, so contractors opened more mines. In the frenzy, mine operators did not properly ventilate the tunnels. That would have taken time, time that could be used to dig ore. The men labored hunched over inside narrow, choking holes.

In some mines they worked on their hands and knees, the reason the tunnels were called dog holes. Mine supervisors never told the men the dangers of mining uranium. Little Joe suspected something was wrong, but the bosses assured him it was safe.

"There was a spring that used to run through the mine," said Joe's son, 33-year-old Eric Joe. "They used to drink from it."

They worked with drills and dynamite, and clouds of radioactive dust billowed from the tunnels. Joe and the others came home covered in the pale yellowish powder. The smaller children would hide, because they looked like ghosts.

After a few years, the first men started to die.

"It is hard for this generation to understand how the nuclear establishment felt it had the right to cut corners and sacrifice these people," said Stewart Udall, the Secretary of the Interior for Presidents Kennedy and Johnson. "They felt they were the frontline protectors of the national security, and all that bulls— "

When Udall left government work, he went home to his law office in Santa Fe to represent the Navajo in their claims. He is an ornery old man who has spent the last 20 years of his life trying to make right what he sees as an inhuman, inexcusable act. It was never only a case of a government turning its back on unsafe working conditions, Udall said. It was a conscious and informed decision to let them die.

"That's the haunting, horrible thing," Udall said. "In 1948, industrial experts went to Colorado mines and saw the problem. They knew there was an easy solution: ventilate the mine. They started to develop a plan, but the Atomic Energy Commission said leave it alone. They wanted it simple, cheap. They were in a hurry.

"They knew what the assault of radiation would do to the lungs, and they never did anything."

In the 1950s, government mining experts knew that the high cancer rate of Navajo miners was caused by exposure to high levels of radiation, mainly the breathing of radon, an invisible, odorless gas created from the decay of radium in uranium ore. But the government did not warn miners until the late 1960s. By 1971, the government had 1,000 uranium mines on Navajo land.

There was 20 years of silence, in the name of patriotism.

In Pitted Rock in 1955, Little Joe had started to cough through the night. By the time he quit the mine a few years later, he was already dying. He was a strong man with arms like iron bars, said Eric. He took a long time to die.

No one is sure exactly how many miners were exposed to lethal levels of radiation. Udall believes that at least half of the 1,500 Navajo worked deep enough underground to be bombarded with radioactivity — about 750 men who are dead, sick or in danger of being diagnosed with cancer.

"The people who perpetrated this are mostly gone," Udall said. "The people (in government) who deal with it now are dealing with the human debris."

WOODEN INDIANS

The mines stare blindly from the sides of mesas and mountains, empty holes still tainted with traces of radioactivity.

"We don't even like to send people inside them, even now," said Bernadine Martin, who works with the Navajo miners' uranium compensation program. "The law says we can't go in more than 8 feet . . . and to do that they have to crawl.

"It's ridiculous, that anyone ever worked in that."

People like to use the word "stoic" when they talk of the Navajo because they are not prone to have their emotions stenciled across their foreheads. White people mistake this as a kind of woodenness, as if pain does not hurt them so much. Paul Belin, the miner who may be dying, hides his pain behind dark glasses.

"It hurts us," said Irma Livingston, whose father died when she was a child.

She knows the government can't wipe away this ugly part of its history any more than it can forget atrocities at Wounded Knee or the Trail of Tears, but this massacre offers a chance for — if not redemption — at least some kind of restitution.

She, her mother and her seven sisters share $100,000 for what they see as the murder of her father. They have placed it in a bank to pay for college for their children, but what it has mostly bought is satisfaction — that the country admitted its crime. Most relatives of the dead don't have even that much.

Many of them never will.

Udall helped write the Radiation Exposure Compensation Act, in which Congress officially acknowledged that the U.S. government failed to protect the miners who furnished the uranium for America's nuclear arsenal. The act apologizes to them and to their families.

It is a compassionate piece of legislation that has been administered in a bureaucratic, uncompassionate way.

No one is sure exactly how many Navajo have applied for compensation. But because the mines were mostly located in and around Navajo land, most of the 1,100 miners or survivors who applied likely were American Indians. So far, 300 claims have been approved — just 54 of them have been Navajo.

Some of them, Livingston said, had been waiting 20 years.

Udall said the compensation program is being slowed or denied by a system that requires pounds of documentation on health, marriage and other family history — written evidence, required of people who did not know how to write, who married without license or state approval, and lived their lives without paper.

Even divorce was accomplished without paper. If a man came home and saw his saddle sitting outside the home, it meant his wife no longer wanted him. There were no lawyers because there were no lawyers the day they were married. There was a ceremony of eating, singing and praying — but no blood tests and no gold band.

Because the written proof of their loss does not exist, the bureaucrats in Washington, D.C., may never approve the claims. U.S. Justice Department officials did not return phone calls.

"It's 40 years later, and how does the country respond? Does it prick our conscience?" said Udall. "We sacrificed these people. Let's be generous. But they're hard-hearted. Maybe this new administration will intervene and place compassionate people in charge."

Or, as many Navajo see it, their people can sit and wait for hell to gently freeze over.

NEVER AGAIN

The Navajo are patriotic for a people who were once massacred, brutalized and left to starve. Outside Window Rock, Ariz., the cemetery for Navajo veterans is ablaze with American flags. A sign says: *Please do not put big flags on graves. Small flags are OK.*

Paul Belin served in the Pacific in World War II. Little Joe and many of the other miners were veterans. Of all the tragedies brought by the mines, this may be the most cruel: They got first chance at jobs in the mines because they had served their country. They were considered good security risks.

Sometimes Mary Ann Joe wonders if the government let Joe die because he was a Navajo, and did not matter as much in their eyes as a white man. Other times she wonders if color mattered at all, if the government men were just vacant inside.

She prefers to believe it had nothing to do with color, because the other alternative is too evil. White men died, too, but they were poor and may not have counted as much as rich white men. That is what breaks her heart most, that Little Joe may have died because he was just an Indian.

She hopes it will never happen again.

But if the government learned a lesson from the mines, it has forgotten it. The U.S. Department of Energy, desperate to find dumping grounds for growing mounds of high-level radioactive waste from nuclear power plants, has offered Indian tribes multimillion dollar economic aid in return for storage space.

Private waste management companies — with governmental blessing — have approached several tribes for permission to bury hazardous and radioactive wastes. Indians, largely impoverished, are again being asked to accept what other Americans would never accept.

Mary Ann is through thinking about Little Joe today. She wants to go to the birthday party down the road, and forget for a little while about all this sad history. But she could walk for days and never get away.

She puts on a dazzling silver and turquoise bracelet Joe made for her and walks down the hill, to mingle with the other relations of dead men.

Four Walls to Hold Me

There are all kind of prisons. Some people are held prisoner by walls and time, some by their own sadness.

Where Alabama Inmates Fade into Old Age

New York Times, November 1, 1995

DATELINE: Hamilton, Ala.

Grant Cooper knows he lives in prison, but there are days when he cannot remember why. His crimes flit in and out of his memory like flies through a hole in a screen door, so that sometimes his mind and conscience are blank and clean.

He used to be a drinker and a drifter who had no control over his rage. In 1978, in an argument with a man in a bread line at the Forgotten Man Ministry in Birmingham, Ala., his hand automatically slid into his pants pocket for a knife.

He cut the man so quick and deep that he died before his body slipped to the floor. Mr. Cooper had killed before, in 1936 and in 1954, so the judge gave him life. Back then, before he needed help to go to the bathroom, Mr. Cooper was a dangerous man.

Now he is 77, and since his stroke in 1993 he mostly just lies in his narrow bunk at the Hamilton Prison for the Aged and Infirm, a blue blanket hiding the tubes that run out of his bony body. Sometimes the other inmates put him in a wheelchair and park him in the sun.

"I'm lost," he mumbled. "I'm just lost."

He is a relic of his violent past, but Mr. Cooper, and the special prison that holds him, may represent the future of corrections in a time when judges and other politicians are offering longer, "true-time" sentences, like life without parole, as a way to protect the public from crime.

This small 200-bed prison in the pine-shrouded hills of northwestern Alabama near the Mississippi line is one of only a few in the nation specializing in aged and disabled inmates, but that is expected to change as prison populations turn gradually gray.

While the proportion of older prisoners has risen only slightly in recent years, their numbers have jumped substantially. In 1989, the nation's prisons held 30,500 inmates 50 or older; by 1993, that number had risen to almost 50,500, according to the American Civil Liberties Union's National Prison Project.

But experts say the major increases are still to come.

"Three-strikes" sentencing for habitual offenders and new laws that require inmates to serve all or most of their sentences, instead of just a fraction, will mean "an aging phenomenon" in American prisons, said James Austin, the executive vice president of the National Council on Crime and Delinquency in San Francisco.

"There are going to be huge geriatric wards," said Jenni Gainsborough, a lawyer with the National Prison Project of the American Civil Liberties Union.

The older inmates will fill beds needed for younger criminals who are more of a threat, said Burl Cain, warden at the Angola State Penitentiary in Louisiana, the nation's largest maximum-security prison. "We need our prison beds for the predators who are murdering people today," he said.

Locked away for good, inmates will need special medical care and will have to be housed inside separate cellblocks, or separate prisons like Hamilton, to protect them from younger, stronger predators, said W. C. Berry, the warden at Hamilton.

"What else can we do with them?" he said.

ONCE DANGEROUS NOW HELPLESS

One Hamilton inmate, Thomas Gurley, has Huntington's disease. He sits in a chair all day and shakes and stares. He was a kidnapper, but now he has trouble holding a spoon.

It may seem cruel to lock a man away and watch him slowly die, Mr. Berry said, but most of the men in his care could not survive in the general population. Some are missing legs, some have misplaced their minds, some are just too old. They have heart, kidney or liver failure and need machines to keep them alive.

Sentences, especially life sentences, used to be like rubber bands. They stretched or snapped short depending on the inmate's record in prison, crowding and, sometimes, whether the inmate could convince the parole board that he had found the Lord. Inmates like the 76-year-old Mr. Hatcher could usually walk after 20 years, even with a murder conviction. But that was before it became so popular for politicians to run on pro-death-penalty, throw-away-the-key platforms.

"I'd like to be free," Mr. Hatcher said, "for a little while."

He has a feeling he will be, he said, and winks, as if some higher power has whispered in his ear that this will happen.

Warden Berry, standing beside him, looks away. It is common for a man doing life without parole to have that feeling, even though he knows chances are he will leave on a hospital gurney, or with a blanket over his head.

"They think, 'I just want a few years at the end of my life, free,'" he said. "You'll see them, men in their 70's, suddenly start walking around out in the prison yard, trying to take care of themselves, to save themselves for it.

"And some we have who wake up in the middle of the night in a cold sweat, because the thought of going out terrifies them."

They know that they have lived so long inside, everything they knew or loved outside will be gone, he said. So when they walk out the door, they will be completely alone.

The Birmingham jail was full of martyrs and heroes in the 1960's. The Rev. Dr. Martin Luther King Jr. made history locked behind its walls.

William (Tex) Johnson, who snatched $24 from a man's hand and got caught, was in fancy company. But as the civil rights heroes rejoined their struggle, a white judge gave him 50 years.

He escaped three times. "You can't give no 21-year-old boy 50 years; I had to run," he said. While he was out, he committed 38 more crimes. Now he is at Hamilton, finishing his sentence. He will be released in 1998, but two strokes have left him mostly dead on one side. "I believe I can make it," he said. "I believe I can."

There will be nothing on the outside for him. Warden Berry said that when an inmate reached a certain point, it might be more humane to keep him in prison. Wives die, children stop coming to see him.

"We bury most of them ourselves," on state land, he said. The undertaking and embalming class at nearby Jefferson State University prepares the bodies for burial for free, for the experience.

"They make 'em up real nice," the warden said.

Inmates Find Brief Escape in Rodeo Ring

New York Times, October 25, 1996

DATELINE: Angola, La., Oct. 20

Nick Nicholson dreamed of being a cowboy when he was a child in Walkill, N.Y. He had to kill a man in Louisiana to see that dream come true.

It is rodeo day in Angola Prison, and the wild bull he has drawn even smells mean, a trembling 2,000-pound mass of muscle, hooves and horns. But as he eases himself carefully onto its spine, there is no fear that he will lose his life. Life, to a man sentenced to forever, is pretty much lost already.

There is only the glory of that moment as the gate swings open, as the bull twists like a Texas cyclone, as 6,000 people in the tightly packed grandstand gasp, clap and roar for a man who can never walk free among them.

A former all-around champion of the Angola Prison Rodeo, he has served 16 years of a life sentence in a prison where more inmates will die of old age than be set free. He is 33.

"I beg for a bull," he said.

The Angola rodeo is a tradition in this pocket of Louisiana and has been for 32 years, a bizarre annual event that may be as close to the Roman coliseums as is available in the 20th century. Like gladiators, the inmates — some of whom have never been on a horse in their lives, let alone a bucking bull — are thrown, stomped, gored, pawed, kicked and bitten in Angola's modified version of the traditional rodeo. First, they sign a legal release saying that they take part in the rodeo of their own free will, and absolve the prison and State of Louisiana of all culpability.

The prize money for the events — bull riding is one of the safest — is usually $50, which is a lot of money to a man who makes four cents an hour picking cotton on the prison farm. This week an inmate won $300 for picking a poker chip off a bull's forehead as the animal tried to skewer him with horns four-feet across. The horns were painted bright red, for effect.

But Mr. Nicholson and most of the other inmates said they do not do it for the money, but for the joy of it. The years drag so slowly. A few seconds on a bull's back is the only escape in the vast, dull flatness, where the inmates are expected to work in the giant fields and the Mississippi River is the only thing that runs free.

"I always wanted to ride when I was a kid, but there weren't horses there," said Mr. Nicholson, a handsome man with sun-streaked hair and a big blond mustache. He looks just like Robert Redford in "Butch Cassidy and the Sundance Kid," except that a collision with the ground has scoured a dot of skin from his nose.

"This prison is a bad place to find it," he said of his childhood dream. "But I found it."

But this rodeo is unique. The bull and bronc riding are traditional rodeo events, but some of events are modified, to compensate for the lack of skill and experience of its competitors. In bulldogging, the Angola cowboys do not jump from a horse and wrestle the running steer to the ground. Here, they stand almost face to face with the thing, just a few feet from the chute, and hurl themselves at it as it comes charging out.

Others are just made up, like "Guts and Glory," where all the inmates in the competition enter the arena and a wild bull is turned loose among them. Then there is "Convict Poker." Four men sit at a card table painted brilliant red, on red chairs, as a wild bull is given a jolt with a cattle prod and let loose on them. The winner is the last one to get up and run, or the last one tossed or hurled from it. Seating is determined by lottery. The man who loses sits with his back to the gate and only knows the bull is coming by listening to the pounding of its hooves, or the fear in the eyes of the man across from him.

The rodeo is a show. People pay $8 a head to see it, four Sundays in October. It draws more than the grandstand can hold, and people pour into the prison from Tunica, Solitude, Hardwood, St. Francisville and other small, quiet places, to eat cotton candy and watch men try to master beasts or, at least, survive the encounter. On Sunday, just one inmate had to be carried off on a stretcher, a man whose forehead collided with the whipping head of a bull.

In 32 years, no one has died. Getting hurt is expected, the inmates said.

"It takes four things to run a good prison: good playing, good praying, good food and good medicine. This is good playing," said Burl Cain, the warden at Angola. "They're king for a day."

The broncs burst wild-eyed out of the stalls, whipping the riders from their backs in a few seconds, sometimes landing almost on top of them with slashing hooves. The massive bulls may be more frightening, the cowboys say, but a bad horse will kill you. "A bull won't stomp on you," said Mr. Nicholson, who breaks horses at the prison farm. His bronc does the unexpected. Instead of leaping around the center of the arena, it races, bucking, toward the fence made of steel poles and thick ropes of wire, and hurls Mr. Nicholson over its neck, head-first into the unyielding fence. People in the front jerk back, instinctively. He gets up and limps back to the gate. The crowd cheers. "When you ride," he said, "everything blacks out around you." For a few seconds, he forgets the fence outside the fence, that one that keeps men in their place.

One of the cowboys has dreadlocks. One has on a pair of Nikes. One, a skinny, long-legged black man of many winters, rides like an expert but wears a brown cloth cap that would be more in place at a Detroit pool hall. Angola, home of Louisiana's death row, has 5,000 inmates; 85 percent of them are here because they murdered or tried to murder, raped, or robbed with violence. The cowboys, one after another, refuse to talk about their crimes. Not today. The stands are full of pretty girls, children and gray-haired old women who could be their mothers, if their mothers still came to see them.

It is a big crowd; prison officials had to turn people away. For a few inmates, it will be a chance to see their wives and children, if only from the stands, if only for a glance or a wave. Others, like Mr. Nicholson and a young man from Baton Rouge named Dale Langlois, will perform for strangers.

"I just want to feel it, feel free for just a little while," said Mr. Langlois, his head bound in a blazing orange headband, his arms and body crossed with jailhouse tattoos. "Maybe it'll take my mind off this 50 years I got." He is 35.

Like the other contestants, he does not feel he is being sacrificed or exploited for the enjoyment of the crowd.

"Maybe people think it's crazy," said James Flowers, a city boy from Gretna who would climb on his first bull — and rapidly come flying off — a few hours later. "I think it's something positive." He is doing life for murder. He is 36.

Major Shirley Coody, an officer at the prison, was the first woman to transverse "The Walk" through the prison's main inmate population. She never forgets that the men inside committed serious criminal acts, but also that they are still men, with dignity.

"The inmates were kinder to me when I first started than the free people," said Major Coody. One inmate told her why.

"'If you can pull a 12-hour shift,' he told me, 'and make it home, then the people on the outside will know we're not the animals that people think we are.'"

The rodeo is just another chance to show that, she said. The inmates think the risk is worth it.

The "Convict Poker" event has drawn a bull with split personality. He comes out of the gate a little unsure at first if he is mad or not, and then decides, as he spots the card table with the four inmates, that he is. He takes a few running steps and rams one horn into the inmate with his back to the gate up high, across his shoulders, just below his neck. The inmate's face twists in pain, and the impact of his body against the table almost crumples it. The inmate who is hit runs away, and so does Mr. Flowers, the murderer from Gretna. Two other inmates refuse to leave their seats, and the bull seems to have lost interest. He snorts around a little, and ignores them. The judges rule that, since the bull has turned timid, to call it a draw. "Them fellows ain't brave," said a trusty in the press box. "They just stupid."

There are ambulances standing by and professional rodeo cowboys in the ring to draw the bulls and bad horses away from fallen men.

"We don't want anyone to get hurt," Mr. Cain said, but there are risks, as in any rodeo. Claude Roberson, a convicted murderer from Baton Rouge, said he is doing it for a Christmas present.

"If I win something, I can send my son a present, maybe even get something for my momma. She's 60," he said. He is 34, and he is doing life.

The bull riders are flung one by one by one, until the question is not if, but how high. Only one rider stays on the six seconds it takes to qualify, so the judging is easy, and only one is carried off in a neck brace, injured but not seriously. "He's talking, and that's a good sign," the announcer says. "I know he can hear you," and he exhorts the crowd to show their appreciation for his valor. The inmate is carried off to cheers.

The inmate spectators are kept separated from the free people by a tall fence, and guards. A young woman with a little girl stands by it, and scans the rows of inmates, searching. She finally gives up.

The atmosphere is like a county fair. Inmates peddle beautiful leather crafts and gleaming cedar chests, along with paintings of women the inmates have never seen and landscapes they will never see again.

With so many people milling around, it would seem that escape would be inevitable. A few years ago one inmate stowed away on a horse trailer, but was recaptured.

There was a time when men would have drowned themselves in the river rather than spend one more night in Angola, one of the most infamous prisons in the nation. Men were whipped for coming up light in their cotton sacks. That era is past.

It is still a place where inmates grow much of their food and work money crops and cattle, where guards keep watch from horseback.

Warden Cain is determined to keep modern-day problems, like gangs, out of the prison. "You have a gang, you make the gang leader a toilet orderly. That way no one wants to follow him."

The rodeo heroes are highly regarded as tough men, men not to be messed with. It is a way to show that you are no one's punk.

"Guts and Glory" is the last event of the day. The contestants file slowly into the arena, and for a second or two you almost expect the announcer to blare: "Those of you who are about to die, we salute you." Then the bull charges in, and with every slash of those wide, red horns, the crowd gasps more than it cheers. Then a man in a red bandanna weaves in and, with a flash of his hand, manages to knock the poker chip into the dirt. He raises it high in his hand. Inside the fences, where a convict makes four cents an hour, Angola has a new rich man.

October still has one Sunday left, one Sunday to ride and fall and tease mean bulls and show off for the free people, for men who grew up to be cowboys in the strangest of places.

A Thief Dines Out, Hoping Later to Eat In

New York Times, May 19, 1994

Every now and then, Gangaram Mahes slips on his best donated clothes and lives the high life. He strolls to a nice restaurant, sips a fine aperitif, savors a $50 meal and finishes with hot black coffee. The waiters call him sir, but Mr. Mahes could not dig a dollar from his pocket for a bus ride to heaven.

He is a thief who never runs, a criminal who picks his teeth as the police close in. To be arrested, to go home to a cell at Rikers Island, is his plan when he unfolds his napkin.

Homeless off and on for several years, he steals dinner from the restaurants because he wants the courts to return him to a place in New York where he is guaranteed three meals a day and a clean bed. In a prison system filled with repeat offenders, the 36-year-old Mr. Mahes is a serial diner.

He has committed the same crime at least 31 times, according to his prison record, always pleads guilty and never urges his lawyer to bargain for a reduced sentence. In his eyes, he is just tunneling inside again, with a knife and fork.

"It's tough on the outside," said Mr. Mahes, who is serving 90 days for stealing a swordfish steak from a midtown Manhattan restaurant.

Prosecutors say it is not their job to consider whether locking some criminals up actually gives them what they want: refuge from poverty or hunger. But Legal Aid lawyers, while they have no statistics, said they had seen a small but growing number of people who commit petty crimes with the intent of going to prison. Mr. Mahes is unusual because of his method, and his persistence.

It is life in a cage, sometimes violent, often demeaning, but to Mr. Mahes it is better than drifting from shelter to shelter or living in cardboard boxes. There is order to prison, and you always dine on time, he said.

"I like to live decent," he said. "I like to be clean."

Christina Swarns, a young Legal Aid lawyer defending a man who does not want her help, faces Mr. Mahes through the wire screen of the holding pen at criminal court and does not know whether to laugh or cry.

"It's funny at first, 'The Serial Eater,'" she said. "But it's a very sad thing. How bad is it, his life, that he would prefer prison?"

On one hand is a man who goes to jail at will without hurting anyone, who steals only expensive New York restaurant food. Instead of throwing a rock through a window, he orders a T-bone.

On the other hand is a man who seems to have abandoned hope of ever having anything better, who prefers society's idea of punishment to his place in the society, said Ms. Swarns. In the past two years, he has seldom been free more than a few days before enjoying an illegal entree.

NOT TOO CHEAP

He has patronized the American Festival Cafe and the Taj Mahal in Manhattan, and Tony Roma's in two boroughs. He chooses restaurants that are not too cheap, not too expensive. If a restaurant is too pretentious, it might not seat him. If it is too cheap, he might not be arrested for stealing its food.

"If they really wanted to punish him," said Ms. Swarns, "they would stand outside Rikers and say, 'You go away.'"

Instead, Mr. Mahes does 90 days for stealing fish.

It costs taxpayers $162 a day to feed, clothe and house Mr. Mahes at Rikers Island. His 90-day sentence will cost them $14,580, to punish him for refusing to pay the $51.31 check. In five years he has cost them more than $250,000.

Louis Fasulo, a supervising lawyer at Legal Aid, said the real shame was that Mr. Mahes was returned to jail over and over before anyone questioned if it was the right thing.

"No one took the time," he said.

His lawyers have asked for alternative sentencing, including counseling, but prosecutors denied it. If Mr. Mahes wants to live in prison, the City of New York will let him.

Barbara Thompson, a spokeswoman for the Manhattan District Attorney, said Mr. Mahes was returned to prison because he was a thief, with a long record of stealing.

"He does belong in jail," she said. "It's the same as if it were a string of shopliftings."

Ms. Thompson said Mr. Mahes was not snatching bread crusts to keep from starving.

"One of his meals cost $100," she said.

All around Mr. Mahes in the holding cages at criminal court are inmates who just want to go home. He is already there, said Ms. Swarns.

She said her client had no expectations, so there were no disappointments: he did not envy people who were free, because they were free to suffer.

Once an inmate accepts where he is, what he is, jail has its good times, Mr. Mahes said.

"Last night," he said, "we had beef stew."

Even in the open room he sits with his arms close to his body and his knees together: people who do time, who share space, sit that way. He tells his life story in a detached monotone, as if he were just some vague acquaintance he used to know.

Raised in poverty and fear as a child in Guyana, he left for the United States in 1976, when he was 18. His myth of New York shimmered in the distance.

"I thought it was going to be milk and honey," he said.

What he found was a country in a recession, with lines for gas, lines for work.

Looking for refuge again, he joined the Army. The Army took care of its own; clothed them, fed them. He would have stayed, but five years and one drug addiction later — to hashish — he was on the street.

He wandered to Florida and Virginia to pick collards and peaches in migrant camps where conditions were barely human. One camp fed its workers just once a day.

He went home to Guyana, and returned to the South Bronx with a wife, who left him. For years he drifted, homeless, drinking himself happy.

"I would drink to forget how the day passed," he said.

By the late 1980's, the one constant in his life was jail. He had done time for a string of misdemeanors. Jail took care of its own; clothed them, fed them.

Getting inside was easy. All he had to do was pretend to be part of the mainstream, the middle class. Then, when the waiter brought the check, he told the truth.

In that golden space of time between being shown to his table and the second the check arrives, he is as good as anybody.

He has the same rights, the same respect, the same choices between fried cheese sticks and French onion soup. He can ask for a table near the window, or send back a steak if the center is not pink enough.

He likes a glass of Johnnie Walker and the chicken and rib platter at Tony Roma's.

"No dessert," he said. "But they did offer."

He was fond of the buffet at an Indian restaurant in midtown, but it closed.

"The curried lamb," he said. He almost smiles.

HE KNEW WHAT HE WANTED

On April 10, he visited the American Festival Cafe at Rockefeller Center. He ordered swordfish, lightly grilled, delicately seasoned.

"He had very good taste," said Paul Sharpe, the cafe's manager.

Mr. Sharpe said Mr. Mahes did nothing to attract attention at first. "He didn't order 50 lobsters to go," he said.

Instead, he acted like a man who knew what he wanted and expected to get it.

"I think he was drinking Chivas Regal," Mr. Sharpe said.

That was a Sunday. He had been released from prison on Thursday.

Court has become purely a formality for him. But in that, he is nothing special.

Arraignments in criminal court in New York are not personal things. An army of blank-faced men and women wait in the pews or in the holding pens for their cases to be called. Most plead guilty and wait for a blank-faced judge to rule on a negotiated sentence.

Over and over, he glided through without complication, accepting 10, 40, even 180 days. Most times they did not even bother to spell his name right. He is also known as Gram Mays, Gangaral Mahez, Gangaram Males and Reggie Mays.

He expected this time to be no different, that he would be assigned another charity lawyer who would glance at his file and cut a deal with thinly disguised indifference.

In walked Ms. Swarns, for the defense.

Fresh from law school at the University of Pennsylvania, a 25-year-old in her first job, she bothered to ask why he did it.

Christina Swarns would argue paint off a wall.

Members of her family on Staten Island have learned to agree with her. That, or leave the room and shut the door. Her voice carries.

"I love to argue," she said.

It was clear to her and to Mr. Fasulo that punishing Mr. Mahes by putting him in jail was like throwing Br'er Rabbit in the briar patch.

Mr. Mahes could commit more serious crimes and go to prison for years, but that is not who he is, said his lawyers. He does not want to hurt people or rob a bodega or hold up a taxi driver. He just wants to eat well and sleep in peace.

Mr. Fasulo fears that jail is becoming a warehouse for the poor. The courts dump them into Rikers because it is the easy thing to do, he said.

In winter, "they take batteries out of cars and stand there waiting, so they can be out of the cold," he said.

Before his arraignment in April, the prosecutor wanted Mr. Mahes to serve a year. Mr. Fasulo and Ms. Swarns argued for placement in a halfway house, where he would have food and counseling.

"We felt that, given his record, it was appropriate to ask for a year," said Ms. Thompson, the District Attorney's spokeswoman.

His lawyers knew that would just continue the cycle.

The judge offered 90 days in jail. Mr. Fasulo and Ms. Swarns did not want to take it, but behind them Mr. Mahes chanted, "Take the 90 days."

She said it was maddening to defend him. Every time she gives him her card and tells him to call, so she can help when he gets out, he throws it away. She cannot compete with prison. The food at Rikers is tasty, said Mr. Mahes. For supper, he had pork chops.

He said he was thinking of quitting this life someday. But when the bus came to take him back to Rikers, he was content. It was almost lunchtime.

"Fried chicken," he said.

He does not have a family to miss him. He does not have an old neighborhood where people know his name.

The bars at Rikers Island are there to hold him in, and to hold onto.

Man Imprisoned for 30 Years
Is Rid of Bars but Not Fears

New York Times, November 23, 1998

Hayes Williams is haunted by closed doors. In the long, narrow house on Lopez Street, what people here call a shotgun house, every inside door is ajar, cabinets are open, kitchen drawers are pulled half open.

His fiancée, Linda Wilson, will come home from her job at the pharmacy and find the house this way, and she thinks about scolding him a little. "But I'll stop when I think about why he does it," Ms. Wilson said. He is not messy, she said. He is just a man who knows what the inside of a box looks like, when it closes shut.

"I don't like closing up nothing," said Mr. Williams, who served 30 years in Angola Prison for a killing he played no part in, except to stand outside a filling station as an argument between two acquaintances and the station owner escalated into a gun battle that the courts called second-degree murder.

A Federal judge, taking into consideration a 1997 state court ruling in which a judge found that prosecutors withheld evidence from the 1967 case that could have proved Mr. Williams's innocence, freed him 18 months ago. Mr. Williams, who has a prison tattoo of a cross on his right forearm, went straight to Rampart Street and lit a candle at the shrine of St. Jude, the saint of lost causes. He prayed, and wondered why, in the grip of such joy, he was so afraid.

The next day, as he thought about going for a walk, as his fingers touched the doorknob, he knew.

He knew, Mr. Williams said, that being turned loose and actually living free, free in his own mind, were not the same. He walked into prison at 19. Now he is almost 50, living in a world he does not remember, constantly afraid some minor blunder, some innocent mistake, will make people laugh at him, and even more afraid that a trivial brush with the law, some bad luck, will steal his freedom again.

"Inside, I used to pray," Mr. Williams said. "I wanted freedom. I didn't care if I lived face-down in a sewage ditch, if I was a bum on a railroad track. Lord, let me be on a corner, begging for food. But let me be free.

"That first morning, you go to the door, your hand hits the knob, and you say, 'I can do this.' And you open it, a crack, but you don't go out. You peek. Because you don't know how to act. So you just stand there, looking out. I'll go out, you say to yourself, eventually."

It is freedom, but 18 months later it still feels brittle and paper thin.

"You're afraid someone will say, 'Look at that fool,'" he said, if he is seen reaching for the handle of an automatic door that has already opened, or seen walking for blocks along Canal Street with a wadded-up sandwich wrapper in his hand, because he did not recognize the new garbage cans.

"It's important to me," he said, "not to look like a fool."

Inside, he had become a hero. A trim, thoughtful man, his name is now synonymous with prison reform in the state of Louisiana. The son of a middle-class family who pleaded guilty to second-degree murder to spare his family the embarrassment of a trial, Mr. Williams and four other state prisoners filed landmark lawsuits in the 1970's that forced an overhaul of the prison that the Federal courts called the most brutal and corrupt in the country.

Rape, stabbings, sickness, bodies stuffed under barracks, pieces of rat in biscuits, all swirl in his head.

"Imagine the worst moment of your life, and then think of living that moment every minute, every hour, every day, of every year, and that's Angola," said Mr. Williams, who carried a rolled-up magazine with a six-inch blade inside to survive the first day. As the reforms he helped force took hold, he only got older.

"I go to sleep and I dream about Angola," he said, sitting in that house with the open doors, where a man can stand inside the front door and throw a baseball all the way through it. "I guess I'll dream about it till the day I die."

But like any dream, of falling off a cliff or stepping on a snake, he wakes to a reality, to a house where doors lock from the inside. And freedom, he has learned, is just another dream he has awakened from.

"You always feel," he said, "like you're not living up to the expectations of the free people."

He walks through it so, so softly, determined to do everything right. In 18 months, his only offense has been a parking ticket. He has a good job, on an oil rig out in the Gulf of Mexico. He has Ms. Wilson, and friends, and some family. It will take time, his friends believe, for him to feel at home again, for that anxiety to fade.

"That's a hellish transition, when you're trying to show you can belong," said John Lewis, the assistant deputy director of Project Return, a program at Tulane University to help former inmates make the transition to the free world. "You're lost, completely lost."

Mr. Lewis knows. He served 20 years at Angola on a narcotics conviction.

"It's just that everything is so new," Ms. Wilson said of Mr. Williams.

Neighborhoods that once rang with rhythm and blues now throb with rap, and whole streets, whole sounds and sights and sensations, just seem wrong: crack dealers working the sidewalks of neighborhoods where he used to go to fish fries; houses, the ones in his old neighborhoods that people worked a lifetime to buy, in ruins; his father and mother dead, long before his freedom; interstate highways, which he is still afraid to navigate, crisscross the city on elevated lanes, their giant concrete columns reaching up from where neighborhoods had stood. Some days, New Orleans is like the dark side of the moon.

"Who ever heard of a carjacking?" Mr. Williams said.

UNDER PRESSURE, A BAD BARGAIN

He grew up in the Ninth and Seventh Wards, the Catholic-school son of respected parents. Until that night in 1967, he had never been in trouble; no one in his family had.

According to trial records, he was standing outside the gas station when Larry Hudson and John Duplessis, men he had been out drinking with, argued inside with the station owner, Oscar Meeks, over the price of fixing a flat tire. Mr. Duplessis and Mr. Meeks pulled pistols and fired at each other, according to trial testimony. Mr. Meeks was mortally wounded.

Mr. Williams said there was no robbery, but all three men, on the word of one witness, who later changed his story, were charged with robbery and murder. The three were black. Mr. Meeks was white.

A lawyer, who was later disbarred for alcoholism, told Mr. Williams he could be free in 10 years and 6 months if he pleaded guilty, and he warned him that if he did not, he could get the electric chair, said Mr. Williams's new lawyer, A. F. Armond, who handled the case for free.

Mr. Williams said he had heard that the electric chair "made the blood in your body boil," but he still refused to plead guilty until his family, embarrassed by news accounts and afraid he would get the chair, begged him to put a stop to the publicity.

But Mr. Williams's 10-year sentence stretched into life under his sentencing guidelines. The two other men were given the death penalty, but as it turned out, both were released from prison long before Mr. Williams was. A state judge ruled that witnesses had lied and prosecutors had withheld other evidence in the case. Mr. Duplessis, the shooter, was pardoned in 1988. Mr. Hudson's conviction was overturned in 1993.

Mr. Williams rode to Angola in chains on March 27, 1968, sitting on the floor of what seemed to be a converted ice cream truck.

As the new inmates lined up, a guard with tobacco juice running down his chin started using a racial epithet as he ordered one black inmate to tell another "to run and look on the dash of my truck and bring me my tobacco knife," said Mr. Williams, who, as one of the lighter-skinned blacks in the New Orleans social strata, had seldom heard the epithet in his presence. "I said to myself: 'Lord have mercy, Jesus. Where am I at now?'"

An inmate who had befriended him in the parish jail in New Orleans, Arthur Mitchell, handed him a magazine with a sharp blade inside. The other inmates noticed how the magazine seemed not to bend the way a magazine should, and left him alone in those crucial first days, when new inmates either fought for their lives, or became someone's "gal boy," Mr. Williams said.

An escape attempt, a year later, taught him the true brutality of Angola. He was thrown into what some called the dungeon, a tiny cell supposedly for one man but sometimes packed with so many prisoners there was room only to stand, with just a hole in the floor for a toilet and bread and water to eat. It was pitch-black, and at night the rats and roaches swarmed.

Marked as a troublemaker, Mr. Williams felt sure he would become one of the inmates who just disappeared or were beaten or stabbed to death. He felt he had nothing to lose when he began collecting information about the abuses at Angola, information that would become fodder in a series of successful lawsuits.

In 1975, Judge E. Gordon West of Federal District Court ruled that conditions at Angola "shock the conscience," and he placed the prison under Federal control.

After that, Mr. Williams was rejected again and again by the parole board, still under state control, even as his lawyers piled up evidence that he had had no direct involvement in the killing and even after his co-defendants had been released.

Finally, two years ago, lawyers won him a new trial, and the District Attorney's office in New Orleans decided not to prosecute him anew. A judge then dismissed the murder charge. It took a few more months for a Federal judge to order him released, for time served, on charges relating to one of two escape efforts.

He walked out in May 1997, to see a daughter, who had been 6 months old when he was locked away, and a niece, and a few other people who had not forgotten him.

THE LONG ROAD TO TOTAL FREEDOM

When he was freed, The Angolite, the respected prison publication at Angola, wrote this: "Williams, during his confinement, earned a place in penal history by becoming the catalyst that turned Angola from a slaughterhouse into the safest maximum-security prison in the nation."

When Mr. Williams walked from the Federal courthouse in New Orleans a free man, he paused and closed his eyes. "I didn't want them to see the fear," he said.

It did not matter that it was unreasonable, that he would not take a walk because he was afraid some woman would point him out at random and yell "rape." The fear was real. As a sort of shield, he held his niece's infant in his arms when he went on walks. No one could accuse him of a crime, he reasoned, with a baby in his arms.

Finally, he walked alone, then walked farther, then got a car and drove tentatively around neighborhoods half-remembered. He attended group therapy sessions in the Project Return program at Tulane. He inched back into freedom, inched away from fear.

He was terrified of women, of intimacy, he said. It had, after all, been 30 years. He needed work, real work, to build a life.

This past summer, through a friend, he met Ms. Wilson, who understands the bad days. He got the job on the oil rig, hard, real work. Most people work 14 days on and 7 off, because it is confining and lonely at the same time, men marooned by all that blue water. Mr. Williams has worked as long as eight weeks in a row. He is an expert at confinement.

But before he goes to his cramped bunk, he sits on the deck at night, black sky melting into black water, 300 miles out in the Gulf. "And all I can see are twinkling lights of another rig, in the distance," he said. He thinks about what was lost, and tries, as he tries every day, to keep his bitterness buried deep inside.

"I have my freedom," he said, but of being truly free, "I pray to God that can happen."

Even free people, he knows, are prisoners of their own anxiety. But they, he said with a smile, are not usually terrified of a department store. "I hate," he said, "those revolving doors."

Prisoner's Pittance Is Meant
As Reminder of a Great Loss

New York Times, December 26, 1996

DATELINE: Gulfport, Miss.

Ann Lee wakes up to her dead child's memory every morning. Pictures of Whitney, forever 4 years old, adorn almost every wall. The child's room, home to abandoned Barbies and teddy bears, is the same as the day she died almost two years ago.

On the floor is a single pink crayon, left behind by the little girl who almost, but not quite, followed her mother's instructions to clean her room. Mrs. Lee sees it every day, but cannot bring herself to pick it up.

"When I wake up, that is the first thing that hits me: 'God, how am I going to get through another day,'" said Mrs. Lee, who lost her daughter when a drunken driver plowed into the rear of her car on Jan. 29, 1995.

It is not asking too much, she said, to require the young man who caused the death of her child to think of her, too, one afternoon a week.

Every Friday for the next 10 years, as part of his sentence, Brandon C. Blenden must write a $1 check and mail it to Mrs. Lee and her husband, Jack. Included on every one of the checks, in that space where most people write memos to themselves like "for rent" or "electric bill," are the words "for the death of your daughter, Whitney."

This fall, Mr. Blenden, 17 at the time of the crash on Old U.S. 49 near Gulfport, was convicted of driving under the influence and causing death, the Mississippi equivalent to vehicular manslaughter. He was sentenced to 20 years in prison by Judge John H. Whitfield of Harrison County Circuit Court.

To make certain that Mr. Blenden did not forget the child whose life he had taken, the judge also ordered him to pay a $520 fine, in weekly increments mailed to the family of the victim. The $520 fine will take 10 years for the inmate to repay, and week by week by week he must face up to the devastation he caused, Judge Whitfield said.

The penalty, part of a trend of alternative sentencing by judges who have found that jail time is not a strong enough message for criminals, would never have been levied if the Lees had not agreed to it, the judge said.

Mrs. Lee not only agreed. She welcomed it.

She knows that some parents would not want to be reminded, week after week, of their child's death, the manner of it or the person who caused that heartbreak. But in a house that has become a shrine to a dead child, for a 37-year-old mother who uses giant photographs of her dead daughter in a tireless war against drunken drivers, there is less pain in it than a sad satisfaction.

"It's not like I don't remember that she is gone until I see that check," said Mrs. Lee, who has traveled the Deep South to give speeches and successfully lobbied the Mississippi Legislature for tougher laws.

She made her daughter a promise in the 49 hours Whitney lay in a coma in the hospital. "You will not die in vain. I will not let anybody forget you, or how you died," Mrs. Lee said.

"I keep the checks in a drawer. I haven't cashed them. What do you do with a $1 check? But at least I know that he has to be reminded of her once a week. He will have to think about her, and what he did.

"But no one has won. No one wins, in this."

She has a 3-year-old son, Jackson, and a 16-year-old stepdaughter, Lauren. The 3-year-old roams the house pretending to be Captain Hook, and shouts, "Take that, dragon," as he stabs the floor with his plastic sword. There is plenty of warmth in Mrs. Lee's life, still, but even wrapped in it, she feels the cold of her daughter's death.

Her daughter died because a young man, working his way through a six-pack on Super Bowl Sunday, did not notice the line of cars stopped at an intersection as he drove to his girlfriend's house, Mrs. Lee said.

It somehow did not register in Mr. Blenden's mind that the cars he approached were not moving as he came up behind Mrs. Lee's car, and he slammed on his brakes much too late, she said. The impact crumpled her car. The trunk and rear bumper were forced through the back seat, crushing the child.

Whitney was correctly strapped into her car seat. Her body showed little of the trauma that was inflicted upon her. She was damaged inside, especially in her head. Her mother knew her child was dying when a young doctor told her he would pray for her. In the second day after the wreck, Whitney's brain began to swell, rapidly.

Mrs. Lee asked for a camera.

"They thought I was crazy," she said of the nurses in intensive care. "I said, 'I am going to take pictures of my baby, and I want whoever did this — at the time I did not know the boy — to know what they did.'"

After Mr. Blenden's eventual conviction — the case is under appeal — the judge said he considered ways to "make him constantly reflect upon the severity of his conduct." He once considered placing a photo of Whitney in the cell.

"As we have seen, just incarcerating people does not force them to actually address the conduct itself," the judge said. "I am just trying to find some alternative, and not just with drunk driving, to the traditional form of sentencing. It doesn't work."

He is satisfied that this sentence is working.

"The first week that he had to write that check, his attorney said that it was very difficult for him to do," the judge said. "He actually started crying and was very nervous."

Mrs. Lee has met with the young man, and they have cried together. She said she believes he is sorry, and she is sorry for him. Mr. Blenden has a wife and baby, the child conceived after her own child was killed.

"I made a bad judgment," Mr. Blenden said earlier this year, after his sentencing. "I am truly sorry. I just pray for forgiveness."

But Mrs. Lee wants to be sure that he, at least for the near future, does not push her daughter out of his conscience.

Every week, she reaches into her mailbox and finds her proof.

Wayne Woodall, Mr. Blenden's lawyer, declared, "Remorsefulness is not a question."

His client has placed flowers on the child's grave, Mr. Woodall said, without a court order to do so.

If his conviction stands, Mr. Blenden will serve at least a quarter of his jail time. The judge also tacked on five years probation, in which Mr. Blenden must talk to youth groups once a month about the "effects of his decision" to drink and drive.

In the meantime, Mrs. Lee is traveling somewhere every week, pleading with young people not to make such a decision. She carries poster-size pictures of Whitney, alive and dead, to drive home her argument.

She was one of the victims of such crashes who persuaded legislators to tighten drunken-driving laws earlier this year, making it more difficult for offenders to avoid losing their driver's licenses.

The crusade is how she holds herself together, Mrs. Lee said, because she is fighting back.

"I want my children to know you don't have to be a victim, then do nothing," she said.

But it seems a sad place to exist. Even the bumper sticker on her car screams her pain: "MY CHILD WAS KILLED BY A DRUNK DRIVER."

It is harder than ever now, at Christmas. There is one less stocking hanging over the fireplace. Mrs. Lee had to force herself not to put one up for her dead child.

She cannot go on this way forever, she knows. She thinks of giving away the toys in her daughter's room, but not now. Meanwhile, every place she goes, everything she does, reminds her of her child.

Some days, Whitney wanted to be a doctor. Some days, she wanted to be a country singer. One day, she asked her mother if she really could be anything she wanted to be. Her mother said, sure.

"I'd like to ride on back of the garbage truck," her daughter said. Now, when Mrs. Lee passes a garbage truck, she wants to cry.

Her little boy swirls around her as she talks.

"I can't lay around feeling sorry for myself," she said. "He's the reason I get out of bed."

Captain Hook skewers another invisible dragon, and shouts, "Ta-da!"

Hurtful Things

I should have a handle on cruelty by now,

after writing about so much of it. I don't.

New York's Bodegas Become Islands under Siege

New York Times, March 20, 1994

One man has already died behind the counter of the West Harlem grocery where Omar Rosario works, murdered in a tiny business where customers pay in pennies and promises. Before he goes to work he slips on his bulletproof vest, slides a black 9-millimeter pistol in his waistband, and gives himself to God.

It is early on a Wednesday night and the store's lights gleam like new money among the dead street lights at the corner of 139th Street and Edgecombe Avenue. The door opens and a young man with a puny mustache walks in, one arm hidden deep inside his baggy, half-open coat. Mr. Rosario thinks he has a machine gun or sawed-off shotgun.

Mr. Rosario takes out his pistol and eases it halfway into the pocket of his pants, his finger on the trigger. He faces the man and lets him see the gun in his hand. He wants to make it clear that if the young man pulls a gun, he will be killed.

The young man drifts around the front of the store as the last two customers walk out, but everywhere he goes Mr. Rosario is beside him, as if in a dance. They stare into each other's eyes for five minutes, silent, and the tension is sickening. Finally the young man turns and goes out. Mr. Rosario stares out the door, gun in hand. His face is pale.

In the last year, 50 workers have been killed in robberies in small stores like this one in New York, more than in any other line of work. The cramped shops have become stages for the city's most vicious crimes, played out week after week in wild gunfights and cold-blooded executions. People kill for $100, for $20, or for fun.

"If I do not resolve it, if I do not act first, he will take my money, make me lie down on the floor, and shoot me in back of the head," said Mr. Rosario, a 28-year-old Dominican native who manages the store. There is no macho posturing here, only a young man who is tired of being scared every time the door opens.

"Not one bullet will I use to protect a piece of candy," he said, rubbing his weary eyes with a shaking hand. "But I will kill 10 before I let one pull a gun on me."

IMMIGRANTS' DREAMS

In Spanish the shops are called bodegas, a word that over the last decade has also come to mean respect and independence in immigrant enclaves. For some new Americans the shops are an avenue to riches, at least compared with Santo Domingo and San Juan and other towns where people dream. Most of the owners are Hispanic, but there are Chinese, Koreans, Haitians and Middle Easterners, too, looking for the same thing.

If America needs more proof that killing is easier now, that life has less value, the evidence is here between rows of candy and cigarettes. The old days of stick-'em-up are long gone in a city where empty-eyed teen-agers kill without provocation, trembling crack addicts lose their nerve and shoot at anything that moves, and robbers torture store owners to make them give up cash boxes.

Robbers display a seemingly bottomless brutality now, even murdering people as they kneel in supplication, say bodega owners in places like Washington Heights, the South Bronx, East Harlem and Bushwick Avenue in Brooklyn.

"When I leave here, I am like a bird in the air, flying," Mr. Rosario said. "I am free."

The previous owner of the store, Henry A. Medina, was killed on Nov. 16, 1992, by two men in ski masks. Mr. Medina was opening the register to give them the cash when one man shot him in the heart. His killers were never found.

It seems too great a risk for a job selling Baby Ruths to children who are a nickel short, but this is more than work.

It is a chance to be the boss, to build a business that might someday be more than a cash register behind a blurry plastic shield. The employees are usually brothers, mothers and distant cousins, sharing the dream.

Here as in the islands, bodegas are meeting places and gossip out-lets for the neighborhoods, where the clerks know their customers and old women rest their feet on empty crates before heading home with sacks full of Cafe Bustelo and green plantains.

Old men argue Latin American politics at Julio Then's bodega in Washington Heights. Sizzling tropical music pours from Domingo Leon's bodega in Bushwick.

LOOKING OUT FOR HOLOPES

The bodegas warm the streets. But they draw criminals. Bodegas deal in cash and stay open late. If the people behind the counters are killed, there are sometimes no witnesses.

"These are people trying to live the American dream, and they will take risks," said Deputy Inspector Joseph E. Lovelock, executive offi-cer of the Police Department's Office of Management Analysis and Planning. "They are risking their lives."

The crime has its own name, a Spanish-English variation of holdup. The bodega owners call them holopes (oh-LO-pays). The men who rob are called holoperos; when the word is uttered it sometimes is fol-lowed by the sign of the cross. The number of killings has been rising steadily over the past few years. In 1992 there were 47.

Outside the bodega on Edgecombe Avenue, Mr. Rosario stands in the cold rain with an employee, Pablo Mendoza, scanning the streets, wishing the street lights were working. They are afraid the young man will come back with friends and more guns. A half-hour later they are still there, watching.

Sometimes Mr. Rosario thinks he can sense the spirit of the previ-ous owner wafting around the place late at night. He and Mr. Mendoza believe in God and like to think that it is an angel. But there are no an-gels on Edgecombe after dark.

SURVIVORS: "I CANNOT RUN AWAY"

The difference between rich people and poor people is that poor peo-ple still wear the clothes they were wearing when they were shot. They save them from the emergency-room floor.

Domingo Leon, the 40-year-old owner of Leon Bodega at 289 Bushwick Avenue, has a bullet hole in the arm of his leather jacket. The dry cleaner took the blood stain out. Domingo Angeles wears the pants he wore when he was shot in the hip. He still has the bullet, lodged deep in his lower back.

Along with a friend, Manuel Celado, who was shot twice in the chest, the men are survivors of a violent bodega robbery last year. But no one died.

"Milagroso," Mr. Leon said.

Miraculous.

The men are all members of an extended family that draws much of its income from the bodega. It does not make anyone rich, but it is exactly what Mr. Leon was searching for when he left Moca, a village in the Dominican Republic, more than 20 years ago. He saved his money and opened in 1982.

"This is a dream to me," he said.

No one holds the keys to his livelihood, so no one can make him bow his head. People who have never been poor, who have never had to live on their knees, do not understand what it means to him, he said. But he is afraid that one day he might die there. The city has changed so much, he said, as if it had misplaced its soul.

On Feb. 23, about 10 P.M., four young men burst into the bodega and one put a gun to Mr. Celado's head, witnesses said. Mr. Leon grabbed at it, in reflex, and the robbers started shooting.

Mr. Angeles grabbed the gun of one young man and the hammer chewed a groove in his hand as the man jerked over and over on the trigger. Finally one of the bullets hit Mr. Angeles in the hip. He lay on the floor, pretending to be dead, quietly praying the man would not shoot again.

One robber dragged the bleeding Mr. Celado into a storeroom and started beating him in the head with a gun, trying to make him tell where the store kept its money. When Mr. Leon ran into the room the man shot him in the arm and ran.

The police later caught all four robbers. The report called them "youths."

A few hours after being shot, while Mr. Celado and Mr. Angeles lay in the hospital, Mr. Leon was back at the cash register of his bodega. Blood still seeped from the bandage.

"I have nine children," he said. "There are bills."

Mr. Angeles was back at work a few days later. He is still in pain, the bullet grating against muscle tissue. He thinks of finding safer work, but refuses to leave his friends in danger.

"This is my family," he said. "I cannot run away and let something bad happen to them."

Now Mr. Celado, still looking frail from his bullet wounds, sits in a dark car outside the bodega. It is his job to spot suspicious people on the street, and warn his friends. He will shout "holope."

"Then we run inside," Mr. Leon said, "and lock the door."

He plans to get a gun. Too much depends on his doors staying open, at any cost.

SHIELDS: FIGHTING THE URGE TO FIGHT BACK

The inch-thick, bulletproof plastic shield surrounds Antonio Mueses like a security blanket, but he still feels cold inside it.

Mr. Mueses and his brother, Rafael, used to run the bodega at 1725 Fulton Avenue in the Bronx. Afraid of the killings and shootings they read about in the newspaper, they hired a man last summer to put up a shield. The man took the money but did not build it, and on July 25 his brother was shot dead.

The brothers were tending store that afternoon when two armed men walked in. One man took the 32-year-old Antonio to the back of the store while the other held a gun on 34-year-old Rafael at the counter. The man tried to club Antonio Mueses in the head, and he struggled. He heard a shot from the counter. His brother was dead.

Mr. Mueses grabbed a gun from a hiding place and shot one robber, Fernando Rodriguez, in the arm. Mr. Rodriguez went to jail, but the other suspect is still on the street, Mr. Mueses said.

"My brother has two children," he said. "We look out for them now. If the man had built the shield . . ."

He might also be alive if his brother had not fought back, but it is hard to let a man repeatedly bash you in the head, say bodega workers who have been attacked.

Mr. Mueses says he does not feel guilty about fighting back.

Andre Gonzalez fought back. The 60-year-old Mr. Gonzalez, a Puerto Rican native who said he would never give up a penny without a fight, grabbed the shotgun of a man who tried to rob his bodega at Manhattan Avenue and 103d Street on Feb. 24. The robber killed Mr. Gonzalez, and Mr. Gonzalez's son killed the killer with a revolver. Now the shop Mr. Gonzalez built from nothing is closed and covered with graffiti.

Not fighting, doing as the robber says, has not saved others this year. It is in those cases, where the people trusted their attackers not to kill, that the increasing brutality of the robbers is most apparent.

The best-known case was that of 19-year-old Marlon Chin of Brooklyn, accused of leading four teen-agers — the youngest was 14

— on a string of bodega robberies and killings. Police officers said the group forced a 40-year-old Bedford-Stuyvesant grocer to kneel before shooting him in the back. They killed two others without provocation, the police said.

In a separate case in January, two employees of a bodega on East Houston Street in lower Manhattan were made to lie down on the floor by six men, who shot them both. One died.

Three years ago, Julio Then's father was abducted from his bodega at West 184th Street and St. Nicholas Avenue, taken to his home and killed, after he gave the robbers all his money. He did not resist. There was no reason to kill him, his son said.

Mr. Rosario has a frightening theory about that, though it is not a new one.

"They kill so they will not be identified," he said.

Mr. Leon talks almost fondly about the days when he first came to New York, when robbers were slow to kill. They were professional.

"They would take the money and would not even hit you," he said. "But in the last three years the robbers are children. They're not experienced. They are nervous and scared."

And worse, he said, "they have no experience living."

They do not appreciate their lives, he said, or his.

THE YOUNG: WHY ARE ROBBERS SO WILLING TO KILL?
Kenneth Carlson, a police lieutenant, does not wonder why so many young criminals are drawn to the bodegas.

"These are not supermarkets with 30 witnesses," said Lieutenant Carlson, who investigates robberies in Queens. "They just look inside and see how many customers are there, and wait for them to leave."

He also knows that the availability of guns makes killing more likely and more frequent. What he cannot figure out is why the bodega robbers are so willing to kill.

So many are young, he said, and know they will not do much time if caught.

"They think if they get caught, it doesn't matter," he said.

Deputy Inspector Lovelock wonders if they would pull the trigger on the human being behind the counter if they understood all that it meant.

"With maturity comes an understanding of what a gun can do," he said, "and the irreversibility of pulling the trigger."

No one has figured out a way to put the bullet back in the gun.

"I Never Seen Nothing Like That"

New York Times Magazine, November 6, 1994

The heroes of the third platoon fumble toward history with canteens full of grape Kool-Aid, scanning the rooftops for snipers and trying hard not to run over their admirers. Their deep-green Humvees weave along streets packed with ragged but cheering people who believe these young men have delivered them from evil.

From high in his machine-gun turret, Pfc. Matthew Gunn of Houston waves to the people below like Miss Texas from a float in the Cotton Bowl Parade. On the filthy street, a bone-thin old Haitian woman blows him a kiss, then stretches both arms to him, eyes closed, head thrown back, face alight with a wide and beatific smile. If he never gets any closer to love and adoration for the rest of his life, he has seen it on this garbage-strewn sidewalk in Port-au-Prince.

"Y'all got to help me wave," yells Gunn, an orange-haired, liberally freckled young man who will be old enough on Jan. 27 to purchase beer legally. "I can't watch for the damn tree limbs and the snipers and do all the waving too."

"We're waving," says Sgt. Paul Stevenson, a blond, blue-eyed 24-year-old from Midland, Mich., who enlisted in the Army to escape the inertia of his hometown.

"Wave," he orders the soldiers. Laughing, leaping, half-starved children chase the Humvee for six blocks. Stevenson knows only a few words of Creole (a rich mix of African dialects and French), yet he understands what the crowd is trying to tell him. "What they're saying," he says, "is 'Thank you.'"

The soldiers, military police with the 101st Airborne Division out of Fort Campbell, Ky., have orders to be friendly, courteous and as unlike an occupying army as possible. The soldiers in the Third Platoon will wave anyway, because they believe what they are doing is right. Here, in the muck and murk of the poorest nation in the Western Hemisphere, a few young soldiers of the post cold war have found something not too far from glory.

"We go where they tell us," Stevenson says, "but this is a place we need to be. The people want us here. They dance for us and serenade us. I've been in this Army since I was 18 and I've seen countries get their freedom in the Eastern Bloc: the East Germans, the old Czecho-slovakia. But this . . . you ride through these slums and see people starving on the streets. The next thing you know they're running be-side you, cheering, making you feel like royalty."

To the Third Platoon, the Haiti mission is an American interven-tion that, for once, comes down on the side of the people. It removed a de facto government that sanctioned the gang rapes and mutilations of women and girls, the torture of old men and the killing of more than 3,000 supporters of the man whose power it had usurped. The men of the Third Platoon might not agree with their Government's real-estate deal with Lieut. Gen. Raoul Cedras, who ruled Haiti with terror for three years, to lease his mountain villa and beach-front re-treat. Or the C.I.A. having a member of Fraph — the Front for the Advancement and Progress in Haiti, a collection of coldblooded killers allied to Haiti's military — on its informants' payroll. They only know that the people feel safe under their guns.

How often in a black man's life, asks Pfc. Vondrain Smith, does he walk through a crowd of people of his own color and see them throw flowers at his feet? "It's a good feeling being cheered," he says. "I've never been cheered before." Smith, 19, has never been so far away from home and he did not expect to feel any love for Haiti. His kin in Hampton, S.C., said black people had enough to worry about at home. "I like these people," he says, looking out on a group of children who stare at him like he fell from the sky. "They like me back."

The others echo him. "We're doing good," says Pfc. Paul Brady, from Billerica, Mass., who is 19 but looks 15. "We know what they've done to people here. We're here to make sure that it doesn't happen anymore. It stops now." Brady, a recruiter's poster boy, is well spoken and mannerly, from middle-class parents in a nice, peaceful middle-class town. When he goes home, he will probably go back to college. But he has the sense that, whatever happens after Haiti, this will be the most important thing he ever does.

They sound too good to be true, angels with M-16's. They are not. They curse in Technicolor. Some speak fondly about being knee-walk-ing drunk, of regrettable trifles with mean women and general all-around sorriness. Yet, when seen against the backdrop of cruel and exotic Haiti, they are innocent. Haiti at once makes them feel like they are doing something pure and scares them half to death.

"I've heard they have this powder," says Gunn, referring to a mix-ture of poisons that voodoo priests are supposed to use to create the walking dead. But it is the base meanness of Haiti, the blank-faced cruelties that people here have inflicted on their neighbors, that chill them.

This is a place where thugs chased away the Argentinian Ambassador by setting two live roosters on fire and flinging them, smoking and squawking, over the consulate wall. Here, until the American troops arrived, bodies were found each morning in the open sewers and streets, their faces sliced away. Here, political prisoners disappeared into mass graves and pigs still root for their bodies after every hard rain. Here, a popular priest was riddled with machine-gun fire at the gates of his order's motherhouse.

This is a place where the gleaming Mercedeses of the ruling class blow past little boys with protruding empty bellies and where horribly deformed children walk on all fours through the streets like animals. Here, the police killed the poor at random, then charged their families $100 to reclaim the bodies. Here, the largely light-skinned aristocracy of a coldly racist society looks with contempt on the darker-skinned poor.

This place, where the American soldiers will play peacekeeper and God, is as different from their experience as voodoo is from dinner on the ground at the Baptist Church. Most of the men in the Third Platoon have never been outside the United States. They are middle class to lower middle class, miss their moms and believe in God — not enough to forgo sin but enough to feel guilty about it. They enlisted to get away from one-stop-sign towns and dead-end jobs, to see the world — and for the adventure.

They patrol Port-Au-Prince in Humvee caravans of two, three and four, guns loaded but not cocked and ready to fire, since this is a peacekeeping mission. The gunners in the turret, the most exposed and most at risk, wear two bulletproof vests. The drivers and navigators keep one eye on their windows, afraid someone will drop in a grenade. And always there are the Haitians pressing in on them, curious and friendly but so many and so close that the men know they would never see an attacker coming in time.

"You can never relax," Brady says. "The one place you come close to relaxing is in the compound," safe behind chain-link fences and razor wire. Then, after five hours' sleep, they are back on the streets, their Humvee rolling past rotting gingerbread houses that look like they tumbled from the pages of a Gothic novel, past slums where the stench and flies waft on the warm breeze, then up into the upper-class suburbs where slave children, called *restaviks*, care for the rich.

The Third Platoon knows it has helped slow and all but stop the atrocities that had been routine here since the Sept. 30, 1991, coup that sent President Jean-Bertrand Aristide, the poor people's prophet, into exile. The killing now is furtive, unlike the blatant daily murders of the past. But what the armed thugs have left behind is the dried-out husk of a country that offers America little except leaky boatloads of desperate people and, for a few enterprising American businesses, people who are willing to work like dogs for $3 a day.

The men of the Third Platoon know most people back home think their presence in Haiti is a mistake. They may even have thought it, too, before their first glimpse into hell, and hope. The Haitians have immortalized them with murals on the walls of the city, heroic scenes of tanks and helicopters and soldiers, next to pictures of the beloved Aristide.

"They look at us and think everything is gonna be O.K. now," says Gunn, who enchants the children with his freckles and with his ability to spit a good 10 feet if the wind is right. "We've given them a sense of safety."

Things do not always go as planned, but the Third Platoon has endeavored to persevere. They helped capture a member of a hated paramilitary group and controlled a mob that wanted to tear his head off and put it on a stick. They invaded, quite by accident, the Haitian officers' club. They taught a 10-year-old boy to count, dreamed of young love and chocolate cake, and waved.

Ask Richard Rice, the 38-year-old platoon sergeant, what he thinks of the morality of his mission and he barks: "Sir, I don't think. I react. If my Government tells me I am here to do good, I'm here to do good." He has enough trouble watching out for his 27 overgrown children in a military operation that has no precedent.

In a year, Rice will retire. He plans to sit on his front porch in a rocking chair, in the center of 105 acres of rich bottom land in Maysville, Ky., and watch the chickens peck. Haiti will seem a distant memory, but he can only have that peace of mind if all the young soldiers in his command leave Haiti alive.

"I came here with 27," he says, and the words seem riveted in the air. "And I'm by God gonna leave with 27."

Rice — a lean, tall, hard-looking black man with arms like telephone poles — is worried. He was for most of his career a soldier of the cold war. He worked a fence line in Korea, where razor wire divided friends and enemies, where soldiers were not expected to ride through towns drumming up good will. This post-cold-war mission seems to write new doctrine each day. Helicopters pound through the blue sky and blare a taped message in Creole on the humanitarian, democratic and peaceful intent of the 20,000 armed soldiers here.

"These guys are more at risk because it is a walk-in mission instead of a forced occupation," Rice says. "If it had been a forced occupation, we would have just taken all these weapons out there, instead of buying them back." He is talking about the plan to buy back weapons, like police departments in crime-infested American cities. "My job is to make sure they are prepared," but for what, no one is quite sure.

The Third Platoon has no fence line. Their enemies look just like their cheering friends, or at least they think so, since they have seen just one confirmed bad man — a member of Fraph. He was a skinny old man in yellow patent-leather shoes and a clip-on tie.

They were told when they got to Haiti that they would work in tandem with the Haitian soldiers, who, as one member of the Third Platoon says, "are the same guys we came to kill, right?" Yet the Third Platoon was trained for this, whatever this is. They were trained to listen politely to people who want to talk, to control and even soothe mobs, to disarm gunmen without killing them. They carry pepper spray, clipped to their uniforms like grenades, to use on looters. They have orders to help anyone they see who seems hurt or sick.

On one patrol, as they pass through the dockside slum of La Saline, the soldiers find a man lying in the street, badly beaten and bleeding. As they walk him to one of their own compounds to get treatment, he tells them his attackers were Fraph, who control places like this with rape, arson and murder.

Near the gate of the compound, a herd of television cameras thunders toward them. Rice has so many cameras stuck in his face he is unable to watch out for his soldiers. After the injured man has been taken inside, Rice spends a minute on hair-curling, white-hot cussing. But he does it when the cameras are gone. Cooperation with the news media, when possible, is part of the directive, to promote positive P.R.

More than anything, the men are afraid of a repeat of Somalia, where crowds first greeted American troops with smiles and later dragged their mutilated bodies through the streets, laughing as they did so. That image is burned into the mind of every soldier in the Third Platoon.

The soldiers have heard stories about Pere Lebrun, sometimes called the flaming necklace, that the poor people use to burn their enemies alive. It is a tire soaked with gasoline that is wedged down over a person's shoulders and set aflame. The burning victim thrashes through the streets, screaming. The poor of Haiti, the soldiers know, have their cruel dark side.

But when the soldiers write home, they mention none of this. The thing Pfc. Jeff Harris hates worse than anything else is lying to his momma. In elegant script, he writes long, heartfelt letters home to Columbus, Miss., that describe Haiti as being safe as church, so his mother will not worry.

"You only write your momma the good stuff," says Harris, who turned 21 in Haiti. He has the soft accent of the Delta.

He writes the same reassuring letters to a dark-haired beauty named Amanda Smith, whom he plans to marry if she will have him. He has two photos of her. He keeps them next to his Playboy magazine.

President Clinton has said he does not want the United States to get involved in nation building in Haiti, but no one in the platoon expects to be home by Christmas. "You know what they say about the M.P.'s?" says Specialist Ernest Jaen-Guardia of Beltsville, Md., a veteran at 27 who served in the Persian Gulf war. "You turn the M on our sleeves upside down and it stands for World Police."

The man sits buck naked in the dirt at the side of the winding road, face painted mustard yellow. His fingers tap the ground in time to a song only he can hear.

"Is that some kind of voodoo?" says Private Gunn, after the Humvee has crawled past. He thinks he has seen his first zombie.

"No," says the squad's interpreter. "Just a crazy person."

Gunn is not afraid of much that is mortal. The Humvee is his chariot, and with his two machine guns — one made for distance shooting, the other for close street fighting — he can sweep an area of any living thing. But he is wary of voodoo, of priests who turn the living into walking dead and hold souls prisoner in empty rum bottles.

Thugs loyal to the de facto government promised to use voodoo to shrivel the livers, burn out the eyes and freeze the hearts of invading Americans. They painted *veves,* voodoo symbols, on the intersections of main roads to stop the American tanks. But a hard rain washed away the veves and the Americans did not really invade, so no one will ever know what would have happened if the forces of evil had clashed with Private Gunn.

He always wanted to be a soldier. When the gulf war broke out, he was too young to enlist. "I was still in high school," he says. "I was crying, wishing I could be there." Haiti did not give him a war, only something like it.

When the Third Platoon is ordered to quell a disturbance downtown, they find the skinny man in yellow patent-leather shoes surrounded by some 300 Haitians. Some hold rocks and yell that they will tear his heart and eyes out and kick his skull along the street like a soccer ball.

The Humvees back against the curb, and Gunn and Brady train their weapons at the crowd, as other soldiers wade in. They shove the Fraph member to his knees and handcuff him. The crowd that seemed ready to kill the Americans to get at the man suddenly cheers. Some even sing. The American soldiers carry the man away, to more cheers.

In the turret, Gunn lets out a rebel yell.

At every meal, the Haitians circle and stare at the soldiers' M.R.E's (meals ready to eat). "I'd like to give something," says Harris, as the men stop for breakfast. They have orders not to share food. It could start a riot. After the platoon finishes its meal, it packs its trash away. If they leave it, street children will fight over the wrappers, to lick them clean.

One noonday, Sergeant Stevenson searches for a place to have lunch away from the hungry crowds. The soldiers carry detailed maps of Port-au-Prince, but sometimes rains wash the roads away or pigs cut a new path through the weeds. On one patrol, Jaen-Guardia took four Humvees into the walled circle drive of a large private residence, mistaking it for a warehouse. He knew he had made a mistake when servants came running to surrender. "The master of the house is in Miami," a servant said, "waiting for the invasion to be over."

Similarly, on this hot day, Stevenson leads his men to a closed double gate marked "Haitian Military," thinking it is a base. Inside is a palatial estate.

"What is this place?" he asks.

The interpreter tells him it is the Haitian officers' club. Stevenson politely asks if they can eat here. The guard, eyeing the machine guns, says, "No problem."

For the next hour, several Haitian officers lounge in Bermuda shorts on one side of a patio, watching disdainfully as Stevenson and his men lounge on the other, eating freeze-dried tuna. Before the Third Platoon happened on them, the Haitians had apparently been trying to learn English. Many Haitian officers have American passports and are expected to go there. There are too many witnesses to

Hurtful Things (59)

their brutality here. On a blackboard are words like "See you tomorrow," "Greet your family for me" and "The same to you."

After lunch, the soldiers take a tour of the estate. In one huge room they find a life-size knight in shining armor and an armored horse. There are colonial muskets on the wall and pool tables and, out back, tennis courts and a curved swimming pool that is bone dry. The soldiers pose for pictures beside the horse.

The only real conversation between the two sides comes when a Haitian officer walks up to complain about the planned downsizing of the Haitian Army. "I have 22 years in, and what happens to me now?" queries the man, a captain.

One of the members of the Third Platoon mutters, out of earshot, that he should be glad they don't shoot him.

Sunday is holy here. In a country that is 99 percent Christian, God swings a certain amount of weight. The streets fill with women in gleaming white and men in funeral black, all carrying dime-store, dog-eared Bibles. They walk miles to hear the Word in small pastel churches, a remarkably devout people for a place with so many unanswered prayers.

It is an odd sight, this pilgrimage flowing down both sides of the street as Gunn, his eyes hidden behind dark glasses, his finger on the trigger of his machine gun, watches from the turret. It is late afternoon and the Third Platoon is on its way up the mountain to take a short siesta. The neighborhood they choose is a pro-Aristide area of middle-class and lower-class-houses, where persecution has been heavy.

A thin, slight man with a camera around his neck walks timidly to the soldiers and asks if he can show them some photographs. The man's name is Greg St. Cyr and for three years he has documented atrocities in this neighborhood, hoping that someday the people who committed them will be brought to justice. The stack of photos is two inches thick. The soldiers flip through them, then go sit quietly, some alone. No one looks at anyone else.

The photos show gunshot wounds to the head, horrid mutilations and bodies, some alive, that have been hacked and burned. One is a young, beautiful woman, her breasts and shoulders crisscrossed with machete slashes. "Fraph," says St. Cyr. "I wish you could have come sooner."

A few feet away, Private Harris is staring at the tops of his boots. "I knew they killed people," he mutters, "but I didn't know they done that." He looks disgusted, like he needs to hit someone. "I never seen nothing like that. How can you do that?"

Brady does not say anything. He just stares out into the trees.

Later, as the Humvees crawl slowly back down the hill, a little boy chases them for a mile. He shouts, "Hooray."

Living in Another World

St. Petersburg Times, June 16, 1991

DATELINE: Miami

Overhead, the cars glide by on the way to places better, cleaner, safer. Down here, in the shadows of Shantytown, roam the ones who have been left behind.

Ed Washington lives in a refrigerator box under the interstate with an emaciated black cat named Two-Lane. He sleeps with a kitchen knife in his blankets because he had a dream once that someone killed him and no one noticed.

"The only reason it ain't happened is the right fool just ain't come along," he says. "Things happen here. Things you wouldn't believe."

Around him, the dirt floor is dotted with mattresses. A skeletal man stares up at the concrete ceiling with eyes as still as marbles. AIDS is Shantytown's final indignity.

Men in drag beckon from the corners. One raggedy man giggles, then covers his head with a sheet. Everybody begs, for a dollar, a dime, a little attention.

Washington's friend, Rollo Williams, squats in a square of dust Washington calls his patio. "Ain't you afraid that black cat will be bad luck?" he asks.

Washington looks around him, at his cardboard condominium, at his neighborhood.

Both men start to laugh.

Shantytown is a society all its own, a homeless colony of makeshift huts and mattresses shielded from heat and rain by the Interstate 395 overpass to Miami Beach. To the city commission's discomfort, it is one block from scenic Biscayne Boulevard and Miami's No. 1 tourist attraction, the Bayside marketplace.

When tourists get off the interstate to shop, go on a cruise or stay at a downtown hotel, Shantytown's castoff humanity is the first thing they see.

They see Jandra Johnson, who will do anything for a ride in their car; and Richard Walbridge, who fought in Vietnam and wakes up screaming; and Wheelchair Man, who blocks traffic until somebody puts a quarter in his cup; and the one they call the Invisible Man, because even when you look right at him, he says he isn't there.

There are about 100, just a few of the city's 5,000 homeless. But these are not just people unable or unwilling to rejoin the outside world. They have formed an alternative, a subculture with its own loosely enforced code of morality and punishment.

The city would move them if it could, but the federal courts have made it illegal to evict the homeless or destroy their property, a tentative victory for Shantytown.

Its residents greet tourists at stoplights, peer into the startled faces behind the glass and say: "Welcome to Miami. Can you spare some change?"

Sometimes they smash the windows, if they need a lot of money for crack cocaine. The crackheads are looked down on by other homeless, giving this place one more element of a true society: Its own class system.

To some people on the outside, everyone here is less than human. In April, a group of men in a van pulled up to Shantytown and beat to death a homeless man, apparently for sport. No one has been arrested.

In this society, Washington is a wealthy man. He has a good box, an AAA magazine with tips on traveling on a budget, and Two-Lane.

Ask him what his most prized possession is and he pulls out a faded birth certificate. It shows he had a mother, a father, an address.

"I keep it with me," he said, "so I don't forget who I am."

"The strangest thing I ever seen was this dude in this brown station wagon, who pulls up and just starts handing out money, folding money. He gave you more if you was pregnant and more if you was crippled. It wasn't long before all the people here was walking around limping."—Rollo Williams

Pinto Green has a long, wicked knife scar on the side of his face, the kind of face children run from in nightmares.

He has lived under the interstate for three months, begging. He has been called a bum, a ne'er-do-well, a dope fiend and once an old woman called him a vermin. "That's a rat? I knew it was something bad," he said.

Now Pinto has new names. He is an obstacle, a social stumbling block, an impediment. He is in the way of Miami's development as a true international city.

Or, as Miami Mayor Xavier Suarez put it, the homeless are "the single remaining issue keeping Miami from being truly a city everybody looks up to around the country as an exciting doggone place."

But this Great Embarrassment is entrenched in its four-block span of I-395. Word has spread over the homeless grapevine: The cops can't touch you here. Phillip Brown heard about it in Philadelphia, where he spent time in drunk tanks.

It started in December 1988, when the American Civil Liberties Union filed a class-action suit to stop Miami police from maliciously arresting street people and burning their property.

Two years later, when Miami police burned belongings of the homeless, a federal judge told them to stop. His order was ignored. On Feb. 11 of this year, police destroyed a camp in two downtown parks. Two weeks later, they forced 200 homeless people out of the parks.

The homeless settled in the cool darkness under the interstate. The next day, Florida Department of Transportation (DOT) workers ran them off and burned their belongings. The DOT called it routine enforcement of right of way.

The homeless came back. Police and DOT tried again to evict them.

"I wonder," said Rollo Williams, "how many of those guys realize they're just a few paychecks ahead of being here in my world."

On March 18, the judge held the city in contempt.

Shantytown had a legal right to exist.

"People see things on the side of the road they don't like, and they call us," said Miami police Sgt. David Rivero. "But we can't do anything."

"My woman had a baby here last week. The prettiest thing you ever saw . . . but I don't know about keeping it. Not here. If I had a place I would. All I got is a box. But it is a pretty baby."—Rollo Williams

Everyone had a home. No one was born here. Some drank, snorted or smoked their way here. Some were just one paycheck short of rent.

It's what people talk about when the daylight fades. They gather around a candle, because no one likes to talk to the dark, and tell stories about homes and families. Almost everyone has a relative who would take them in, but while it's fine to beg strangers for nickels, it's hard to beg someone you know.

"And deep in your guts you're a little afraid," said William Phillip Burden, who has been homeless a long time. "Because you become satisfied having just this much."

In a world where an address is a finger pointing to the last direction a man was seen walking, Shantytown is permanent. People build living rooms out of circled shopping carts. They do their cooking on barbecue grills or tap into electric lines to power hot plates and even televisions.

They get their water from a sprinkler system, and someone modified one sprinkler into a shower. Privacy is a problem.

"Hell, this ain't the Marriott," Pinto Green said.

A grassy area nearby, the designated toilet, has a powerful stench. The homeless wait and watch for signs of disease, which is bound to come.

A downtown shelter feeds them, gives them old clothes. The odd thing, in a place where people beg, is that everyone is wearing new shoes.

"These people from the church come by now and then and take our shoe size, and we get new shoes," said Chelly Bulnes, who lives here with her husband, Salvadore. "That's nice. Isn't that nice?"

Some have been here so long they have five or six pair.

"When our parents were maids and servants here in Miami, they were working to put us through school, planning on us someday getting good jobs and running businesses. But when the refugee influx came, there were Cubans who were just as well educated as us but much more experienced. They already knew how to run a business . . . and they were the right color. Now we live under the bridge."—William Phillip Burden

The Marielitos lived here first, 10 years before it was Shantytown. When Fidel Castro flooded Miami under 125,000 refugees almost overnight, many were housed under the same bridge Burden calls home.

"Man, they gave 'em food and clean clothes. . . . They even gave 'em money," said Burden, who worked at a bank, lost his job and his home and now says he is addicted to crack. "They brought it to their *bedside.*"

Burden is so mad he shakes. In 10 years, he has seen Cubans go from the Mariel Boatlift to camps under the interstate to the dominant culture. Now they are embarrassed to have Miami's homeless in the place they left behind, he said.

There are Hispanics in Shantytown, but only two or three at any given time. Most of the faces are black.

Burden believes the city owes him something, if it's only an unmolested patch of dirt. "Because I was already here," he says. "We were here."

"There was this one guy got cut real bad one time, and this copy comes up. He looks at the guy and says, 'Look, if you die here it's my problem.' So the guy walks on down the road. We never did see that guy again."—Ed Washington

The law, at least the law enforced by Miami police, does not apply here. "They have their own," said Sgt. Rivero.

Prostitution is accepted. There is no sex act imaginable $10 won't buy.

Jandra Johnson says she has been homeless a year, that she sells her body for crack, that she doesn't worry or wonder or hope much anymore. She drops her price to pocket change if she has to, to make a sale.

Sometimes she does it for change and a ride in the car.

"Do I worry about the future?" she says. "Honey, nobody worries about the future down here. We're here because nobody bothers us much anymore, 'cause we know that long as we don't do nothing to nobody but each other, they'll let us alone."

Shantytown, like any town, has its bad neighborhoods. The good neighborhoods are paved and close to well-lit Biscayne Boulevard. The bad neighborhoods are deeper into the city, darker, more private. The floor is powdery gray dust, like old graveyard dirt.

"Normal people don't go in there. They may pull up to the fence and throw out some things, clothes and food and stuff," said Cheryl Thomas, who lives with her husband, Ben, in the bad neighborhood.

But even here, there are rules.

- Don't touch anybody else's stuff. If someone takes your stuff, you can beat them. A friend can help.
- Don't touch anybody's mate. If someone touches your mate, you can beat them.
- Don't do anything to bring in The Man or soon He will run the place.

They have their own police. The people form co-ops, cells of five or six who leave someone behind to watch their stuff. Sometimes they select sheriffs to patrol a bigger part of camp.

But at night, no one is really safe. The crackheads will crawl in a box and beat the person inside to death, for pennies. "It happens," Washington said.

There is no real leader here, although Williams is head of the financial district. He collects clothes, sells them to other homeless people. The fact the clothes were donated by a charity does not enter into his thinking.

That is an outside law.

Arguments are settled in a secluded corner of the camp.

"They just call it Thunderdome," Williams said. "Two men enter, one man leaves."

"Man, I don't think you can say that we're lost. I think we're just sort of misplaced."—William Phillip Burden

The Invisible Man materialized for a few seconds last week, then vanished again inside his own mind.

He is about 50, with gray hair and beard, harmless looking. He stares at the ground a lot. People don't talk to him because when they do, he is prone to blurt out: "I'm not here" and walk away.

One day last week he sat in a chair near his blankets, slowly straightening a tangle of wire.

"I'm just messing with this wire," he said. "I'm not here."

He tuned out Shantytown and the planet. Talking to him when he is invisible is like conversing with a fire hydrant.

It would be unusual behavior in the real world, but not Shantytown. Most of them are invisible one way or another. People see only the dirt, the intruding presence on their parks and rights of way.

Some deny their classification as homeless altogether, because it embarrasses them.

Alex Wright is a tall, thin Californian, cool as the other side of your pillow. He has a begonia in a ceramic pot and some kind of fern.

His bed, on a well-swept square of asphalt, is immaculately made. He says he is a professional musician, says he can whup the blues on the guitar so hot it makes the strings stand up to testify. The pawn shop man holds his music ransom for $120.

He said he played for Carlos Santana once, in San Francisco. "That's what I am, man. I'm a musician, an artist. I'm not homeless. I'm just here until I get my guitar."

"I'm not homeless. I'm just camping out."

Some chafe under it, letting it skin away a little more of their pride every day.

Every morning at 5 A.M., Vietnam veteran Richard Walbridge gets up from his mattress and walks to the labor pool, where business owners select people for odd jobs. He stays until 4 P.M., then walks back.

"But at least I try," Walbridge says. "By God I try, not like these other lazy sons of bitches here."

He likes to keep moving, never naps in the daytime. He dreads sleep the way some people dread dying, because it takes him back to Vietnam. The people who sleep close to him say he screams all night, warning people with names they don't know to duck.

Some embrace it, like windshield-washer Ozzie Hill.

He makes as much as $50 a day from weak-willed tourists who can't tell him no when he jumps in front of their cars and covers their windshields in blue Windex. He wears Porsche sunglasses.

And some just flow with it, like Ed Washington.

He works the groves when the oranges don't freeze, works the labor pool to get cigarette money. A half pack of Winstons is a fine day.

He is asked what he does when the dirt and despair get to be too much, when it seems like he really might die here someday in a box marked THIS END UP. He thinks a minute, hard.

Then: "I go to Fort Lauderdale."

Where a Child on the Stoop Can Strike Fear

New York Times, December 2, 1994

DATELINE: New Orleans

Once, before the children had guns, she could send them running from her stoop as if her voice were thunder and her accusing finger were lightning. Louise Layton and other old women in the St. Thomas housing project held power and respect, keeping watch on the courtyard from their high windows and rusted screen doors.

"I remember when we had flowers in St. Thomas," Mrs. Layton said recently. "You can't go out now to tend flowers. I'm afraid. I'm afraid of the young ones."

Mrs. Layton, who is nearing 90, said things started to change in the mid-1980's. Now the windows the women watched from are punctured with bullet holes and patched with cardboard. The young people they watched over now frighten them so much that they refuse to go outside even in daylight, and at night the gunfire flashes like fireflies through this barren, crumbling place.

In New Orleans, where violence by young people has grown so severe that the police have ordered a dusk-to-dawn curfew for juveniles, the epicenter of that fear is the impoverished public housing projects. Here, boys of 14 shoot grown men in drug deals gone bad, children of 11 tote guns too big for their hands, and old people and mothers with small children sleep under beds, because big children fire guns indiscriminately just to hear them go "bang."

The most recent trend among the young criminals is to pre-pay their own funerals, because they do not expect to live past 16.

There has always been violence in New Orleans, where the underclass lives within pistol-shot of opulence, of Greek revival architecture and 300-year-old oaks in the Garden District. New Orleans's homicide rate was the highest of any city in the country in 1993, and billboards with the words "Thou Shalt Not Kill" plead for the violence to end.

But there is a sense of sanity to the crimes of adults, say the people who live in the deadliest neighborhoods, the projects like St. Thomas, Desire, Florida and Cooper. The childlike criminals chill them.

"I want to run out in the yard and say to the kids: 'Stop it. If y'all can't play without killing each other, then just go home,'" said Ethel Noel, a 29-year-old mother. But instead she just closes her door and tells her 5-year-old daughter to lie with her on the floor.

It has become a cliché to say an inner-city American neighborhood is held prisoner by its crime. In wealthy neighborhoods in New Orleans, people hire security guards to follow them home from work and check the closets before the owners step inside the house.

In the projects, violence is not something that reaches for residents, but something that lives among them, in size 5 sneakers.

There is something almost sociopathic about the young criminals here. "Children with adult faces," said the Rev. Marshall Truehill, who was born in a New Orleans housing project, earned a Ph.D. in urban studies and has worked most of his life in the inner city as a teacher and social worker. "Children who only feel secure with a big wad of money in their pockets, who don't care how they get it. Children who have a complete depletion of moral values. This is not white phobia. This is real."

It is why Mrs. Layton, who used to love to go to church and sing "I'll Fly Away," now gets her preaching on the television, from a man with perfect hair who needs a donation to send her to Glory.

It is why maids who work in $150-a-night hotels on St. Charles Avenue and live in the projects hurry to catch the clattering old streetcar home at dusk, because waiting even a minute for the next car may mean they will have to walk the courtyard after dark.

It is why the two tiny bicycles in Ramona Boyd's house still gleam a year after she bought them. Mrs. Boyd, who lost one 4-year-old boy to a stray bullet, will not allow her other two children, a 6-year-old and a 4-year-old, to ride the bikes outside, because so many young people lurking there are armed.

It is why Diana Mason's days drag past in a haze of grief over a son, Nicholas, who is charged with murdering a man who, the police said, came to the projects to buy drugs. In the last year, Nicholas has also been charged with two assaults, two armed robberies, attempted murder, gun possession and more, 14 crimes in all, one for every year of his life.

And it is why, when the leader of a Christian missionary group asked a group of children in the Cooper housing project to name some things they worry about, a 7-year-old girl raised her hand and said, "Dying." After the class, the children ran screaming from the playground when the sound of a machine-gun ripped through the air. It was 11:57 A.M.

In 1993, 31 of New Orleans's 389 murders were committed by people under the age of 17, according to Police Department statistics. So far this year, 18 murders had been committed by people under 17 out of a citywide total of 391. The police who patrol the projects say the curfew is what has kept the 1994 homicide figures down among juveniles.

About one-third of all New Orleans's killings come inside the projects. Here, about 1 in 5 killers is a juvenile. In 1993, the youngest was 11.

"It's them 13- and 14-year-olds you really got to watch out for," Mrs. Layton said.

The residents of the projects say they think things will get better. They see an advocate in the new Mayor, Marc Morial, who calls the violence among the young a crisis. For years, people here felt that City Hall saw them, the poorest of the poor, as expendable, as if their lives did not count as much.

The Police Department is opening substations inside some projects. Black officers in the New Orleans Police Department, while admitting that officers are a little afraid of the projects, say it had to be done.

"I remember when I chased these two juveniles up three flights of stairs, but I got them," said one officer, eating pork chops over red beans and rice in Eddie's restaurant on Law Street.

"You should have," said his partner. "They were 7 years old."

THE SHUT-INS: FEAR IMPRISONS PROJECT RESIDENTS

St. Charles Avenue is a banquet for the eyes.

On almost every block are the towering, dazzling old homes with fat columns and broad porches, surrounded by a perfume of flowers and old money. Sandwiched between those mansions are the smaller but still beautiful homes, dressed in a lace of wrought iron. The people of New Orleans call it, "The Avenue," and Mrs. Layton loved to ride the streetcar along its median and dream.

"I haven't been on that streetcar in five years," she said. She is afraid to walk through her project. She has lived in St. Thomas for 30 years, just a few blocks off the grandeur of St. Charles. If St. Thomas has a historian, it is she.

Unlike so many of her neighbors who have been shot, assaulted, robbed, raped and threatened by the juveniles who live among them, she has been spared. It is her fear of violence, not a memory of it, that imprisons her.

"That shooting, Lord, it's all around you," she said. "You can't rest at night, and now there's shots during the day. I hear it and I just say, 'Our Father, who art in heaven, hallowed be thy name. . . .'"

In the 1980's, when crack spread through inner-city New Orleans like cholera, older teen-agers and grown men snatched purses and broke into the homes of their own neighbors to feed their addiction. But life still seemed to mean something, Mrs. Layton said. Now the children treat their guns like toys, she said, as if the person they shoot down will get up, as in a cartoon, and say "Ouch!"

"I'm old and crippled now," said Mrs. Layton, who has arthritis, "and I can't get out of their way. It's drugs, some say, that's made the children so terrible. Some say it's because the mommas had them too young, and didn't raise them right. Some say it's just because they're poor, and don't have any hope."

Like those of other elderly women in the project, her life is contained by the walls of her little apartment. There are dust-covered beads from a Mardi Gras years ago, pictures of children she has not seen in years. She did not attend the funeral of her best friend. "I don't even go out to make my groceries," she said.

Her only son is in prison. A Roman Catholic nun brings her groceries. One day is pretty much like another inside. She does not read much but always holds an old, dog-eared prayer book because she likes the way it feels. She still keeps vigil, sometimes, from the window, but it is a silent one.

She was born in Maynard, La., to sharecroppers and cut sugar cane as a child. When she was in her teens, her Aunt Tea brought her to New Orleans, to "work for the white ladies," as a maid in the nice houses uptown. In all those years of hard work, she thought she earned, if nothing else, some peace in her old age. To hide from the children hurts her pride. She would leave if she could.

"It's a shame when the grown people have to hide," she said. "But when you're poor, you got to act like you're poor."

Like other subsidized housing in New Orleans, this is far from a welfare community. At dusk, the women in their maid's uniforms and men in mechanic's coveralls filter in through the half-light and disappear into tiny rooms where, if the electricity, water and heat all work at the same time, it is a tiny miracle.

The projects are mostly two- and three-story brick, featureless buildings in long rows, like warehouses. In some of the projects, whole blocks are too far gone for human habitation, and the buildings sit vacant and dark, home only to rats and palmetto bugs and crack users.

But it is still a neighborhood, if a wasted one. Mrs. Layton used to like to sit outside and pass the time with the neighbors, but more and more the older residents go straight home and lock their doors.

She has a picture of a streetcar on her wall. It is a trolley in San Francisco, not the one in New Orleans. Still, she likes to look at it.

THE TURNAROUND: WHEN A GOOD BOY GOES BAD
The manifestation of Louise Layton's fears is a 14-year-old boy who used to ride his bicycle down Apple Street, till the New Orleans police charged him with shooting a man in the head.

The boy, Nicholas Mason, is in a juvenile detention center, charged with murder and 13 other crimes, most of them violent. The police said he killed 32-year-old Michael Barngrover just outside a housing project on Phalia Street on Oct. 28 in what appeared to be a botched drug deal.

The killing was the culmination of one of their most puzzling juvenile crime sprees so far. In one year, said a police officer, Nicholas went from being a normal junior high school student to being a cold-blooded killer. He robbed people at gunpoint and shot at others and missed, the officer said. When the police came to arrest him, he fled in a stolen car.

"He was a sweet little boy," said his mother, Diana Mason. "For 13 years he didn't cause me any trouble. He was my baby."

She talks about him in the past tense, because she knows the boy she had is lost to her for a long time, if not forever. She has already lost one son this year to the violence of New Orleans.

Mrs. Mason said Nicolas's best friend was his older brother, Troy, in his 20's. He was shot dead in a housing project in March. His killer has not been arrested.

"After that happened," she said, "was when Nicholas went bad."

Clifford Hubbard, who went to the aid of a woman as Nicholas stole her car, will always remember the look in the boy's face when he shoved his gun in Mr. Hubbard's face.

"There was evil in that boy's eyes," Mr. Hubbard said. "I hope they don't let him out anytime soon."

When Nicholas pointed the gun at Mr. Hubbard, he put his arm around the woman and they fled.

Nicholas's mother does not believe her son is evil. She just believes he gave up.

He spent most of his life in the projects. "I moved us out, a while back, to get out from the meanness. But my sons kept going back."

Her sons, she believes, did what they thought they had to do to survive. They got guns. They took their place in a culture of violence "'cause it's too hard to be good," she said. "They know they ain't gonna get no decent job and no good life."

She has a daughter, 17, but her house seems empty to her now. "It's always too quiet here," she said. "Sometimes it gets so quiet I start to cry."

There is a recent family photograph on the wall. It shows a round-faced smiling Nicholas and his young-looking, pretty mother.

Now Mrs. Mason, in her 40's, looks half in shock, used up. An out-of-work nurse's assistant, she struggles every day to find a reason to take off her housecoat.

"Sometimes my daughter asks me if I'm going to cook dinner," she said, "and I say, 'Why?'"

THE MESSAGE: NO PROTECTION IN GOD'S WORDS
Every Saturday at 10 A.M., a missionary group takes children in the Cooper apartments into the project meeting room, to teach them

songs and let them play games and slip in a little prayer. The oldest are 8 and 9, the youngest 3. The missionaries tell the children that God loves them and is watching over them, that they should not live in fear and should never give up hope.

When the missionary, a young white woman from the suburbs, asks what they worry about, one child says, "Eating."

The missionary says God will provide.

Another little girl says, "Dying."

The missionary says God will shield them.

Then everyone sings a song.

The missionaries are barely out of the parking lot when the sound of an automatic weapon booms through the dusty courtyard. The children, who had gone outside to play, scramble for their homes to hide under beds and inside bathtubs, the way their parents taught them. They say it happens every day.

"There's been shooting here ever since I was born," said 7-year-old T. Darryl Cabalier. "It's the big kids. We run from the big kids."

Another little boy says his cousin was killed and his sister was raped by boys still in high school. Another says his mother found three pistols in his older brother's room. "She threw them away," said the boy, 9. "She was mad."

Earlier that morning, when four little boys were asked what they would do if another child pulled a real gun, they answered immediately.

"Duck," said one.

"Duck," said the second.

"Duck," said the third.

"Go to the hospital," said the fourth.

"They have such fear for their lives, that they eventually get real guns of their own because they think they have to protect themselves," said Barbara Martin, who lives in the St. Thomas project and works with a support group for the mothers of homicide victims. "They don't expect to live past childhood, many of them. It's children killing children."

And, because they are children, they act rashly. The shoot without aiming. They shoot without thinking.

"I got a letter from this one little girl," Mrs. Martin said. "She said her goal in life was to live to graduate high school."

Outside, in the Cooper project playground, a showdown is coming.

A little boy named Antonio Jackson and another named Cedric have toy pistols in their pockets. It is really just one, but they broke it into two pieces so both could have one. They chase each other around the yard, shooting with the unlimited ammunition of their imagination. No one dies for more than a few seconds.

The Story of Dirty Red

St. Petersburg Times, September 1, 1991

DATELINE: Fort Lauderdale

The neighborhood has low rent and no trees, a leaky bucket of a place where dreams seem to run right on through. Dirty Red's mother pries the boy's fingers from the hem of her dress and tells him a hundredth time: "Baby, it's okay to play."

Dirty Red knows if he goes outside children will call him names and punch and pinch him, like the day before and the day before that.

To please his mother he walks outside, but instead of going to play he doubles back up the stairs and sits just outside the closed door.

Dirty Red can't face the neighborhood, not today. He curls up in a ball on the concrete steps and sticks a thumb in his mouth. People step over him like litter.

"They don't like me," he said.

It started May 20, 1990, when the police car came and took Red away for a crime he didn't do. It was just another dirty sex crime, but this time the suspect was reaching for his momma as they took him away. This time, the arrest left an empty desk at Peters Elementary kindergarten class.

The deputy said Red had poked a little girl between the legs with a stick, hurting her. Red shook his head, NO. Then the deputy took him to the car and locked him in. All his momma could see as they drove away was the top of his head.

James Montgomery Dicks Jr., who everyone called Dirty Red, was accused of sexually assaulting the 7-year-old girl. He didn't know, as his feet dangled over the floor mat, that it was either the beginning or the end of everything.

It was the end of the 6-year-old boy who turned his momma's dish towel into a turban, who had friends on every corner of the housing project, who traveled from his front door to the playground unhindered by anything, not even his shoes.

It was the beginning of a year of contempt and confusion, of mothers who snatched their little girls away when they walked close to him, of big boys who beat him and called him a pervert, of whispers and stares and cruelties without end.

The fact that it was all a mistake, that the Broward County Sheriff's Department arrested the wrong person on evidence no stronger than a smattering of lies, never registered in Red's neighborhood. He was tried by rumor, found guilty by gossip, and sentenced to suffer.

He surrendered to it. He became a recluse, who clutched his mother like a drowning man, who ran screaming from strangers and did not go outside unless his mother forced him. Now, more than a year later, he still has not emerged from his shell. He is still an outcast, still treated like dirt.

"You see Dirty Red now," said 13-year-old Juliette Logan, "you see him by himself."

His momma, Mary Dicks, doesn't know who to blame. Maybe the deputies who took him away and never made an effort to clear his name. Or maybe the State Attorney's Office, which decided not to formally charge her son — but never bothered to tell her.

No one — not sheriff's deputies, not prosecutors — ever said they were sorry.

It was more than a month after her son's arrest that she discovered the charges were dropped. She received a summons to testify against a man named Troy Mosely, the boyfriend of the little girl's mother, the man who would go to prison for the crime. He was charged one day after Dirty Red, one day too late to save Red from the character-crushing lies of the rumor mill.

She knows how she feels about her neighbors, a sick feeling of rage that begins like ice in her stomach, then telegraphs up her spine to squeeze the hot tears from her eyes.

"We started calling James 'Dirty Red' way back when he was a baby, because he couldn't go three minutes after I gave him a bath without gettin' dirty all over again," she said. "When he was a baby his skin had a red tinge to it so we all just called him Dirty Red . . . It wasn't meant to be nothin' dirty."

The neighborhood children have turned his nickname into a needle to jab him with. Dirty Red's teachers say he is a little slow, but he is normal. He is at a critical stage in his development, where everything that happens to him will be carried like baggage into the rest of his life.

One day last week, a girl of about 5 saw him walking down the sidewalk and started to chant: "Dirty Red, Dirty Red, Dirty Red." Two girls with her moved over to the edge of sidewalk so they wouldn't have to walk close to him. One of them said her momma told her to.

"He Dirty Red," said the little girl. "Momma say he bad."

LONG WAY FROM THE BEACH

The apartments at Driftwood Terrace are the same, the same rust-red color, the same telltale signs of sorry luck and too much damning history. But this is not a slum, not a place where the poverty spills out into the streets for everyone to see.

It has rules and fences to keep it as clean and characterless as the inside of a Clorox jug.

No one can walk on the grass. No one is allowed to put out a chair to visit with neighbors, or to catch the evening breeze. A guard keeps a list of people who visit. Overnight guests have to pay $25 a night. Tenants say it takes what little fun there is out of being poor, the difference between a real community and a warehouse for strangers.

Dirty Red's life has been here, on a treadmill of tiny steps from a small apartment to school to playground and back again. His momma used to say he was the apartment mascot, because she brought him home to this.

Mary Dicks is a mother of six, separated from her husband and living on a government check. It's because of who she is, she believes, that the Broward County legal system felt it could arrest her son with no real evidence, then discard him.

It is beyond her imagination that this would have happened to anyone with more money, more influence. The apartments and small homes of northwest Fort Lauderdale are a long way from the beach.

Sheriff's deputies and prosecutors said it's not their job to tell someone when a charge is dropped, or apologize if a mistake is made.

That makes Mary Dicks laugh. "If this had been a rich white family, do you think this would have happened?" she said.

"Do you think they wouldn't have fallen all over themselves saying they were sorry?"

Sheriff's spokesman George Crolius said his department does not operate under a double standard, of color or income.

"We felt we acted entirely appropriately," he said. "We brought the true suspect to justice in a short period of time, and we don't feel we have anything to apologize for."

Broward Detective Carol Dansky visited Mary Dicks two days after Dirty Red was arrested, to tell her about Mosely's arrest. But she did not say if Red's case was dropped. Mary Dicks asked: "What happens now?"

Crolius said Dansky couldn't answer that question, because it's not her decision whether to drop a case or pursue it. That left Mary Dicks still wondering.

Assistant State Attorney Sherry Haagenson said detectives never presented the case to her, so there was never a formal charge against Dirty Red. But again, no one told Mrs. Dicks that her son had been cleared of the crime. Haagenson refused to say anything else about the case.

The boy's name doesn't exist in the office's computer. Technically, it never happened.

Susan Aramony, assistant state attorney in charge of the juvenile division, called Red: "A victim of the system."

Mrs. Dicks said she is tired of people telling her what a damn shame it is, that it's just the way things happen sometimes.

"They told me my boy fell through the cracks," she said. "I wanted somebody to write a letter, maybe, to the people who live here. I wanted somebody to tell them my boy is all right. But nobody has done it, maybe because they just don't care about him."

Mrs. Dicks is not an educated woman, and doesn't know anything about the law. She never got a lawyer because the case was not prosecuted.

"The whole thing was resolved in a little more than 24 hours," Crolius said. "We assumed everybody knew why he (Mosely) had been taken to jail."

The weeks dragged by. Every few days Dirty Red asked his momma if he was going to prison, if they had prisons for little boys, and withdrew a little deeper.

The legal system may have started it, but it would be the community that would never let Dirty Red forget.

Geneva Logan, who lives two doors down from the Dicks, said people in the neighborhood never heard about Mosely's arrest but talked about Red's arrest for days. She says they never heard he was cleared and that most of them still think Dirty Red committed the crime, but didn't do time because of his age. They think it's up to them to punish him.

"They might treat the boy different if they know," she said. "But they don't know. . . . No matter what you tell them, they only believe what they saw that night."

A door-to-door visit in the housing project bears that out. People do not remember all the details in the case, but they remember a little girl with a towel wrapped around her, and blood running down her legs. They remember the boy the deputy took away.

"I know the boy," one of them said. "I don't want him nowhere around my babies."

Troy Mosely started it with a lie, trying to save his own skin at the expense of a little boy's whole world.

Mosely was 27, a sometimes salesman for a meat company who spent his days hanging around the housing project. He lived with a woman who had five small children. He told people he was the babysitter. "I raised those children," he said.

The story is told in two police reports, one day apart. In the first, dated May 20, police were called to the housing project after the little girl's mother came home from church to find her daughter bleeding badly from between her legs.

The little girl told her Dirty Red did it with a stick. Her 4-year-old brother and another child said the same thing. The deputy, acting on their word, arrested Dirty Red that night.

Red was fingerprinted and photographed and released into his mother's custody.

"He didn't understand any of that," said his mother. "But he knew he was blamed for doing something bad to that girl, and didn't know why."

The second report, dated May 21, explained how it happened.

Detective Carol Dansky was suspicious of the children's statements. She went to talk to the little girl in the hospital. The girl — safe away from Mosely — told her the truth.

Mosely had caused the bleeding by forcing his finger inside her, tearing the wall of her vagina. He tried to stop the bleeding by putting the girl in a tub of cold water. When that didn't work, he threatened the children and made them make up a story about a little boy he had seen outside the apartment.

"He told me . . . to say Dirty Red stuck a stick up her," the 4-year-old said, according to the report. Mosely also had assaulted two of the 7-year-old girl's sisters.

Mosely picked Dirty Red at random. Mary Dicks wonders if the women who despise her son, who tell their sons not to play with him, know how easily it could have been their child Mosely chose.

Mosely is serving a 10-year sentence for sexual battery at Apalachee Correctional Institution in the Florida Panhandle.

He said he is sorry. He said he never expected people in the neighborhood to respond so viciously. He thought they would forgive Dirty Red, because he is just a child.

"I never meant for the little boy to have so much trouble," he said. "It's bad for a boy to grow up with trouble."

He whispers as he talks on the telephone in the prison dormitory. Inmates do not like child molesters.

THE SIN EATER

Mary Dicks is like a lot of people in Driftwood Terrace: a black Southerner who left small towns for South Florida on the off-chance all that paradise pap was true. They speak with red-clay accents from Georgia and South Carolina and Mississippi.

They know about Sin Eaters here.

In almost every one-dog Southern town there is a Sin Eater, someone who is either dumb or weak or miserable enough to absorb all the petty meanness, all the guilt and shame and blame of a community. It is always someone who can be abused without fighting back.

Dirty Red is the Sin Eater at Driftwood Terrace. If anything happens, a rock thrown, a baby pinched, a dirty handprint on a wall, people here just blame Dirty Red.

"You hear it all the time, 'Dirty Red done it, Dirty Red done it,'" said Juliette Logan, who starts junior high this year. "Most of the time he was a mile away, but people know — especially the little kids — that if they say it was him, their mommas will leave 'em alone."

Worse than the blame is the contempt. This is Dirty Red's life the past six months:

A woman from the project sees him in the local Winn Dixie and starts cussing him, calling him names and screaming for her children as everyone in the store turns their eyes on him. He stands there and lets it wash over him, and starts to shake.

Two boys from the neighborhood trap him outside his apartment. One holds his arms behind his back as another boy tries to put his penis in Red's mouth. Other children told his momma what had happened. Red, ashamed, wanted to just let it pass.

A woman sees him on the sidewalk. She slaps him, because he was there.

He plays at the school playground by himself, because his classmates' parents have told them not to play with him.

A police cruiser rolls into the project on a disturbance call. Dirty Red sees it and runs screaming for his mother, thinking they've come to get him again.

"You see the little boy growing up with all that hurt, and it breaks your heart," said Geneva Logan, who tells her children to treat Dirty Red right. "He knows he ain't done nothing wrong, and these people still treat him the way they do.

"He's got to wonder what's wrong with him. Think about it. What would it be like to grow up believing that nobody likes you?"

One little boy, who said his name is Martin, used to play with Dirty Red. "I can't now," he said.

His momma calls and he runs away. He stops at the door to wave to Dirty Red, who sits on the steps. Dirty Red, his eyes two mirrors of indifference, doesn't wave back.

THE BIG PICTURE

Teachers at Peters Elementary have noticed a difference in Dirty Red from the other children. He has no self-esteem.

To build it back, Principal Linda Springer and guidance counselor Barbara Lazear have put him in special program. They think it's helping.

He is not retarded. He doesn't qualify for special state programs that could help him. A test for learning disabilities showed him to be only a little slow, they said. What is wrong with Dirty Red, he wasn't born with.

He needs more time and more attention. The problem, they agree, is that there are so many children who are so much worse off than him, children in physical danger from their parents, suicidal. Red has problems, but in the hopelessness of the big picture, he is categorized as walking wounded.

His father, James Montgomery, said the solution is to just take the boy out of the project. Mary Dicks said she would if she could, but doesn't have money for a decent place. The only alternative is something worse, a slum without fences and guards to keep children safe from stray bullets.

She has the other children to think of.

He looks fragile for a little boy.

He is about as high as the belt-buckle on a good-sized man. The police report said he weighed 50 pounds. "Maybe if he was holding a sack of 'taters," his momma said.

He sits on the floor in his apartment with his head on his momma's knee. He is not as bad as he was, right after his arrest, when the abuse from Driftwood Terrace's tenants first started.

Then, he never turned loose of his momma, staying in physical contact with her at all time. Things are better now, but his mother is scared to death that this may be as good as it gets.

Before he was arrested, he slept by himself. Now he can sleep only if he's with his momma. She doesn't have the heart to force him to sleep in his own bed.

If she gets up, he follows her like a dog. If she goes to the bathroom, he stands outside the door.

"Finally, we got him to go outside by himself," Mrs. Dicks said. "But that's when the people get him."

If he goes out in public now, he keeps a hand twisted in his momma's dress. If he sits on the porch, he clings to the bars of the stair railing. His intent is plain: No one is taking me away from here again.

"Every time it seems like he's pulling out of it, he just keeps going back inside (himself), over and over and over," said his mother.

"He don't trust too many people any more."

The neighbor, Geneva Logan, said the thing that frightens her most is the way the little boy reacts to police. When he sees them, no one can hold him, not even his momma. He finds a place to hide, and buries his head in his arms.

It is a fact of life in this world that young black men are challenged by police, sometimes just because they are young black men, said Mrs. Logan. She sees a time when an older version of Dirty Red is confronted, and the officer draws his gun.

Dirty Red starts to run.

Secrets

The best stories in the world are of people who reach back into the past, into sometimes dark places, and tell you what they find. Sometimes, they find what they were hoping for. Sometimes, they just prick themselves again on the sharp edges of a past that should have been left sheathed in mystery. And some answers, like in the story of an autistic boy who somehow survived for days lost in a swamp that had killed grown men, we will never have.

Town Secret Is Uncovered in Birth Quest

New York Times, August 23, 1997

DATELINE: McCaysville, Ga.

The day the child was born, to a woman who might have briefly loved her, a small-town doctor in northern Georgia passed her through the back door of his office to a tire maker and his wife from Akron, Ohio, who wanted a baby badly enough to buy one.

She had dark brown hair and emerald eyes, and cost $1,000 on Jan. 15, 1965. The doctor threw in a fake birth certificate that listed the buyers as birth parents, erasing the real mother from the child's past.

They named her Jane, wrapped her in a blanket and drove due north for eight hours, far away from the South, to a place where the winter winds pick up speed on Lake Erie and make people curse the cold.

The man whom Jane Blasio came to know as her father told her all of this, after she had grown up and married, after the death of the woman she called her mother. She had been told when she was 5 years old that she was adopted, but in 1988 she learned that she was purchased in the drowsy little town of McCaysville, Ga., just across the Tennessee line.

She came back to McCaysville in 1989 to search the faces of people in this lovely, picture-postcard mountain town for a woman with emerald eyes. She never found her, but the search for her mother shook loose a secret.

With the aid of a Georgia probate judge who became her friend, she learned that Dr. Thomas Jugarthy Hicks, beloved by the farmers, miners and townspeople he had healed, sold as many as 200 babies from 1951 to 1965, according to county birth records.

"When they handed me out the door, I still had the blood on me" from the delivery, said Mrs. Blasio, who is now 32 and living in a green suburb of North Canton, Ohio. Her adoptive father said he wanted a boy, but the doctor told him it was a girl or nothing. "There won't be any more," Dr. Hicks said at the time.

Her birth is believed one of the last in his black-market business, but just the beginning of an unusual understanding between the aged doctor and many in his loyal town, one that would last until Mrs. Blasio came here for answers.

"This is just too bizarre for real life," said Judge Linda Davis of Fannin County Probate Court, who has risked the ire of people in her county to help Mrs. Blasio in her quest through county birth records. "If I wasn't so personally involved, I'd think they were making it all up."

The doctor, who also performed then-illegal abortions, persuaded young women who came for abortions — many from out of state — to carry their babies to full term, then sold the newborns to people who wanted a baby with no questions asked, the judge said. The Akron couple who bought Mrs. Blasio had already bought one baby from Dr. Hicks, Michelle, for $800 in the fall of 1961.

The doctor kept no known records of the birth mothers, who discreetly vanished.

Mrs. Blasio, a former insurance claims investigator who knows how to follow a trail, has come here five times, drawn by the slim chance she might connect with someone across a lane of Georgia asphalt, or in the I.G.A. grocery, where the parking lot is partly in McCaysville, partly in Copperhill, Tenn.

She does not know if her mother held her, or even saw her face. She wonders if her mother gave her away because she did not want her, or

— and she hopes this is true — that her mother did want her, but had to give her up.

"I used to fantasize about my mother," Mrs. Blasio said. "As a child, I pictured her being a doctor, a writer, an intellectual, a gorgeous woman, of course," she said, smiling. "I thought my mother must have been like Katharine Hepburn."

Her expectations have changed with time. "Now I just want somebody with a good heart, who would like to know a little something about me, about what happened to me."

In McCaysville, it is no scandal. The way some townspeople see it, Dr. Hicks was saving the life of an innocent with each infant he sold on the black market.

In a sense, Mrs. Blasio sees it that way, too.

"The villain is the circumstance" that made a young mother feel she had to abort her baby in secret in the north Georgia mountains, or else give it away because community mores would have branded her forever for having an illegitimate child, Mrs. Blasio said.

Through a confidential registry, Mrs. Blasio and Judge Davis want to try to reunite as many as possible of the now-grown babies with their real mothers, fathers or siblings. DNA testing, impossible a decade ago, can now make the connection, and plug the holes in the past.

Seven mothers have come forward, quietly, and about 50 bought-and-sold "Hicks babies." There have been no positive matches between parents and babies so far, but Judge Davis and Mrs. Blasio believe it is only a matter of time as more possibilities join the pool.

This week, a small group of the Hicks babies gathered in the town of 1,065 to search the streets as Mrs. Blasio had, for a sign of kinship in the faces of the people who live here.

"All those years of looking in the mirror and wondering where I came from, where I got the hair and the eyes, not one moment did I ever have any anger toward her," Mrs. Blasio said. "I will never say anything bad about her. I don't know why it happened. I don't know what it was like to be in her shoes. If she wants to come forward, there are no strings, no blame. I just want to know.

"All my life, I've felt like I didn't belong, like I didn't fit in. To know," she said, "would complete me."

She accepts the possibility that it may never happen. Dr. Hicks died of leukemia in 1972, when he was 83. His secretary, nurse and lawyer are all dead, as is the police chief who investigated the doctor and ultimately charged him, not with selling babies, but with running an abortion clinic.

A DOCTOR REVERED BY TOWNSFOLK

The trails all seemed cold until Judge Davis, a tiny woman who once threw a man in jail for missing an appointment, searched the county's birth records and grew puzzled at the number of women who had come from as far as Ohio and Arizona to have their babies at the clinic of a country doctor.

His respectability, 25 years after his death, still has a sheen to it. People buff it all the time, with their selective memories.

"He saved my life," said Herb Hood, 69, who had pneumonia when he was a boy. Dr. Hicks nursed him back to health. "He made house calls. I don't care where you lived, day or night.

"Over all, he done more good than otherwise."

Dr. Hicks was viewed as a caring aristocrat, a member of the Adams Bible Class of the First Baptist Church and the Copperhill Kiwanis. He had a large house in town and a nice farm, and he gave medicine away sometimes, from a black leather bag.

Everywhere, in this little pocket of the world, are testimonials to him.

One man points to a hand as he shakes with a stranger and tells how that hand would not be there if Dr. Hicks had not operated on it, for free. In the Fannin Inn restaurant, a waitress praises his kindness to children.

"He gave the most terrific Halloween candy," said Tina Golden, the waitress and a former neighbor.

This town seems to have either collectively turned its head from the other legacies left by the doctor, or interprets them not as shameful things, but kindnesses.

It was known as far away as Atlanta and Chattanooga that if a boy got his girlfriend pregnant, Dr. Hicks could fix it quietly, Judge Davis said.

"Back then, it was a horrible disgrace," said Doralese Tipton, who is in her 60s now, and knew a boy who would bring girls up from the University of Alabama when they got pregnant. But it was only a disgrace, the people here say, if anyone knew. Dr. Hicks charged $100 for the abortion, but what is the price tag on respectability?

People even flew in, to a red-dirt airstrip, for abortions. In the town, people said it was better than seeing young girls butchered in filthy, back-room abortions. At least one prominent young woman died in that way. At least Dr. Hicks was a professional, who sent his patients away alive.

People knew. But they also knew he gave a piano to the Baptist church.

"It was always a little secret thing," said Ms. Golden, that everyone knew.

But it was only one of the doctor's sidelines. Sometimes, with poor girls from the Tennessee mountains and with big-city girls from Atlanta, he persuaded them to carry the child to term, to give it up for what he called adoption.

No one knows if he paid them, but at least once, he asked the buyers to give the mother a new suit of clothes.

FOR WORKING FAMILIES, AN AFFORDABLE ADOPTION

Word spread. Even as far away as the rubberworkers union hall in Akron, men with lunchboxes talked about how a childless couple could, for $1,000 tops, buy themselves a baby, a child without strings. There was no paperwork, no lawyer, no child welfare agency to peek over their shoulders. They plunked down their money and got a baby, and a birth certificate that was genuine, except for the lies.

But it gave the child their last name, and one by one, they came for them. Birth records show that 49 babies were born in Fannin County to parents in Summit County, Ohio, alone. They also came from Pennsylvania, Illinois, Michigan.

Most of them, Judge Davis believes, were not rich, but working people.

For reasons no one is quite certain of, the doctor demanded that the women who bought the babies go through an odd charade.

When Mrs. Blasio's adoptive parents, James and Joan Walters, went to McCaysville to buy their first baby in 1961, Dr. Hicks told Mrs. Walters to put on a hospital gown and lie down in a bed in his clinic. Then, he handed her a baby girl.

Her husband walked in to see her nursing the baby from a bottle.

The birth mothers were believed to have never met the people who bought their babies.

"It was much better for the birth mothers to do this than to have an abortion," Judge Davis said. The townspeople agreed.

"It was the simple way" to save the baby and make sure it wound up in the arms of a loving parent, said Mr. Hood, who owns a restaurant.

But Dr. Hicks would see his practice come to an end in 1964, when charges were finally brought against him for performing illegal abortions. The court papers made no mention of the black-market babies.

He sold at least one more child. Mr. and Mrs. Walters made the drive down in January 1965. This time there was no play-acting. He handed an infant through the door.

The date was the 15th. When Mrs. Walters got home, she knitted a pillow for her baby Jane with her birth date. But when the child's birth certificate arrived, it showed the birthday as Dec. 6, 1964.

Mrs. Walters hid the pillow in the attic.

Neither Mrs. Blasio nor Judge Davis wants to cause harm to the doctor's legacy. They only want to give the Hicks babies an opportunity to find their parents, if they can, and if the parents want to be found.

"I would be able to stop wondering," Mrs. Blasio said. "I don't want anything from her. No strings."

She just wants to look in a stranger's face, and find herself.

Woman, Sold as Infant in '65, Grasps at Clues to Her Roots

New York Times, December 22, 1997

DATELINE: McCaysville, Ga.

Not even the red clay can keep a secret if memory is stronger than time.

Jane Blasio, sold as a newborn for $1,000 in a black market baby ring 32 years ago, had long feared that the search for her mother would end in the hush of a hilltop cemetery here on the Tennessee-Georgia line. Then, it would be too late to ask her mother why she gave her away, and whether she was ever sorry that she did.

"I was hoping for a fairy tale," said Mrs. Blasio, whose decade-long search for her mother pried the lid off a small-town doctor's lucrative baby-selling operation and laid bare the town's long-held secret. Now she has found the woman she believes to be the one, in the cemetery clay.

Yet even at this seeming dead end, there were footprints, impressions left by a dead woman who had lived a hard, often desperate life but who endeared herself to so many people that she was unforgettable. That trail, through the memories of the woman's family and friends, seems to have led Mrs. Blasio to the answers she craved.

Her name was Kitty Self, the oldest of nine children in a dirt poor family, and she was barely 15 in the winter of 1965 when she gave birth to a girl in this tiny copper-mining town in the mountains of northern Georgia. She gave her baby to the town doctor who delivered it, as many desperate young women did then, not so much because of scandal but because keeping it meant one more mouth to feed.

About that time, the doctor sold a baby, the baby Jane, to a couple from Akron, Ohio. She was one of about 200 such transactions from 1951 to 1965 for the doctor, Thomas Jugarthy Hicks. The babies, whose births were never officially recorded, vanished from here with the taillights.

Ms. Self died in November 1987 at the age of 37, when the brakes on her car failed on a four-lane mountain road. Mrs. Blasio's search might have died with her were it not for a startling physical resemblance between them, a resemblance that convinced Ms. Self's friends and family that Kitty's girl had come home.

For years she had been coming here, walking the streets, searching the faces of the people there for her own features. But it was an old friend of Ms. Self, Carlynn Manning, who saw Mrs. Blasio on a television program this past summer about the baby-selling operation, made the connection and introduced her to possible relatives.

"She's Kitty," said Mrs. Manning, who was also her social worker.

While her mother was beyond touch for her, Mrs. Blasio learned from Mrs. Manning that there was a living link, a child of Ms. Self who still lived in the McCaysville area, on the Tennessee side.

"It was like looking at a ghost," Jamie Goss, 20, Ms. Self's son, said of the first time he saw Mrs. Blasio.

Although DNA testing has failed to either prove or disprove the link between the two women — further tests are planned — Mr. Goss is convinced that "I have a sister." His aunt says the same thing, as does Mrs. Manning, her 91-year-old mother, and others who carry images of Ms. Self in their heads.

Mr. Goss, who bears a striking resemblance to Mrs. Blasio, said: "If it looks like a duck, walks like a duck and quacks like a duck, it's a duck. She looks just like my mom."

The most startling resemblance, say the people who have seen the two women, so many years apart, is in their eyes. Kitty Self's eyes flashed from blue to green, like sea water running from sunlight to shade.

"The eyes, the face, even the way they giggle, it's all the same," Mrs. Manning said. "I can see it, feel it. I don't need DNA. I just feel it."

The most encouraging evidence may have come when Mrs. Manning recently took Mrs. Blasio, unannounced, to see her 91-year-old mother, Edith. "That's Kitty's child," the old woman said when they walked into the room.

But feelings are not science, and the DNA tests could still prove that the link between the two women may be some lesser kin, or perhaps just a coincidence of nature. Photos of them, taken at the same age, are startling — both have dark hair, emerald eyes, even the same cheekbones. Both had sharp, boney elbows.

Both had slightly hooked noses, until a broken nose in her 20's led Mrs. Blasio to undergo plastic surgery. Pictures of the two women laid side by side, before the surgery, appear to be of sisters. Even through the filter of Mrs. Blasio's Yankee accent, out of place here, their voices have the same timbre, the same lilt, said people who remember Ms. Self.

Mrs. Blasio wishes she could be sure, but "if I didn't believe Kitty was my mother, I wouldn't be here." She has put much of her life on hold — she is a former insurance claims investigator studying law — to pursue her past. Yet she acknowledged that her desires might have clouded her judgment.

"I want somebody to be my mother," she said. Both the man and woman who bought her — she calls them Mom and Dad — have died.

"If she wants to stay here and be Kitty's daughter, she can," said Linda K. Davis, the Fannin County probate judge who helped Mrs. Blasio in tracking down her own past. "It's very plausible that she is."

Judge Davis and Mrs. Blasio set up a registry to help other "Hicks babies," named for the doctor, find their birth mothers. Two have been matched, through DNA and other evidence, with their birth mothers, although one has refused to meet with her child, or acknowledge it.

Ms. Blasio has already become a part of Kitty Self's family, and won over her old friends. They treat her not as a long-lost child but as a second chance to love the woman who had so little luck and who left them too soon.

As a child in a poor family that worked in borrowed fields and in odd jobs, Ms. Self had almost nothing. As a young woman, after the birth of her daughter, she married a man who she said beat her and tried to make her life mean and small.

It is one reason that Mrs. Blasio can live with the notion of Kitty Self as her mother. Ms. Self, her friends said, did not give away her baby because she wanted to — it was because she had to. She regretted it, they said, for the rest of her life.

"That's all I ever really needed to know," Mrs. Blasio said.

Mrs. Manning became Ms. Self's social worker after she married, after she said her husband started to abuse her. The two women had to meet at night, clandestinely. Ms. Self would hide in the woods. Mrs. Manning would drive by and flash her headlights, to signal her that it was safe to come out.

"They were living in an old school bus," Mrs. Manning said. It gets cold here in the north Georgia mountains, so high up, she said, adding, "She was stuffing newspaper in the cracks of the windows."

In time, the two women became friends. While she lived part of her life in terror, Ms. Self loved to laugh, to talk. "Bubbly," Mrs. Manning said. Often, they talked about the girl that Ms. Self had given away, that January in 1965. Ms. Self believed that the child would have a better life than she could give her, no matter who took her, Mrs. Manning said.

Many of the babies went to blue-collar families in the North, who wanted children but did not have the time or money for adoption.

Mrs. Manning said Ms. Self once told her: "If I could find her, I wouldn't want to disturb them. I'd just go watch her. Maybe I could stand behind a tree."

Mrs. Blasio learned that she had been sold, not adopted, after the woman she knew as her adoptive mother died. The man she knew as her adoptive father then told her the story in 1988.

As a child, Mrs. Blasio often daydreamed about what her birth mother was like. She had no idea that the woman who may well be her mother was daydreaming about her. Mrs. Manning said she and Ms. Self would "go to the store and we'd see dresses, and she'd say, 'I bet my daughter would look pretty in that.'"

"She talked about her daughter doing things that she never got a chance to do," Mrs. Manning said, "like graduating from school, going to a prom. She hoped for all that, for her."

Mrs. Manning stared across her kitchen table to Jane Blasio, the smart, tough, attractive woman that looked so much like her friend, and her eyes teared up.

"Delight," she said. "That's what Kitty would feel. I wish she could have been alive and seen this."

Through Mrs. Manning and others, Mrs. Blasio has found some of the peace she was searching for. Her mother — if the link between them turns out to be solid, true — did not toss her away, without thought. She was a woman, Jane Blasio believes, without choices.

"Jane has what she wants now," Judge Davis said. "All her life, she could paint her own picture of her mother," choosing anyone, anywhere.

"I guess she still can," she said, because the DNA evidence will probably never be 100 percent certain, one way or another.

Mrs. Blasio would prefer to look at old black-and-white photographs of a woman who once lived in a school bus, and to boss around that woman's son, as any older sister would.

"I'd heard stories that I had a sister, but I never believed it until now," Jamie Goss said. Of course, he said, "I am better looking."

Mrs. Blasio said she had never felt any anger at Dr. Hicks, who died in 1972, for making a profit on the exchange. She only wished that he had kept records, which would have provided a paper trail to follow.

"It's the only thing I've ever wanted so badly that it fogs my thinking," Mrs. Blasio said.

Dr. Hicks performed illegal abortions in the 1950's and 1960's at a small clinic here, but sometimes he would persuade a young woman to carry her baby to term. Then, he would quietly sell the baby, charging $800 to $1,000.

Word spread as far as Ohio and Arizona: Babies for cash, no questions asked.

Many people say that Dr. Hicks was doing a public service by putting so many babies into the arms of parents who wanted a child.

He made sure that there would be almost no way for people to find one of the babies he sold. He falsely recorded the birth, listing the people who bought them as birth parents.

No one seemed to wonder why — at least until Mrs. Blasio and Judge Davis began their search into his past a few years ago — why people came from around the country to have their babies delivered by a country doctor in Georgia.

Mrs. Blasio's long-sought answer may turn out not to be true. It may be that friends of Kitty Self want her daughter to walk among them so badly that it colors their memory. But science seems to count for less than feeling here in the hills and hollows along the Ocoee River.

"Every once in a while I look in her eyes and I see this flash" as the colors change, Mrs. Manning said. "And I know. I never thought I'd see Kitty's child, but I do."

New Development Stirs Old Case

Birmingham News, July 19, 1987

Blond, pretty Betty Culver Renfroe was strangled in her home near Lincoln in Talladega County, sometime in the morning of June 24, 1971. She died on the kitchen floor with one of her husband's white shirts knotted around her neck.

Her husband, Congregational Holiness minister and part-time used car salesman Harvie D. Renfroe, was charged with murder. He said he was innocent — and loved his wife too much to hurt her.

Defense attorneys claimed state evidence was weak, circumstantial. The state's primary witness was Sheriff Luke Brewer — who later would be impeached and eventually plead guilty to felony charges. Brewer told the court the Renfroe marriage was failing, and Renfroe killed his wife because she was about to leave him.

A Talladega County jury in 1972 found Renfroe guilty of murder. The appeals process took years, ending in a five-year sentence for manslaughter in 1980. The Rev. Harvie D. Renfroe picked up his Bible and went to prison. He served two years.

The State of Alabama closed the book on the Renfroe killing.

On March 12, 1987, 42-year-old Beverly Ann Caster was found dead in her home in the tiny South Georgia town of Lennox. She had been strangled. A shirt was knotted around her neck.

Georgia authorities say they have a suspect they won't name — a man linked to suspected serial killings in Alabama, Florida and Georgia, a man who was in the towns when the women victims were strangled, a man who was in Lincoln when Betty Renfroe was killed.

"Harvie never confessed," even in confidence, said Sylacauga attorney Lyndol Bolton, who defended Renfroe.

WRONG MAN IN PRISON?

Now an investigation into a Georgia murder has refueled Renfroe's claim that the state judicial system imprisoned the wrong man.

Renfroe served his time. He is 63 — a free man again but one stripped of his license to preach by the state Congregational Holiness Council. Living again in his hometown of Centre, he has been shunned by people who once called him friend and is ignored by church congregations.

He is a big man — 6-feet-tall, 210 pounds — with a ruddy face, pale blue eyes and snow-white hair. He sits in the office of his used car lot in Centre and thinks back 16 years, flipping through a well-worn Bible. An air conditioner and electric fan duel the heat. It's noon in a little town in the summertime, and not much moves.

"Betty was a beautiful woman — physically and spiritually," said Renfroe, looking out on a parking lot filled with 4-year-old Chevrolets and a few "like-new" foreign cars.

"She didn't deserve to die. I don't deserve to carry the brand of a killer. It's just a lie. And I been waitin' a long time to see it told right."

David Kelley, chief assistant district attorney in Cook County, Ga., said he is re-investigating the Renfroe case as part of his probe into the Beverly Ann Caster murder. That case could ultimately help clear Renfroe, Kelley said.

Kelley said the FBI, Georgia Bureau of Investigation and Cook County law enforcement agencies are "looking into a murder in South Georgia which has necessitated my looking into other murders in other jurisdictions.

"I believe Mr. Renfroe has reason to hope that he will one day be vindicated."

Kelley said he is "not at liberty to mention names, specifics. I don't want to jeopardize anybody's rights.

"But I have a key suspect in a South Georgia murder that we're focusing on, and I have reason to believe there is an Alabama connection," Kelley said.

For the past month Renfroe has been furnishing Georgia investigators with information on his wife's killing — court documents, photographs and his own testimony of what he remembers of the crime and the man under investigation.

Renfroe and others connected with the case have said the man under suspicion in Georgia was in Lincoln at the time his wife was killed.

The suspect is a transient laborer who has served time for attempted murder in a case in Florida where he tried to strangle a woman, Renfroe said.

Investigators said they can't release anything more about the case or their suspect because it could hamper their investigation.

Kelley would not comment on how his suspect is linked to other strangling cases — including the Betty Renfroe killing — or how many cases there are.

But according to the files of the *Adell News Tribune* in Adell, the

Cook County seat, at least two other murders by strangulation similar to the Lennox murder are being investigated in South Georgia.

In those cases, too, the women had been strangled with articles of clothing. The method of murder is the same as in several other unsolved crimes in Alabama, Georgia and Florida, Georgia authorities have said.

Like Kelley, other Georgia authorities said they won't talk about specifics in their investigation. No one has been charged in the Georgia murders.

"I wouldn't be looking into this (Renfroe) case that occurred 16 years ago if I didn't think it had something to do with the Georgia murder. I have other things to do," Kelley said.

"But as a prosecutor — and more importantly, as an individual — I won't stop until I know the truth. And I'm not sure the truth is known (in the Renfroe killing)," Kelley said.

Renfroe is getting old. He said he has faced the possibility of death with the quiet confidence of the pious, a Christian firm in his faith in God and the afterlife.

But he has a very real fear of dying with the reputation of the preacher who killed his wife.

"I just wanted to live long enough to see it end. I've always had faith my name would be cleared. It's what I've lived for . . . to see my name lifted out of the mud," Renfroe said.

Renfroe has been a preacher for almost 40 years, mostly in the strict Congregational Holiness, a Pentecostal denomination that emphasized fire-and-brimstone preaching.

In 1970 he was preaching full-time and selling used cars on the side. He was a popular, forceful preacher who traveled the state in search of potential born-again converts.

He helped found churches and youth camps. He became a trustee in the state Congregational Holiness council, a prestigious position in the denomination.

His first wife died in an automobile accident. In 1970, when he was 46, he married 27-year-old Betty Culver. He built her a new house on Alabama 77 in Lincoln.

"He was proud of her," said Bolton. "He hurried to open doors for her. He wanted to show her off to his friends.

"He was in love with her."

Renfroe's story of what happened on the day of her death has been told and retold to police, lawyers and friends. He tells it without drama and without emotion — like reading from the pages of a play he saw one time too many.

He and his wife had breakfast together the morning of her death. He hugged and kissed her and then left to do some business. "She told me she'd have me some sweet milk and cornbread for dinner," he said.

He said he returned at about 10:30 A.M. and found his wife dead on the kitchen floor. She was in her nightgown. One shoe was off, lying under the kitchen table. One of his shirts was twisted around her neck.

"She was blue, she'd already turned blue," Renfroe says, his voice steady and low. "I covered her up with a sheet. Then I called the coroner."

Sheriff Brewer arrived about 45 minutes later. His investigation of the house and the body was only cursory, "a very poor investigation," defense attorney Bolton contends.

There was no examination to determine the possibility of a sexual assault, Bolton said. There was no analysis of the woman's nightgown, which Bolton said contained stains that may have been semen.

Those tests may have proved that someone else was in the house at the time Renfroe said his wife was killed, Bolton said.

"What the sheriff did was to just put Harvie in jail, thinking he would confess," Bolton argues. "He thought he already had his man, and didn't see any use in doing anything else."

Brewer, who died in 1985, was the sheriff for 14 years. He was thrown out of office in 1972 on charges of embezzlement and challenging a circuit court judge to a duel. During Brewer's impeachment trial, a parade of witnesses testified that he protected bootleggers, used recovered stolen cars for his own use and threatened public officials when they tried to do anything about it.

Renfroe says he didn't get any justice. It was an election year, and Brewer's hold on Talladega County — unshakeable for more than a decade — was threatened.

"The sheriff rigged it just like he wanted to rig it," Renfroe contends. "Brewer was about to be throwed out and he needed something to rebuild his kingdom.

"He would have hung it on Jesus Christ if he could have. He was looking for a man, and I was the easiest one to build a case on," Renfroe said.

In Renfroe's first trial in Talladega Circuit Court in 1972, spectators packed the courtroom, stood in the aisles and lined up outside.

"Everybody for Harvie sat on one side of the room and everybody against him sat on the other side," Bolton said. "They moved back and forth, depending on how things were going.

"It was a good trial if you were a spectator."

"He had an airtight alibi, as I remember," said Yvonne Grice, a Talladega County Courthouse employee. Renfroe was calm, confident, she remembers.

"A lot of people figured he was the coolest man alive . . . and the unluckiest man alive (to be convicted)."

Renfroe had witnesses who said they saw him the morning of the murder. The prosecution said Mrs. Renfroe was killed before he left home that morning. Medical evidence, Bolton said, was inconclusive. With few hard facts, the court battle over the circumstantial evidence raged.

Defense attorneys painted a picture of a man who loved his wife and would have never harmed her.

Prosecutors painted a different picture, of a young wife ready to leave her older husband, of a marriage torn by strife.

"We were happy," Renfroe said, shaking his head. "We had some problems like any other married couple. They pretended there was some divorce action, but there's not a bit of truth in it."

Records in Talladega County don't show any divorce papers. Court records show that the late Mrs. Renfroe had once called a moving van to her house, but later canceled it.

"I lost the case because I could not overcome the fact he was an older man and she was a beautiful woman, that he was a Pentecostal preacher and part-time used-car salesman," Bolton said. "Harvie needed a public relations man more than he needed lawyer."

Jerry Studdard, Brewer's nephew and a sheriff's deputy at the time, now is the sheriff in Talladega County. He said there was no hard evidence to link Renfroe to the murder, but that the circumstantial evidence was strong.

He said Renfroe's five hours of testimony contained statements that weren't true.

"They caught him in a few," Studdard said.

A look at the court transcripts shows one discrepancy. Renfroe said he was in McGaig's restaurant in Talladega one day, but witnesses said they remembered seeing him there on a different day.

It might seem insignificant, Bolton said, but it tainted the rest of Renfroe's story about where he had been and what he had done in the days before the killing.

The jury found him guilty of second-degree murder. Bolton appealed. The Alabama Court of Criminal Appeals reversed the decision and sent the case back to Talladega for a new trial. A change-of-venue motion sent it to Jefferson County where a jury would reduce the charge to manslaughter.

By the time of the Birmingham trial in 1975, Renfroe had information on a man he believed was responsible for his wife's death.

The man, who was working in Renfroe's yard the day before Renfroe's wife was killed, was convicted in the early 1970s in the strangling death of a Florida woman and served a sentence in a Florida prison, Bolton said.

It is the same man, Renfroe said, whom authorities are seeking in the Lennox, Ga., death.

"He was at Harvie's house the day before she was killed, working for a contractor," Bolton said. "I went down there (to Florida) to talk to him, hoping I might get something that would help Harvie, but he refused to see me."

Bolton put together a file on the man and combined information about the murder of a Florida woman with information linking him to the Renfroe killing.

But Jefferson County Circuit Judge Charles Nice refused to admit the information as evidence in Renfroe's second trial. The man's name and his alleged link to the Renfroe killing never came out in any trial.

"Right or wrong, the judge never let me introduce it," Bolton said.

Nice said he wouldn't allow evidence on the other man because "it was just too speculative. They wanted to introduce evidence that on the day she died, there was another man — this (Florida) murderer — who was in town.

"They did not have evidence that this man was ever actually in the house or was in any other way connected. I ruled against it and I was upheld in the appeal.

"It's possible, of course, that it happened just like they (Renfroe) say. But it was just too . . . speculative, I guess, is the word," Nice said.

During and after his trial, Renfroe paid private investigators to gather information on the man. He made those files available to the Georgia investigators last month.

Bolton said Renfroe spent thousands of dollars to get that information. Renfroe kept spending even after he was convicted, Bolton said.

A guilty man, Bolton surmises, would have served his time and saved his money.

On May 26, 1975, a Jefferson County jury found Renfroe guilty on the lesser manslaughter charge. A second appeal, which took five years, was denied. Renfroe, who had been out on bond during the appeals process, was sentenced to five years.

He left in 1980 for the Farquahar State Cattle Farm in Greensboro — where the labor is done by convicts.

"I told the truth, because in the Bible it says the truth will set you free," Renfroe said. "As it turned out, I was sentenced to five years."

PRISON PREACHER

Renfroe became the prison farm's preacher. While he was there, inmate-preacher Harvie D. turned 40 or so people to the Lord.

"I told people it was the best Sunday school I ever had, because they sure weren't going to just walk out on me," he said, smiling. "I had some people come back to the Lord who were way out there, people you would think would never repent . . . there were even a few backslid preachers.

"I remember I baptized this one man in a cow trough. I mean we gave him a good 'un. I told him it was the first time I ever baptized anybody while I was standing in dry ground.

"I always thought you had to have a creek or a pond, but this 'un seemed to take."

Warden Charlie Farquahar said there was something about Renfroe that didn't fit at the ranch: He said he just didn't belong in prison.

"He was kindly on the religious side . . . but we get a lot of people in here who grab up a Bible first thing. He was different. He influenced the younger boys to do right. He had ideals and he had a good background.

"He was a citizen."

RENFROE COMES HOME

Renfroe did his time and came home to Centre. A marriage to a Jacksonville woman before he went to prison failed because of the ordeal, he said. Deep in debt, he sold his home and farm and most everything else he owned.

He went to work at one of the two things he knows most — selling cars — and started rebuilding the material side of his life.

He opened his own used car lot — D's Tradin' Place — near downtown Centre. Last year, Renfroe married again. A picture of his new wife in a white wedding gown is on his desk, beside his Bible.

He says his business is doing well. He sells cars and pre-fab buildings that look like little barns. His narrative of his business comeback was interrupted when a man came to his office to ask about a station wagon.

"It's a good 'un, just as good as it looks," Renfroe says. "I think it's used one quart of oil."

Every day he comes to work until about noon, when he and wife Helen go to eat lunch at Cherokee County Hospital's open-to-the-public buffet. Businessmen walk by and say hello.

He remains a preacher without a home church. He said he has been blackballed in churches both inside and outside the denomination. In some churches preachers refused to look at him. Members of congregations pretended he wasn't there, he said.

"People have sort of been giving ol' Harvie D. the left foot of fellowship all these years," said Edward Fair, a Jacksonville landscape contractor who was raised in the Congregational Holiness church.

"People just ignored me," Renfroe said. "Instead of recognizing me as being there, they just left me out. They never asked me to say a word, like I wasn't even there.

"These are people I had kept in my home, fed and labored with. So I kept moving to churches, looking for a place I could feel close to. I never was rejected, I never was turned away. I was just totally ignored. They had passed judgment on me."

NO GUARANTEES

This is no guarantee, Renfroe said, that the Georgia investigation will clear him.

The fact that the man Georgia authorities are building a case against was at his home the day before his wife died could be nothing but co-incidence.

But there is the *possibility.*

After 16 years of treatment he says he never deserved, he has seized that possibility with both hands.

"How in the world can you ever pay somebody back for what I've been through, for what my family has been through, for what it's all cost me — not in terms of money and property — but just suffering." Renfroe snaps the Bible closed.

"There ain't no way to pay that back."

Autism No Handicap, Boy Defies Swamp

New York Times, August 17, 1996

DATELINE: Fort Walton Beach, Fla., Aug. 16

Taylor Touchstone, a 10-year-old autistic boy who takes along a stuffed leopard and pink blanket when he goes to visit his grandmother, somehow survived for four days lost and alone in a swamp acrawl with poisonous snakes and alligators.

He swam, floated, crawled and limped about 14 miles, his feet, legs and stomach covered with cuts from brush and briars that rescuers believed to be impassable, his journey lighted at night by thunderstorms that stabbed the swamp with lightning.

People in this resort town on the Gulf of Mexico say they believe that Taylor's survival is a miracle, and that may be as good an explanation as they will ever have. The answer, the key to the mystery that baffles rescue workers who have seen this swamp kill grown, tough men, may be forever lost behind the boy's calm blue eyes.

"I see fish, lots of fish," was all Taylor told his mother, Suzanne Touchstone, when she gently asked him what he remembered from his ordeal in the remote reservation on Eglin Air Force Base.

Over years, Taylor may tell her more, but most likely it will come in glints and glimmers of information, a peek into a journey that ended on Sunday when a fisherman found Taylor floating naked in the East Bay River, bloody, hungry but very much alive.

He may turn loose a few words as he sits in the living room, munching on the junk food that is about the only thing his mother can coax him to eat, or when they go for one of their drives to look at cows. He likes the cows, sometimes. Sometimes he does not see them at all, and they just ride, quiet.

Taylor's form of autism is considered moderate. The neurological disorder is characterized by speech and learning impairment, and manifests itself in unusual responses to people and surroundings.

"I've heard stories of autistic people who suddenly just remember, and begin to talk" of something in the far past, Mrs. Touchstone said. "But we may never know" what he lived through, or how he lived through it, she said.

His father, Ray, added, "I don't know that it matters." Like his wife and their 12-year-old daughter, Jayne, Mr. Touchstone can live with the mystery. It is the ending of the story that matters.

Still, they have their theories. They say they believe that it is possible that Taylor survived the horrors of the swamp not in spite of his autism, but because of it.

"He doesn't know how to panic," Jayne said. "He doesn't know what fear is."

Her brother is focused, she said. Mrs. Touchstone says Taylor will focus all his attention and energy on a simple thing — he will fixate on a knot in a bathing suit's draw string — and not be concerned about the broader realm of his life.

If that focus helped him survive, Mrs. Touchstone said, then "it is a miracle" that it was her son and not some otherwise normal child who went for a four-day swim in the black water of a region in which Army Rangers and sheriff's deputies could not fully penetrate. He may have paddled with the gators, and worried more about losing his trunks.

"Bullheaded," said Mrs. Touchstone, who is more prone to say what is on her mind than grope for pat answers. Instead of coddling and being overly protective of her child, she tried to let him enjoy a life as close to normal as common sense allowed.

Taylor's scramble and swim through the swamp, apparently without any direction or motive beyond the obvious fact that he wanted to keep in motion, left him with no permanent injuries. On Wednesday, he sat in his living room, the ugly, healing cuts crisscrossing his legs, and munched junk food.

"Cheetos," he said, when asked what he was eating.

But when he was asked about the swamp, he carefully put the plastic lid back on the container, and left the room. He did not appear upset, just uninterested.

THE JOURNEY

Taylor has been swimming most of his life. In the water, his autism seems to disappear. He swims like a dolphin, untiring.

His journey began about 4 P.M. on Aug. 7, a Wednesday, while he and his mother and sister were swimming with friends in Turtle Creek on the reservation lands of the Air Force base. Taylor walked into the water and floated downstream, disappearing from sight. He did not answer his mother's calls.

An extensive air, water and ground search followed. It involved Army Rangers, Green Berets, marines, deputies with the Okaloosa County Sheriff's Department and volunteers, who conducted arm-to-arm searches in water that was at times neck-deep, making noise to scare off the alligators and rattlesnakes and water moccasins, and shouting Taylor's name.

He is only moderately autistic, Mrs. Touchstone said, but it is possible that he may not have responded to the calls of the searchers. At night, when it was nearly useless to search on foot, AC-130 helicopters crisscrossed the swamp, searching for Taylor with heat-seeking, infrared tracking systems.

In all, the air and ground searchers covered 36 square miles, but Taylor, barefoot, had somehow moved outside their range.

"The search area encompassed as much area as we could cover," said Rick Hord of the Sheriff's Department. "He went farther."

It was not just the distance that surprised the searchers. Taylor somehow went under, around or through brush that the searchers saw as impassable. Yet there is no evidence that anyone else was involved in his journey, or of foul play, investigators said.

Apparently, Taylor just felt compelled to keep moving. Members of his family say they believe that he spent a good part of his time swimming, which may have kept him away from snakes on land.

The nights brought pitch blackness to the swamp, and on two nights there were violent thunderstorms. Lightning would have penetrated his shell, Mrs. Touchstone said.

"I think it may have kept him moving," she said, and that might have been a blessing. Certainly, said his mother and doctors who treated the boy, he was exhausted.

"Do you really think God would strike him with lightning?" she asked. "Wouldn't that be redundant?"

Somewhere, somehow, he lost his bathing suit. His parents said he might have torn them, and, concentrating on a single blemish, found them unacceptable. Mrs. Touchstone compared it to a talk she once heard by an autistic woman who had escaped her shell, who told the audience that most people in a forest see the vastness of trees, but she might fixate on a spider web.

On the third day of Taylor's journey, Mrs. Touchstone realized that her son might be dead. For reasons she could not fully explain, she did not want to see his body recovered. It would have been too hard to see him that way. Even though Taylor is physically fit and strong, friends and relatives knew that this was the same terrain that in February 1995 claimed the lives of four Rangers who died of hypothermia while training in swampland near here.

Instead, about 7 A.M. last Sunday, a fisherman named Jimmy Potts spotted what seemed to be a child bobbing in the waters of the East Bay River. Mr. Potts hauled him into his small motorboat.

Later that day, Taylor told his momma that he really liked the boat ride. In the hospital, he sang, "Row, Row, Row Your Boat."

INDEPENDENCE

Mrs. Touchstone lost Taylor at a Wal-Mart, once. "That was bad," she said.

He ran out of Cheetos once and hiked a few blocks, alone, to get some. The police found him and brought him home.

He decided once that the floor in the grocery store needed "dusting"—he likes to dust — and he got down on the floor and began dusting the grimy floor with his fingers.

But he has never lived in a prison of overprotectiveness. Even though his mother says there are limits to how much freedom he can realistically have and how much so-called normal behavior she can expect from him, she decided years ago that the only way he could have anything approaching a normal life — in some ways, the only way she herself could have one — was to let him go swimming, visit neighbors, take some normal, childlike risks.

He is prone, now and then, to just walk into a neighbor's house. Once, he went into the kitchen of a neighbor, opened the refrigerator, took out a carton of milk, slammed it down on the counter and stood there, expectantly. The woman called Mrs. Touchstone.

"What should I do?" the woman asked.

"Well," Mrs. Touchstone said, "I'd pour him a glass of milk."

The fact that Taylor is not completely dependent on his parents, that he is not treated like an overgrown infant, that he is allowed to swim on his own and roam the aisles of the Wal-Mart and raid the neighbors' refrigerators, may have helped him survive when he was all alone in the swamp, his family believes.

His father offered this explanation: "That's all his mom. I was overly protective."

The phenomenon of his journey has prompted teachers at his school to consider changes in the study plan for autistic or handicapped students. One teacher told Mrs. Touchstone that they would stress more self-reliance.

Mrs. Touchstone, who jokingly calls herself "Treasurer for Life" for the Fort Walton chapter of the Autism Society of America, said her son's journey should clarify, in some people's minds, what autism is.

"I want every inch of that swamp he crossed to count for something," she said.

For now, life is back to normal. He screamed when he was forced to take his medicine, which is not so unusual for a 10-year-old. "We've got a little autism in all of us," Mrs. Touchstone said.

Taylor has always been something of a celebrity in his neighborhood, so his mother does not expect much to change after his ordeal. There was a sign outside his school that just said, "Welcome Home," and many people have called or written to tell her how relieved they are. One elderly neighbor wrote to tell Mrs. Touchstone how relieved she was that "our child" was home safe.

Mrs. Touchstone will not waste time wondering, at least not too much, about her son's strange trip. She can live with the notion of a miracle.

"I guess God was looking for something to do," she said. "I guess he looked down and said, 'Let's fix things up a little bit.'"

Silver Hair, Golden Years

I've heard people say that there is more character in an old man's face

than in a million books, a million songs. I have always loved to write

about the old because they have seen some things, done some things, and

don't mind telling you about it — if you don't rush them.

All She Has, $150,000, Is Going to a University

New York Times, August 13, 1995

DATELINE: Hattiesburg, Miss., Aug. 10

Oseola McCarty spent a lifetime making other people look nice. Day after day, for most of her 87 years, she took in bundles of dirty clothes and made them clean and neat for parties she never attended, weddings to which she was never invited, graduations she never saw.

She had quit school in the sixth grade to go to work, never married, never had children and never learned to drive because there was never any place in particular she wanted to go. All she ever had was the work, which she saw as a blessing. Too many other black people in rural Mississippi did not have even that.

She spent almost nothing, living in her old family home, cutting the toes out of shoes if they did not fit right and binding her ragged Bible with Scotch tape to keep Corinthians from falling out. Over the decades, her pay — mostly dollar bills and change — grew to more than $150,000.

"More than I could ever use," Miss McCarty said the other day without a trace of self-pity. So she is giving her money away, to finance scholarships for black students at the University of Southern Mississippi here in her hometown, where tuition is $2,400 a year.

"I wanted to share my wealth with the children," said Miss McCarty, whose only real regret is that she never went back to school. "I never minded work, but I was always so busy, busy. Maybe I can make it so the children don't have to work like I did."

People in Hattiesburg call her donation the Gift. She made it, in part, in anticipation of her death.

As she sat in her warm, dark living room, she talked of that death matter-of-factly, the same way she talked about the possibility of an afternoon thundershower. To her, the Gift was a preparation, like closing the bedroom windows to keep the rain from blowing in on the bedspread.

"I know it won't be too many years before I pass on," she said, "and I just figured the money would do them a lot more good than it would me."

Her donation has piqued interest around the nation. In a few short days, Oseola McCarty, the washerwoman, has risen from obscurity to a notice she does not understand. She sits in her little frame house, just blocks from the university, and patiently greets the reporters, business leaders and others who line up outside her door.

"I live where I want to live, and I live the way I want to live," she said. "I couldn't drive a car if I had one. I'm too old to go to college. So I planned to do this. I planned it myself."

It has been only three decades since the university integrated. "My race used to not get to go to that college," she said. "But now they can."

When asked why she had picked this university instead of a predominantly black institution, she said, "Because it's here; it's close."

While Miss McCarty does not want a building named for her or a statue in her honor, she would like one thing in return: to attend the graduation of a student who made it through college because of her gift. "I'd like to see it," she said.

Business leaders in Hattiesburg, 110 miles northeast of New Orleans, plan to match her $150,000, said Bill Pace, the executive director of the University of Southern Mississippi Foundation, which administers donations to the school.

"I've been in the business 24 years now, in private fund raising," Mr. Pace said. "And this is the first time I've experienced anything like this from an individual who simply was not affluent, did not have the resources and yet gave substantially. In fact, she gave almost everything she has.

"No one approached her from the university; she approached us. She's seen the poverty, the young people who have struggled, who need an education. She is the most unselfish individual I have ever met."

Although some details are still being worked out, the $300,000 — Miss McCarty's money and the matching sum — will finance scholarships into the indefinite future. The only stipulation is that the beneficiaries be black and live in southern Mississippi.

The college has already awarded a $1,000 scholarship in Miss McCarty's name to an 18-year-old honors student from Hattiesburg, Stephanie Bullock.

Miss Bullock's grandmother, Ledrester Hayes, sat in Miss McCarty's tiny living room the other day and thanked her. Later, when Miss McCarty left the room, Mrs. Hayes shook her head in wonder.

"I thought she would be some little old rich lady with a fine car and a fine house and clothes," she said. "I was a seamstress myself, worked two jobs. I know what it's like to work like she did, and she gave it away."

The Oseola McCarty Scholarship Fund bears the name of a woman who bought her first air-conditioner just three years ago and even now turns it on only when company comes. Miss McCarty also does not mind that her tiny black-and-white television set gets only one channel, because she never watches anyway. She complains that her electricity bill is too high and says she never subscribed to a newspaper because it cost too much.

The pace of Miss McCarty's walks about the neighborhood is slowed now, and she misses more Sundays than she would like at Friendship Baptist Church. Arthritis has left her hands stiff and numb. For the first time in almost 80 years, her independence is threatened.

"Since I was a child, I've been working," washing the clothes of doctors, lawyers, teachers, police officers, she said. "But I can't do it no more. I can't work like I used to."

She is 5 feet tall and would weigh 100 pounds with rocks in her pockets. Her voice is so soft that it disappears in the squeak of the screen door and the hum of the air-conditioner.

She comes from a wide place in the road called Shubuta, Miss., a farming town outside Meridian, not far from the Alabama line. She quit school, she said, when the grandmother who reared her became ill and needed care.

"I would have gone back," she said, "but the people in my class had done gone on, and I was too big. I wanted to be with my class."

So she worked, and almost every dollar went into the bank. In time, all her immediate family died. "And I didn't have nobody," she said. "But I stayed busy."

She took a short vacation once, as a young woman, to Niagara Falls. The roar of the water scared her. "Seemed like the world was coming to an end," she said.

She stayed home, mostly, after that. She has lived alone since 1967.

Earlier this year her banker asked what she wanted done with her money when she passed on. She told him that she wanted to give it to the university, now rather than later; she set aside just enough to live on.

She says she does not want to depend on anyone after all these years, but she may have little choice. She has been informally adopted by the first young person whose life was changed by her gift.

As a young woman, Stephanie Bullock's mother wanted to go to the University of Southern Mississippi. But that was during the height of the integration battles, and if she had tried her father might have lost his job with the city.

It looked as if Stephanie's own dream of going to the university would also be snuffed out, for lack of money. Although she was president of her senior class in high school and had grades that were among the best there, she fell just short of getting an academic scholarship. Miss Bullock said her family earned too much money to qualify for most Federal grants but not enough to send her to the university.

Then, last week, she learned that the university was giving her $1,000, in Miss McCarty's name. "It was a total miracle," she said, "and an honor."

She visited Miss McCarty to thank her personally and told her that she planned to "adopt" her. Now she visits regularly, offering to drive Miss McCarty around and filling a space in the tiny woman's home that has been empty for decades.

She feels a little pressure, she concedes, not to fail the woman who helped her. "I was thinking how amazing it was that she made all that money doing laundry," said Miss Bullock, who plans to major in business.

She counts on Miss McCarty's being there four years from now, when she graduates.

Band Plays On for Class of '39

St. Petersburg Times, June 12, 1989

DATELINE: St. Petersburg Beach

The blond pompadour never turned gray, and the two-tone shoes never lost their shine.

The years didn't mark Bill Nowling the way they did the other members of the St. Petersburg High School Class of 1939. They came to their 50th class reunion with silver hair and seamed faces. They found Nowling the same as on graduation day, his face unlined and body unbent, still the football hero, still the good-looking boy they voted Most Popular.

He still wore his letterman's sweater.

He always will.

Nowling was killed fighting in France in 1944. He came to the reunion as a black-and-white image pressed between the pages of the high school yearbook, and old friends turned to him on Page 25, Page 50, Page 119 . . . over and over again.

They have watched each other grow old, reunion after reunion. But Nowling remains uncorrupted by time, an image of their youth, good, pure and brave. Next to his picture on Page 25 are the words "High School Hero."

It was a class that believed in heroes.

Their childhood was the Great Depression. They left their teens at the outbreak of World War II, flew bombers over the Pacific, danced with soldiers at the USO.

Now they enter the twilight of their lives in a more complex world.

Fifty years to the day after their June 3 graduation, about 100 members of the Class of '39 gathered in the sprawling pink opulence of the Don CeSar hotel.

Valedictorian Bill Emerson and Class President Bob Miller are gray-haired and prosperous now, still living in St. Petersburg. They had been best friends in high school.

At the reunion they talked of class hero Nowling and others from '39, touching them one by one in their memories the way a wandering boy touches fence posts as he walks down a country road.

Would you like to do it all again?" Emerson asked.

"No, not now," Miller said. "Not in this time."

1939–1989

White bucks scuffed across the yellow pine dance floor. The band leader sang, "Yes, sir, that's my baby." A man in a pink sport coat pressed his cheek against his wife's. Then they dipped, just like in the movies.

It was the reunion's grand finale, a dinner-dance in the Grand Ball-room of the Don. They danced until the band stopped playing.

They wore name tags with yearbook pictures attached, young faces under old ones to help them remember. The boys in the photos had hair cut severely short on the sides. Their ears jutted from their heads like a '36 Chevrolet with the doors open.

The girls in the photos all wore pearls borrowed from their mothers or crosses on gold chains.

"I'm Carolyn Taylor Roewe," said one woman to another.

"Is that you? I can't see a thing without my glasses," said Dorothy Willis Ground.

The graduating class numbered 471. Eighty-nine of them have died: 15 in World War II, the rest by common causes such as cancer, heart attacks or car accidents.

The survivors are 67 to 69 years old. Most completed careers. They are old enough to draw Social Security. They drive big cars made in Detroit. Most vote Republican. They are fond of bright green pants. And there is more life behind them than ahead of them.

"Anybody who has lived as long as us will have some stories to tell," said Charles Holt, now a professor of economics at the University of Texas after stops at the London School of Economics, University of Chicago and Massachusetts Institute of Technology.

"I remember skinny-dipping on the beach. I don't think we could get away with that now."

The year they graduated was the year Albert Einstein wrote to President Franklin D. Roosevelt to alert him to the opportunity of an atomic bomb. John Steinbeck published "The Grapes of Wrath."

Stores in downtown St. Petersburg shut down that summer when the winter visitors went home. The Florida Theater showed "The Cat Creeps" with Bob Hope and Dorothy Lamour. Tom Mix shot a lot of Mexican bandits in the matinee.

The dance craze was the "Big Apple," a dance with a lot of strutting and stomping. They stomped so hard one Saturday at the Old Pier ballroom that the manager begged them to stop.

"We don't jump so high now," said '39 graduate Juliet Mastry.

SHADOW OF THE DEPRESSION

When the stock market dropped on Oct. 29, 1929, it left many parents of the Class of '39 on a treadmill of odd jobs and anticipation, searching for steady work.

In a city already dependent on tourists and luxury dollars, hard times lingered for a decade. Gasoline was rationed, and the few students who had cars sometimes were desperate.

"Stealing gas was big," said Albert D. Wallace, a football tackle who went on to make a career with Florida Power Corp. With a can and a siphon hose, they would get gas a gallon at a time. A lot of students walked around reeking of regular and high-test.

"You were afraid to light a cigarette because you'd blow yourself up," Wallace said.

It may have been the greatest sin of the Class of '39. More serious crime was unheard of.

"We didn't have drugs, and we didn't have guns," said Janet Helen Mohr Bohannon, now a grandmother living in St. Petersburg. "We had a mother and a father, and it was a time of great values. Everybody was nice to everybody else.

"It wasn't like today, so . . . I hate to use the word 'corrupt.'"

It was not embarrassing to be poor because everyone was. Emerson's father went from owning his own business to being the janitor at the First Baptist Church.

Emerson, a recently retired high-ranking executive at Merrill Lynch, worked seven nights a week at the Florida Theater as an usher.

Miller, now an architect, worked with him. A four-hour shift paid $1. Most of it went to buy groceries for the family.

In 1939, the line between success and failure was well-defined. Work hard and make your own money, or do without, Emerson said.

Miller's father ran a store, a position that enabled him to provide his family certain luxuries. "We had meat, once a week on Sunday," he said.

TEACHER LOIS GEIGER

The Class of '39 saw education as a way to escape poverty. David Miller, now a retired accountant in DeLand, said teachers did not order them to study.

It was assumed they would. Teachers did not quiet classrooms or clamor for attention. They owned it.

English teacher Lois Geiger purged the students of double negatives and smote them with Shakespeare. She was a favorite of the Class of '39.

"We shall have a grammar test on Tuesday," she would say. "But right now, let us read a little Shakespeare."

The Class of '39 had planned to honor her at its 50th reunion, as it had in years past.

She died last August from injuries she suffered during a burglary of her home on Burlington Avenue. She was 90.

"I guess they never found the one who did it," David Miller said. He shook his head.

MILESTONES IN '39

Bette Herche French, who would marry a doctor and move to California, was caught smoking in the girls' restroom. The track team won a state championship. Then track stars D. L. Hobby and Dick Case raced a horse in the high hurdles and beat it.

Emerson and Miller pooled their money and bought a Model T for $20. It would have been a much bigger boost to their social status if the right rear tire did not frequently go flat in the school parking lot.

Football star Nowling walked the halls hand in hand with the girl he would marry, cheerleader and Most Popular senior Helen Childs.

On Friday nights in the fall, he scored touchdowns. In 1939 the Green Devils went 11-2-1. They gave up only three touchdowns.

Football games were the social event of the week, always followed by a dance. "I wouldn't go if I didn't have a date," said Carolyn Taylor. "But I lived not far from the field, and I would stand in the yard and listen to the crowd."

The Lakeland Dreadnaughts and almost everybody else beat the Green Devils in basketball. By the end of the year, they had won three and lost everything but their britches. The yearbook described the season as "rather ragged."

Joe Hartley, who died of cancer a few years ago, broke all state records in the discus.

Elvida Locke Geegan wrote poetry. Shirley Maring Swaab was always late for class.

There was a dance every weekend. Now and then a few reckless youths drove to Hillsborough County, where a man named Skeeter Johnson sold moonshine by the quart.

Most of them said they didn't drink until the war.

"Mainly, what we did was just sit and talk," Bob Miller said.

They were all white, so there were no racial or ethnic barriers for them to overcome. "We were just poor white Americans, and we latched together," David Miller said.

Tripplett's drive-in across the street from the school dished up 10-cent hamburgers to students who often paid in pennies.

COMMENCEMENT

The Class of 1939 has kept a secret all these years.

Underneath their robes at graduation ceremonies on June 3, 1939, many of the young women were nearly naked.

The temperature in the auditorium was over 100 degrees, still hot and sticky as the processional began at 8 P.M.

"We took off everything we could under those robes," said Carolyn Taylor.

No one knew.

Graduation was staid, somber. Juliet Mastry, who would go on to sing show tunes in performances all over the world, sang Strauss' "Tales from the Vienna Woods." Bob Miller and Emerson gave their speeches, full of hope and promise and opportunity.

"I don't remember it, but it was something about going out and do-ing great things, 'You've got the world ahead of you,' something like that," Miller said. "I said the things everybody wanted to hear."

Emerson doesn't remember his speech, either.

"No, but it was something heroic," he said.

It was rhetoric. They didn't say what was really on their minds, on the minds of their classmates.

The deteriorating European peace brought rumors of war. The United States was uncommitted. Germany's invasion of Poland was three months in the future.

But the students knew about the menacing rise of the Third Reich.

"A lot of us knew, deep down, we would go to war," said David Miller. They did not know that when war came, it would come first from Japan.

WAR

The class scattered in the years after graduation — to junior college, business and trade schools, work. Many of them started families.

The Japanese bombing of Pearl Harbor on Dec. 7, 1941, disrupted their plans and split families that were just getting started. Some men were drafted. Some volunteered. Some were left behind.

Bill Nowling had started at fullback every game of his last three years at the University of Tennessee and played in two Sugar Bowls.

After graduation, he was commissioned an infantry second lieutenant at Fort Benning, Ga., in June 1943, and married his high school sweetheart in July.

He was killed in August 1944, leading his platoon in fighting in France.

"Bill was a hero before he went to war," Emerson said.

"He seemed indestructible," Bob Miller said.

Other casualties touched the Class of '39. BeeBee Dabbs Chandler, a cheerleader, lost her first husband, Oliver Simard. He died fighting with the 2nd Armored Division in Europe.

The survivors talk about the war almost with detachment. They did their duty, that's all.

Marine Lt. Emerson flew bombers over the Pacific with a picture of his wife, and a son he'd never seen, tucked inside his jacket.

He flew a stripped-down B-25 filled with rockets and bombs, searching for Japanese ships. He didn't keep count of the ones his squadron found.

"I was no hero," he said.

Army Lt. Robert Miller fought with the infantry in the Pacific, then served with occupational forces in Japan.

"You could still get shot dead in the street," he said.

They were shot at but never hit, served until they were no longer needed and came home to pick up their lives where they had left off.

Elvida Locke Geegan, now a semiretired secretary in St. Petersburg, danced with servicemen at the Don CeSar. She worried every day about family and friends who were in uniform.

Her brother George Locke, also Class of '39, joined the Coast Guard and transported troops to North Africa. Two men, one on each side of him, were killed when his boat was strafed by German planes.

He survived the war only to be accidentally crushed to death aboard a ship in peacetime in 1948.

David Miller never went to war. Army doctors found an irregular heartbeat and wouldn't accept him.

"Now here I am almost 70 years old," he said disgustedly. "And I'm fine."

The band played until 11 P.M. At 10:55, Charles Holt, the lifetime academician, was dancing in his socks.

His life has been full. He taught at the best schools and traveled the world. And he buried a wife.

Elvida Locke Geegan had been a south-side St. Petersburg girl when it was more fashionable to be from the north side, and she had never been one of the most popular.

Her dream in high school had been a simple one. "I just wanted to be an old maid schoolteacher," she said. But there was no money for a teacher's college. She trained to be a secretary.

If there were bad memories from high school, they didn't show as she danced close with her husband.

It was she who worked the hardest to make the reunion a success. Her classmates had applauded her at their reunion dinner. If there was a Most Popular at this reunion, it was Mrs. Geegan.

BeeBee Dabbs Chandler remarried and now helps run a gift shop in St. Petersburg. Seeing the old faces brought mixed emotions. "It's happy and sad," she said.

Lt. Bill Nowling's widow, Helen Childs Siviter, remarried. She doesn't like to talk about the past. Her friends said it's too painful for her.

Bob Miller and Emerson have had good lives. The promise they showed in high school was realized.

Emerson warned that if you call his St. Petersburg home, let the phone ring awhile. The house is so big it takes awhile to get to the phone.

Miller still works a little in his home. "But I try not to," he said.

In some ways they are all the same — resilient and industrious, God-fearing and fun-loving, patriotic and proud of what they went through to return here one more time.

Bob Miller, the one they elected 50 years ago as their leader, said he knows young people in the '80s may not understand them, may call them naive, even corny.

But in the well-seasoned Class of '39 is a strength of character that may be missing today, he said.

"We all went through a lot, that's true, things few other classes ever did," he said. "Back then if you were strong, you could survive. If you were smart, you could get what you wanted. It wasn't any more complicated than that.

"But now . . . kids have so many things in their way. In some ways, their lives may be even tougher than ours."

All night long, hotel guests curious about what was going on in the ballroom peeked in from the door. A few of the younger ones laughed, discreetly, at the old folks moving across the dance floor.

The last dance of the night was a slow one. A young couple, sun-burned and dressed in finest of yuppie leisure wear, stood in the door and watched the Class of '39 glide across the pine.

The young woman looked up at her husband and smiled. "I wish I could do that," she said.

Woman Clings to Her Paradise

St. Petersburg Times, April 18, 1989

DATELINE: Seminole

A stroke of a pen could destroy it.

With her signature, tiny, frail Margueritte Thurston could trade her citrus grove at 10566 Ridge Road for cold, hard cash.

Developers would divide her 70 acres into lots. Machines would up-root most of the orange, tangerine and grapefruit trees.

In months, houses or condominiums would rise into the skyline where now only a weather-beaten water tower leans drunkenly to one side.

One more piece of Old Florida would cease to exist.

But the power of money and persistence of developers have not penetrated the iron resolve of Mrs. J. T. Thurston, a 5-foot-tall retired schoolteacher with a voice sweet as mango marmalade.

"She'll never sell," said Ted Kay of Kay Development, one of sev-eral land development companies that have tried for years to buy the property. "All the money in the Japanese Empire couldn't buy that land."

It is Mrs. Thurston's paradise.

"My land's going to stay right here, just like it is, like it always has been," she said. "It is not for sale. It has never been for sale. I won't even listen to a price."

Her husband's family bought the land in 1917. It has been a grove since the late 1800s.

Now the property, between Seminole and Largo, is valued at $2-million by Pinellas County property appraisers.

"Developers would pay a lot more than that for it," said appraiser Tom Cheney of the Property Appraiser's Office. "It's in a key area. Developers have been pressuring her for years. But she hangs on."

Kay said $4.2-million is a fair estimate of what the land is worth, but price has never been the problem. No one has ever gotten that far with Mrs. Thurston. She shoos them out before they talk money.

Kay is the second generation of Kays to try. His late father, David Kay, tried for years.

The grove is bordered by Ridge Road on the East and 102nd Avenue N on the South. It has been gradually surrounded by housing developments. Houses valued at $70,000 to $100,000 line streets named after citrus trees.

"It's in the path of that growth," Kay said. "That, and the scarcity of land makes it valuable. You could make money off it."

Residential lots in north Pinellas County are priced out of the range of most wage-earning families. The unincorporated Largo-Seminole area is one of the last frontiers of affordable housing in Pinellas County, Cheney said.

Mrs. Thurston said she can't remember how many developers have asked her to sell the property. She tore up their business cards after they left.

"Every year we have a freeze they call me, thinking I'll be ready to sell" because of damage to her trees, she said.

"In the winter of 1962 we had a bad freeze. Trees all over the state died. All the leaves dropped off our trees."

Not even then did she consider selling.

Mrs. Thurston said she won't stand in judgment of others who chose to sell. She doesn't know their stories, their wants or needs.

If she needed money to live on, her attitude might be different, she said.

She lives modestly and comfortably on savings. The grove is a working farm and makes money. She has two full-time hands who handle planting and cultivation. Contractors pick the fruit.

"It's business," she said.

But it's more.

The one-story white house and its long, neat rows of palm and citrus are her retirement home. There are no children, only the land and the trees.

"My beautiful grove," she calls it.

She has nine birdhouses in the grove for her now-wild parakeets, which flutter around in flashes of yellow, green and blue.

The grove screens the home from the surrounding suburbs. Entering her property from the clutter outside is like stepping into a quiet room.

Phil Davis, 87, has worked at the grove for 20 years. He has been in Florida for 45. A Japanese soldier put a bullet in his back in the Philippines in World War II. Davis' doctor told him he needed a warm climate in which to recover.

"He said, 'Maybe Arizona?' And I said, 'Hell, I don't know anybody in Arizona.' So I came to Florida. But the Florida I came to isn't here anymore," Davis said. He pointed at the grove.

"This is what it used to be like, before the people came. And they're still coming, by the thousands.

"But I'll tell you one damn thing. They won't ever get this place. No sir. They won't ever get this."

The woman who saved this oasis is an unlikely heroine. Last week, she walked her property in a faded plaid shirt that reached almost to her knees. But there was a touch of brown dye in her hair and a trace of red on her lips — elegance in a pair of blue sneakers.

Her hands are the size of a child's — cool, dry and delicate. In her greenhouse, they seemed out of place as she ran her fingers through potting soil.

"We only use natural fertilizer," she said. "We use the St. Petersburg Times in our mulch bed."

She wouldn't let a photographer take her picture. She would not give her age, but bristled when asked whether she might be in her 70s.

"Oh, I'm not that old.

"This is a story about the grove," she declared. "This isn't a story about people."

Then she reached up, plucked a dead leaf off a mango tree and talked almost dreamily about the first time she saw it.

It was when she and her husband J. T. were courting, sometime soon after World War II. He was an Army doctor back from the lines. She was a young teacher.

The trees were heavy with fruit and a breeze wafted in from the Gulf. Two black mules were hitched to a white post.

She fell in love with it all.

Hanging in her home is an old color picture of the grove, taken from the air. It was made sometime after World War II and before the encroachment of the housing developments in the 1960s and 1970s.

It shows a splash of green — the grove — surrounded by palmetto, sawgrass and other groves.

It is the Florida of her youth. It still exists, but only within her property lines.

Cheney at the Property Appraiser's Office said other Pinellas County landowners are holding out here and there, but most have long since sold.

Cheney sometimes wonders what will happen when every square foot of land in the county is developed. "We need some green, a little green, a place for the water to sink into the ground when it rains," he said.

Mrs. Thurston said she hasn't decided what will happen to her land after she dies. She has considered some kind of arrangement so it could only be used for growing citrus.

"I think about all the nice land, all covered with concrete," she said. "It shouldn't have happened. I should say not."

Little Women Look Back on a Lost World

St. Petersburg Times, February 11, 1990

DATELINE: Sarasota

She should have wings. Everything else is in place. The high, lilting voice. The elfin face. The tiny, fragile, fairy-like form.

She should have a name like Tinker Bell. She should have magic slippers that give her the power to spring into the air and disappear back over the threshold of imagination, leaving behind a cloud of enchanted dust.

But the wrinkles in her face and the blue veins in her doll-like hands belong here, in the real world.

Because fairies never get old.

Her name is the very ordinary-sounding Nita Krebs, and she is a little person — what people in a less-enlightened time would have called a midget.

Miss Krebs, 82, lives in Sarasota with Anna Mitchell, another little person and her lifetime friend. Once there was a thriving colony of little people in Sarasota, lured there by the carnival atmosphere of the Ringling Bros. circus and a desire to live among their own kind.

Now there are only Miss Krebs, Ms. Mitchell and a few others around Tampa Bay, aging examples of a people different from everyone else — not in race or religion or economic status, but in size.

They are among the last of their kind. Modern medical science now makes it possible — through growth hormones and other artificial means — to accelerate the growth of children who are perfectly formed but tiny at birth.

"We are antiques," said Ms. Mitchell, 61.

Longtime performers in the so-called midget troupes of the 1940s and '50s, they danced on stage and rode in chauffeured limousines. It was Miss Krebs, more than 50 years ago, who told Dorothy to follow the Yellow Brick Road in "The Wizard of Oz."

Along the way they encountered cruelty and ignorance, were sometimes used and treated condescendingly. They have been looked at as sideshow freaks.

They are not dwarves, with short arms and legs. They are miniature people.

"Are we the last, the last ones like us? I certainly hope not," Ms. Mitchell said. "I would hate to think that no one would ever do the things we did, have the fun we had."

"It was a wonderful life," said Nita Krebs from across the room, her voice sounding thin and far away. "Wonderful . . ."

LIFE IN MINIATURE

Their furniture is mostly child-size. Still, Nita Krebs' shoes dangle from her chair.

She is 3 feet 8. "And a half," she said. She weighs about 45 pounds. Her eyesight and hearing have started to fail, and her tiny steps are uncertain. She does not dance anymore.

Anna Mitchell — 4 feet 2 in a pair of red high-heeled shoes — seems to tower over Miss Krebs. She spent the first half of her life even smaller than her good friend. Then, in an unexplained burst of growth, she grew about a foot after her 30th birthday. But even now, children marvel at her in stores and point to her on the street.

She is a ball of uncontrollable energy, prone to climbing over furniture instead of walking around it. She says "Ta Da" a lot.

Miss Krebs and Ms. Mitchell take turns living in each other's homes and take care of each other — not an unusual arrangement for Florida retirees who live alone.

But they also share a bond that would be impossible with a big person. They talk about people and places and problems unique to their world.

"Why would we want to be big, and have our feet always hanging off the end of the bed?" Ms. Mitchell asked.

A LIVING DOLL

Miss Krebs' father was a shoemaker in Czechoslovakia. Her mother and father were normal-sized. "My mother gave me a doll, a little doll, and said, 'That's how small you were when you were born,'" Miss Krebs said.

She was only about 2-feet tall when she started school. "I always had to sit on the front row."

World War I starved many in her village. Her father fed the family by making shoes for farmers and trading shoes for food.

After the war the only job she could find was dancing in a children's chorus in an opera house. Then a friend invited her to Prague, Czechoslovakia, where she went to see a song-and-dance troupe of little people. It was the first time she had ever seen people, grown people, her size.

She joined the troupe and traveled to the United States, where she would later sign a contract with showman-promoter Leo Singer and become one of the stars of the Singer Midgets. She danced and sang in opera houses and theaters across the country. In 1937 she had her first movie role, as a gangster's moll in "The Terror of Tiny Town."

She was 33 when Singer was hired to provide little people for "The Wizard of Oz." She had two parts, one as a ballerina, another as the Munchkin who darted out to tell Judy Garland to "Follow the Yellow Brick Road."

She loved Garland, even knitted her a crocheted poodle. Yet it was Garland who, in a 1967 appearance on "The Jack Paar Show," started the rumors that many of the Munchkin actors were wild-living, whiskey-drinking, promiscuous hell-raisers.

The rumors were mostly untrue, Miss Krebs and Ms. Mitchell said. It was so long ago it doesn't matter anymore, they say.

Big people always have let Ms. Krebs down. Singer, whom she admired, apparently pocketed half of the $100-per-head he was paid to provide Munchkins for the film.

But Miss Krebs said she has no regrets. She was a star, in the spotlight, in sequined gowns, fur coats. Singer made that possible.

She never seemed to have time for marriage. Asked if she ever had been in love, her eyes closed.

"Oh yes, I was in love. With little people, yes, and big people," she said. "There was one man . . . he could have put his shoes under my bed any time."

ALABAMA KINDNESS

Anna Mitchell weighed 6 pounds at birth and seemed destined to be a normal-sized child. Sometime in her preschool years she just stopped growing.

The daughter of a Canadian farmer, she, too, would find herself on stage with traveling shows and carnivals. She, too, would become a $50-a-week star.

She met Nita Krebs in the 1940s. Later she would meet and marry Frank Cucksey, also a little person. It was Cucksey who told Dorothy, after the death of the Wicked Witch of the West, "You killed her so completely that we thank you very sweetly."

But as Ms. Mitchell grew older — and larger — she left show business for a more normal life. She became a hairdresser and spent several years in and around Huntsville, Ala. She loved Alabama because people were nice to her.

Eventually she and her husband moved back to Sarasota, where they had worked with the Ringling Bros. circus in the 1950s. The city seemed to appeal strongly to the little people.

One by one others came there to retire, including her old friend Miss Krebs. Later, after her husband's death, Ms. Mitchell and Miss Krebs moved in together.

Not even 20 years ago, there were more than 50 little people living in and around Sarasota. Some worked for the circus, some just wanted to live "where they could walk down the street and see people like themselves," Ms. Mitchell said.

Now most of them have died. Those remaining seldom see other little people. Even the circus is gone.

Country Club Meets Enemy: Country Music and Pigs

New York Times, April 11, 1999

DATELINE: Stuart, Fla., April 8

Two worlds collide, on the 15th tee.

On one side of the skinny blacktop road, the manicured fairways of the Florida Club golf course meander through the palmetto scrub, where a solitary golfer with a retirement tan hacks hard at the ball and then chases it down in his golf cart, like a duck after a June bug.

On the other side, 165 mud-spattered pigs wallow, grunt, scratch and squeal under the skimpy shade of the same southeast Florida scrub, and the stench, from the animals, the manure and the mounds of rotting lettuce, tomatoes and moldy bread that they consume, hits the people who turn in the sandy driveway like a punch in the nose.

Country music — at the moment the Dixie Chicks, singing on WIRK radio about crying mamas and wide open spaces — mingles with the smell and the heat and the squeals, and the whole experience drifts across the scrub, across the road and onto the carefully tended greens of the Florida Club course.

The pigs' owner, a big, ruddy-faced, white-haired, sunburned man named Paul Thompson, sits in the shade beside the fly-blown pens and shakes his head.

"Now who," Mr. Thompson said, "would choose to build a golf course next to a pig farm? Didn't they read the sign? It says 'pig farm,' not 'rose garden.'"

He shakes his head again.

"And they say I'm crazy."

Such a confrontation of old and new Florida, here in this corner of Martin County about 30 minutes north of Palm Beach, was bound to lead to lawyers. But it is the music, not the smell, that has Mr. Thompson in court, defending his right to play Merle Haggard, Garth Brooks and Dolly Parton for his pigs. He swears it improves their disposition.

The Florida Club, a golf course and subdivision with homes that sell for around $300,000, is suing Mr. Thompson, 60, and another farmer, claiming that the country music they play bothers the golfers.

Mr. Thompson says he is being told how to live his life by the new, richer residents who are encroaching on what used to be a wild, simple place, "just one more case of the rich developers running over the little guy."

Asked how he knew the developers were rich, he smiled.

"Because I've never seen a poor developer," he said.

A trial date has not been set.

Greg Cotten, the general manager of the Florida Club, insists that its members only want to play in peace, and that the legal challenge is a simple lawsuit intended to halt a nuisance. The club seeks no damages, just reduced volume.

"This guy is persisting with his story of the big developers squeezing him out," which is false, Mr. Cotten said. "He's welcome to stay there."

Lawyers for the club have said that Mr. Thompson and the neighbor who also raises music-accented pork, Tom Rossano, want the club to buy their properties at an inflated price, to gain peace and quiet.

Mr. Cotten said Mr. Thompson also liked being courted by the media. "He's just a lonely guy who's enjoying the attention," Mr. Cotten said.

Asked whether he was playing the country music in an effort to get the club to buy his three acres, Mr. Thompson said no.

He was here first, in 1957, 38 years before the country club, he said.

But when asked whether he would consider selling his property, Mr. Thompson replied that "everything is for sale, if someone is willing to sell and someone is willing to buy.

"But I can't force anybody to buy me out," and certainly, he said, not by playing country music.

"When I pulled up in my car here for the first time, in '57, there was country music on the radio," Mr. Thompson said. Over the years, he read studies about how music made cows give more milk, made chickens lay more eggs and even made small children in day care centers happier.

What was good for humans must be good for pigs, he reasoned. He found that the music soothed the pigs, and made them less prone to attack each other in their tight surroundings.

The pigs, Mr. Thompson said, do not know the difference between styles of music, between Handel and Hank Williams.

"I play country," he said, "because I like country."

The golfers, bent over their Big Bertha drivers, trying to cleanly strike a small white sphere, have found that hard to do with George Jones warbling: "It's that teeny-weeny, itsy-bitsy thing we call the love bug."

Mr. Thompson has no sympathy for them. He does not play golf.

He considers the golfers hypocrites, people who do not want to know where their pork comes from.

"Standing around moaning about me, with a pork chop in their mouth," he said.

The battle with the country club has been raging for the past year, and so far the law seems to be on the pig farmers' side.

Checks on the noise level of the music by deputies of the Martin County Sheriff's Department and the neighboring St. Lucie County Sheriff's Department found that the music at both Mr. Thompson's and Mr. Rossano's farms was below the 60 decibels allowed in residential areas.

"There is no violation," said Jenell Atlas, the public information officer for the Martin County Sheriff's Department. Mr. Thompson has "been out there many, many years. As far as we're concerned, he's not breaking the law."

On the face of it, it seems a lopsided battle. One of the country club's lawyers is State Representative Tom Warner, a Republican from Stuart.

And within the past year, the country club pushed for and won a new ordinance that set a decibel level for residential areas — the very one that Mr. Thompson has been obeying.

But Mr. Thompson is no backwoods farmer, despite the pig flop on his boots. He has his own Web site — www.pigfarmer.com — and now he has his own legal defense fund, the Paul Thompson–Pig Farmer Legal Defense Fund, to be precise.

It will give him a chance, he said, against the country club.

Why not just turn the music down, he is asked. Well, he said, the pigs could not hear it, and, worse than that, it would be giving up.

And when he gives up, he said, it will be only when "they're carrying me out of here, walking slow and singing low."

Appropriately, John Anderson comes on the radio a few minutes later, singing about a dying way of life in Florida.

> Blow, blow Seminole wind
> Blow like it's never gonna blow again

It is hard to tell if the pigs are impressed.

Icons

Sometimes, we do them just for fun.

The King Is Long Dead, but Long Live the King

New York Times, August 16, 1997

DATELINE: Memphis, Aug. 15

How beloved is a man who, two decades after his heart stopped beating, has never been allowed to truly die?

In Memphis, where he grew up lean and poor and then, 20 years ago on Saturday, died fat and rich, the evidence of Elvis Presley's immortality is apparent in motel parking lots, at the Shoney's breakfast buffet and in the clubs where the posers in thick black sideburns resurrect not just a dead man's music but also the pout of his lips and the whirlwind of his hips.

His fans have gathered by the thousands this week — Graceland, his home, drew more than 20,000 for a candlelight vigil this evening — to celebrate that immortality, and to carry on what may be the largest, longest outpouring of devotion any entertainer has ever inspired.

Listen to them.

Cathy Bie, 36, of Memphis, who used to wait outside the gates of Graceland just to catch a fleeting glimpse: "I see him every day. He is in my heart. He is in my home. He is on my refrigerator. That is all that counts. What more do you need?"

Mia Biggs, 15, a cheerleader at the now predominantly black Humes Junior High School, where Elvis failed to make the football team: "There have been people here all week taking pictures of the water fountain, and I heard that some people are going in the boys' bathroom and kissing the bathroom floor."

Oliver Schmidt, a 26-year-old medical student who is a delegate with the Elvis Presley Gesellschaft appreciation organization of Frankfurt, Germany: "I feel good when I hear his music. It is international. There are no borders for feeling."

Sam Phillips, founder of Sun Records, Elvis's first label: "He made five records with me. On each one, one side had real influences of black music, and the other side was leaning toward country music. Nobody had ever done that. But the music came out of the hearts and souls of black and white Southerners."

Elisabeth Cronin, 49, president of the Elvis fan club in Birmingham, Ala.: "I saw 27 concerts. I have 4 scarves and 14 autographs. After the first autograph, he always remembered that my name was spelled with an s and not a z for the other 13."

And Sandy Martindale, now 51, who dated Elvis before the rhinestone jumpsuits and the drugs, when he was sharp and cool and jagged, like porcelain that has been hurled against a wall: "When I was out with Elvis, one time a girl came up and was so excited and saying, 'Oh, Elvis, I just can't believe it's you.' And Elvis said, 'You know, honey, sometimes I can't believe it's me, either.'"

In the year leading up to this anniversary, it has been popular for scholars, writers and others who view Elvis from an academic distance to ponder the meaning of all this. But the people who cry when they hear "Love Me Tender" say meaning is not so important as feeling. Elvis was all about feeling.

"Some people are breast-fed," said Terry Bellis, 36, the leader of the Liverpool branch of the Elvis fan club in Britain. "I was Elvis-fed," by his mother, who loved the Southern boy with the ducktail haircut. "Elvis communicates something very personal to an individual. Without a doubt, he is the greatest interpreter of popular song in this century. He is still communicating."

It angers his fans when they are condescended to by people who see them as unsophisticated, as zealots, even as cultists. Making fun of that strong affection is almost sport for some people, even here in Memphis.

But most of the tens of thousands of people who have arrived here this week did not come to see men with potbellies, in chrome-rimmed dark glasses and bejeweled jumpsuits, mimicking the aging, drug-addicted Elvis in decline, the one who died in the bathroom.

They came from all over the world to celebrate the life of the young man who seemed so wicked on stage but who loved his mama so much that when she died, he too was lost. And all along, there was the music, the mix of gospel, blues, country and something that Elvis himself injected, making it all not something borrowed but something new.

"I saw him on TV," said Megan Murphy, 23, a supermarket worker who is president of Young and Beautiful Fans of Elvis, in Bayonne, N.J., "and I loved him immediately." She was 3 years old then.

Some people cannot settle for adoration. They have to be Elvis. The vast ballroom of the Memphis Airport Sheraton is lousy with Elvises. There are three Asian Elvises, an Elvis in a wheelchair, toddler Elvises in tiny gold lame coats, female Elvises with pasted-on sideburns, young Elvises, old Elvises, short Elvises.

After talking to one Elvis and walking away, a middle-aged woman said to her friend, "What was that one's name?"

"I don't know," the friend replied. "Elvis?"

Elvis impersonators have been around since long before the real Elvis died, the impostors working Holiday Inns, state fairs and Kiwanis picnics. If imitation is the sincerest form of flattery, Elvis would be overwhelmed by what this impersonation of his style, moves and clothing has become.

The gathering at the Sheraton is a weeklong contest to crown the latest pretender to the throne of rock-and-roll. One contestant, Darrell Dunhill, 33, sold his Italian restaurant in Florida so he could be Elvis full time. He does three costume changes in a 12-minute show, carrying the fans through Elvis's incarnations.

At home in Florida, people look at him and laugh when they see him on the street.

"It's like coming home when I come to Memphis," said Mr. Dunhill, who has attended this contest in each of the last four years. "I feel right at home here with sideburns, looking like this. If I didn't have them, I'd feel odd. I don't feel like an outcast here."

Some of Elvis's most ardent fans are disapproving of the impersonators, whose work, they believe, is not respectful.

Yoshi Suzuki, who calls himself the Japanese Elvis, does sing, but a big part of his act is comedy. He tells the crowd that he and his "mama-san" were very poor, just like Elvis and his beloved mother. He says they could not afford cloth for the trademark Elvis scarves that the sweating older Elvis draped around the necks of adoring fans, sometimes with a kiss. Then Mr. Suzuki takes out a roll of toilet paper and drapes it around his neck, to laughter.

On Beale Street, where sharecroppers from the Mississippi Delta first brought their country blues to the big city, another type of Elvis impersonator plays to a younger, hipper crowd.

Here there is El Vez, the Mexican Elvis, who has adapted the music and the persona to fit the parallels he sees between Elvis's humble beginnings and current-day Mexicans and Mexican-Americans. One of his trademark songs is "You Ain't Nothin' but a Chihuahua."

A few doors down is "Elvis Herselvis," the lesbian Elvis. She calls herself the "queen of rock-and-roll" and is backed by her band, the Straight White Males.

"I think they're silly," said Sharon Ott, 58, president of Elvis Fans of Hoosierland, in Indianapolis. And Mr. Bellis, of the Liverpool fan club, believes that the impersonators diminish the legend and turn the memory of Elvis into caricature. "I hate the jumpsuits," he said.

The impersonators, in turn, say they are just loving Elvis in their own way. But that is the way it has always been with Elvis. People have always insisted on making him less or more than he was, even if that means making him alive again.

"He ain't dead — he's at the Waffle House in Peachtree City," said Betty Williams, a travel agent in Atlanta. But she knows that it is not the real Elvis there, just another person who finds putting on his clothes and his face irresistible.

"Elvis is not an icon," said Priscilla Parker, 57, president of We Remember Elvis, one of the largest of the 500 Elvis fan clubs around the world. "He is a man. He was a very human man. He is one of us, a poor country boy who made it and never lost his roots. He respected his fans."

Although "Elvis's memory will stay alive as long as I walk the face of the earth, as long as a fan is alive," Ms. Parker said, "we are not a cult. We do not worship Elvis Presley. We don't call this week a pilgrimage. It is more like a family reunion."

Mr. Bellis, the British fan, has little doubt that Elvis — the voice, if not the man — really will live forever.

"Last year," he said, "an Elvis album went to No. 3 on the British charts."

Savoring a Sweet Taste of Southern Summers

New York Times, July 4, 1997

DATELINE: Mobile, Ala., July 3

They put sweet iced tea in a can, now. Stores sell it in the soft drink section, beside 7-Up and Diet Coke and Evian. People pop the top and savor the brisk chemical bite and the imitation lemon aftertaste.

For some Southerners, the ones who grew up with iced tea brewed in gallon pickle jars by the loving hands of grandmothers and served over crushed ice in tall, sweating glasses, progress is a very, very sorry thing.

In the vernacular of the South of not so long ago, there was no such thing as sweet iced tea. There was just tea, always sweetened in a jug or pitcher with cane sugar, always poured over ice. In a region where the summertime air is thick and hot and still even when it's the dark, where people work hard and sweat rivers, hot tea was senseless and unsweetened tea was just brown ice water.

But now, say true believers in sweet iced tea, this most Southern of delicacies might be in its last generation, as younger people turn more to soft drinks and many of them do not even know how to make it. In time, it may go the way of poke salad and moonshine, a thing of museums and memory.

But down here on Mobile Bay, there is at least one lonely voice crying out, begging to still the hands of time.

"It's an art," said Jay Grelen, a columnist for the *Mobile Register* who is trying to preserve the dignity and sanctity of sweet iced tea. "Now people drink it out of a can."

Mr. Grelen, born in Marianna, Fla., just south of the Alabama state line, persuaded his newspaper four years ago to sponsor a sweet tea–brewing contest, drawing contestants from, well, Alabama mostly. But it just may be sweet tea's world championship, because it may be the only contest there is — at least the only one anyone knows of. In the past few years, it has been a part of the Fourth of July holiday, drawing as many as 40 contestants.

First prize is a handsome pewter pitcher.

"I've got my game face on," said Jean DeSchriver of Fairhope, Ala., who has tried every year and lost. "I am the Susan Lucci of iced tea contests."

The 40-year-old Mr. Grelen, whose columns on ordinary and extraordinary people have won him a broad following of readers, came up with the idea five years ago, after a hot and sweaty day of picking corn outside Mobile.

Mr. Grelen, covered in grime and sweat and all but faint from thirst, stopped at a sit-down catfish restaurant but realized he was just too dirty to sit inside. "I looked awful," he said.

"I sheepishly asked the cashier if I could buy a glass of sweet tea to go," he said. "She came back with a whole pitcher of tea, sat me on the porch in a rocking chair and refused to take any money. I was so struck by her kindness I nearly killed myself, because I felt obligated to drink every sip.

"I knew then that sweet tea embodies all that is good about the South and its hospitality. Life's too short not to enjoy, and it's too hot not to have sweet iced tea."

Mr. Grelen is no white-gloved scion of a rich Southern family trying to preserve mint juleps on the veranda and harp music in the hall. Sweet iced tea spanned race and class; it was one thing Southerners had in common, besides mosquitoes and creeping mildew.

Back when people sat on their porches and talked, back when they knew their neighbors' names, they did so with iced tea, in Mason jars, in antique leaded crystal, in Flintstones' jelly glasses.

People still do that, in some corners of the South, but not as much as before.

"It is a civilizing force in our society," Mr. Grelen said. "I love to sit and talk and drink tea."

Besides, he said: "I'm a Southern Baptist. I can't smoke. I can't drink. I can't cuss. And now I can't go to Disney World. So tea is the only vice left to me."

A generation ago, it was common to see it in baby bottles.

Byron McCauley, who writes editorials at the paper, may have summed it up just right. Iced tea, he said, "is the house wine of the South."

Mr. Grelen was so enamored with the place of iced tea in Southern society that he wrote a column about it, and asked people to send in their favorite iced tea recipes. The contest soon was born.

"I just got seven letters," he said, but he was struck with the feeling with which people described the tea and their experiences. Life itself was flavored by it.

"People who wrote," he said, "wrote poetry."

So what makes award-winning tea? In the beginning, Mrs. De-Schriver tried to get fancy, adding passion fruit and nutmeg. She caught the judges looking at it funny. One judge, she said, held a jar of it and stared at the bottom, as if trying to decide where those unique flavors came from.

"Now I just make plain tea with lots of sugar," she said. "I would love one of those pewter tea pots."

The winner is always basic tea, usually with water, tea and sugar, and skill.

"Major sugar, major lemon," said Scott Steele, whose tea, served at his Sonic Drive-In, is a local favorite. He also adds ice to the tea as soon as it is brewed, and keeps it at 40 degrees.

Mr. Grelen's recipe has a subtle twist.

He begins with a local brand of tea, Hill & Brooks, which is smooth, not bitter, he said.

He lets a half gallon of water come to a boil, then turns off the heat and puts in four quart-size tea bags. He lets them steep for exactly eight minutes. He does not boil the tea.

Then he pours the hot, half-gallon of steeped tea into a jug of cold water, exactly one-half gallon, in which he has dissolved two cups of sugar.

Some people insist on putting the sugar into a boiling tea mixture, then adding cold water. He politely disagrees.

"It makes it a little bitter," he said.

The tea is better the second day. But he cannot resist draining several glasses as soon as it is done, and lets the rest sit in the refrigerator, where it mellows a little.

This year's competition, on the banks of the Mobile River at a downtown park, will also include a contest for best tea cakes. A mild controversy has arisen over what a tea cake is — it is supposed to be a simple, vanilla-flavored cookie — but it is a sideshow to the main event.

There is also a contest to see who can suck a bottle of tea the fastest through a baby bottle nipple.

Some traditions need to die.

A Delicacy of the Past Is a Winner at Drive-In

New York Times, November 10, 1996

DATELINE: Atlanta, Nov. 9

Ponce de Leon Avenue is a fat boy's dream.

In one two-block stretch, just north of downtown Atlanta, the drive-through fast-food restaurants are door-to-door, and the hungry but very busy people are bumper to bumper. A motorist can purchase three different brands of fried chicken, grab a handful of soft tacos, throw a pizza in the back seat, sample four different nationally advertised cheeseburgers and slurp down a butter-pecan milk shake and never get his car out of first gear.

By making right turns only in the block, the motorist could "do chicken right" and "run for the border" and save the Domino's driver a trip. It is typical of Atlanta and America, the too-tired-to-cook person's salvation on the lonely drive home.

But here, among this predictable plenty, rises the unmistakable smell of chitlins. That would be remarkable in itself, in this city that has buried or razed its past, where good Southern food is a precious rarity and chitlins — the proper, virtually unused spelling is chitterlings — are as Southern as Southern gets.

What really makes it remarkable is that a customer can order them by shouting into a drive-up microphone, just as if ordering a burger and fries, and come away with some seasoned, aromatic, honest-to-God genuine chitlins — fried pork entrails — while hardly even slowing down.

Shelley Anthony, a 44-year-old second-generation restaurateur, might be the only drive-through chitlin magnate in the whole world. He owns eight restaurants in the Atlanta area, and some of them — like the one on Ponce de Leon, housed in an abandoned hamburger drive-through — are take-out only.

A plain-spoken man who wants it understood right up front that the only reason his restaurants are doing well is because his wife, Diane, has done such a good job refining old family recipes, he never thought of himself as a pioneer until he was asked if he knew anyone else in the drive-through chitlin business.

"Drive-by chitlins?" said Mr. Anthony, whose mother and father ran a sit-down restaurant in his native Tampa, Fla. "You got a point there. I haven't even thought about that. But that's a serious fact. We might be the only ones in the world."

The name of the drive-through restaurants is just This Is It.

Chitlins, or chitterlings, are testament to the down-home doctrine that nothing in the hog is inedible, except the eyeballs. Chitlins look terrible and smell strong when they are cooking — no one is real sure why that happens, because they are carefully cleaned — but they taste good, said patrons who stopped by to get a mess of them outside the Ponce de Leon restaurant.

"I hadn't had any since I was little," said Alicia Thomas, a middle-aged woman who was visiting friends in Atlanta. "They're good. They're high, but they're good."

Chitlins, with fries and slaw, cost $6.99.

Mr. Anthony sells them from this boxlike restaurant about the size of a delivery van, with double drive-through windows, one on each side.

"We sell a lot of them," he said, but he conceded that a man would go broke selling just chitlins in a city where most people are either from somewhere else or are so citified they do not know what a chitlin is.

"No way," said one young woman at the drive-through, when asked if she had ever had any chitlins. "I don't know what they are, but they're something nasty."

That is why Mr. Anthony also sells barbecued chicken, collard greens, corn bread, fresh potato salad specked with green onions, and real macaroni and cheese, "not that stuff from a box," he said. He sells a chopped pork sandwich for 99 cents, to compete with the 99-cent burgers on the fast-food highway.

But if you really want chitlins, as Ms. Thomas said, you will pay the $6.99.

It is the 90's way of enjoying this traditional pork product.

It is hog-killing time in the South — usually after the first frost — and one of the first things consumed is the intestines. Unlike other cuts of meat that could be salted and put away, at least before refrigeration, the intestines would not keep.

"This is the season," Mr. Anthony said, "and people want them real bad now." People do not seem to mind that they come on a Styrofoam plate.

He refuses to give out his recipe, in fear there would be drive-by chitlins popping up all over. But the first thing, he said, is "just make sure they're clean."

One of his restaurants is in the Georgia Dome, where the Falcons of the National Football League play. He does not sell chitlins there (they are not good stadium food), but people ask for them.

"I think people get tired of the traditional drive-through," he said. "You come here, you get something that sticks to your ribs, something that will help you make it to the next day. I've been wanting to sell things like collard greens and fresh macaroni and cheese from a drive-by window for a long time."

That meant downsizing the menus from the sit-down barbecues and sit-down Southern food restaurants that he opened here several years ago, but he kept the chitlins.

"People ask for them — doctors, lawyers, all kinds of people," he said. "Because they remember them."

A Sugar Bowl Lacking a Certain Sweetness

New York Times, January 1, 1997

DATELINE: New Orleans, Dec. 31

Maybe it will unfold this way:

The University of Florida and Florida State University meet on a field of honor in the Superdome here this Thursday night, and sportsmanship reigns. There is no trash talk, no dirty play or accusations of dirty play. Two respected football coaches gaze at each other across the artificial turf, in mutual admiration.

And the fans, stone-cold sober every one, cheer for their team without cussing the other team, even a little. Then, when the Sugar Bowl game is over, the winners and the losers embrace in fellowship, and all drive home together on Interstate 10, in a caravan of brotherly love.

It could happen.

And swine could fly.

"Last time, there were fistfights in the elevator lobby" of a nearby hotel, Joanne Fleece, University of Florida class of 1953, said of the most recent Sugar Bowl meeting between the two rivals, just two years ago. "It was really bad. I walked up eight flights of stairs" just to avoid the warring fans.

"There was almost too much emotion," said Mrs. Fleece, who lives in St. Petersburg with her husband, Joe, also a Florida alumnus. "I hope it won't be that bad this time."

But as fans filter into the neutral ground of New Orleans to see their teams knock heads for the second time this season, the emotions are more intense, more raw, than ever in a rivalry that is by tradition hot to the touch.

"It is your basic battle between good and evil," said one Florida State backer, Bill Evans, a real estate broker in Jacksonville. "We are good, and they are evil. Evil always loses to good."

The passions run strong any time they play. The schools are just 134 miles apart — Florida at Gainesville, Florida State at Tallahassee. The alumni see each other every day, in company boardrooms and courthouse cafes, and when they turn out the lights to go to bed. In Florida, a mixed marriage might not have anything to do with race.

One Florida legislator, having been splashed with what appeared to be urine at the first meeting of the teams this year, in Tallahassee, called the fanaticism "the dark side of college football." The older alumni, of a more gentle age, shake their heads sadly at what the rivalry has become but are flocking to this game in Cadillacs and chartered planes.

Now circumstances have turned the already intense heat up to a faster boil. Part of it is that this bowl game is a rare major-college rematch — the Florida State Seminoles beat the University of Florida Gators just a month ago, in the regular season — and that a victory would mean a national championship for the No. 1-ranked Seminoles and perhaps for the No. 3-ranked Gators.

But the two teams have met a second time in a single season before, in the game that resulted in the brawl that chased Mrs. Fleece up the staircase.

This particular game is more personal and more important than ever because honor has been assaulted. Florida's coach, Steve Spurrier, known to Seminole fans and some other foes as the Evil Genius, tossed a lighted match into a lake of gasoline when he contended that the Florida State coach, Bobby Bowden, had told Seminole players to injure Florida's Heisman Trophy–winning quarterback, Danny Wuerffel, in the game at Tallahassee.

Making an accusation of dirty football is about the worst thing one coach can say to another, short of calling him a sissy.

"Bobby Bowden is a fine man," sniffed Fanitsa Meehan, an interior designer from Tarpon Springs whose home is adorned with a stuffed gator head, a hatchet buried in its skull.

"That other guy," she said of Mr. Spurrier, "pitches fits on television." She is referring to Mr. Spurrier's habit of flinging things on the sideline when all is not going well.

Even the jokes seem a little meaner this time.

QUESTION. Why do Florida State graduates put their diplomas on the dashboards of their cars?
ANSWER. So they can park in the handicap spots.

Tens of thousands of Gator-haters and 'Nole-bashers will be in New Orleans by Thursday, but the name-calling started weeks ago. Nerds on both sides slug it out with words on the Net; drunks from both sides will almost certainly slug it out this week on Bourbon Street. Already some fans have exchanged four-letter greetings and middle-digit salutations in the French Quarter.

New Orleans, besieged by the latest in a wave of murders and other violent crime — Miss Louisiana was carjacked in front of her home this week — and still recovering from the crash of a freighter into a riverside shopping mall, is not too concerned about the gathering clouds, say hotel clerks, taxi drivers and bartenders.

The city will just absorb them, like any other storm.

QUESTION. What do you get when you go slow through Gainesville?
ANSWER. A diploma.

The oyster bar at Felix's restaurant in the Quarter was thick with cigar smoke and lined with empty shells on Monday afternoon. Seminole fans stood at the bar, their backs to a table of seated Gator fans.

"We don't hate the Gators," said Steve Kalenich, a Florida State fan from Fort Lauderdale whose father played for the Seminoles in the 1950's. "We just hate Steve Spurrier."

"No," said Mr. Evans, the real estate broker from Jacksonville, standing a few feet away. "We hate the Gators, too."

The table of Gators endured it with chilly civility.

"We have to live with them year round," said Bill Brannon, a lawyer from Lake City.

QUESTION. How do Florida State players get their morning exercise?
ANSWER. By fighting over the toy in the Fruit Loops.

The Gators see the game not just as a chance to get even but as a way to vault back into title contention.

"We Seminoles are not enamored of a rematch," said Martin Fleet, a psychologist in Marietta, Ga., who grew up in Tallahassee and is as much a Seminole as a man can be. "I was at that first game. It was an emotionally draining experience. Now we have to do this all over again. We didn't want that."

The rivalry can even strain a marriage.

As a younger man, Dr. Fleet first enrolled at Florida but never felt as if he belonged.

"I tried to root for the Gators," he said, "but I never put my heart in it."

He eventually left — having stayed long enough to meet Susan, now his wife, in 1976 — and later graduated from Florida State. She remained at Florida, took her degree there and is a determined Gator fan.

They will watch the game on television.

"A chance to beat Spurrier twice," said Dr. Fleet, noting the one good thing about a rematch. He may, he said, "do a couple of dances around the couch" if that happens.

"He talks a lot of trash," said Mrs. Fleet, a tax analyst.

"We're going to kill them," she said, not long after her husband had described her as "quiet" and "not that sports-minded."

QUESTION. What does a University of Florida graduate say to a
  Florida State graduate?
ANSWER. Welcome to McDonald's. Can I help you?

The sideshow created by Mr. Spurrier's accusation has in some ways become the show itself.

"He's got to learn some control," said Mrs. Meehan, the Seminole booster.

Mr. Spurrier's contention that Mr. Bowden, who is a preacher as well as a coach, instructed Seminole defenders to hurt the Gator quarterback is a rare thing in major-college football, where coaches are more prone to swallow such accusations than to speak them.

Mr. Bowden said Mr. Spurrier was probably just trying to influence the Sugar Bowl's game officials, making them more likely to penalize the Seminoles for any marginally late hits on Danny Wuerffel. Mr. Spurrier said he was just trying to protect his quarterback.

The fans know who is right, who is just.

Bobby Bowden "is a role model," said Mrs. Meehan, owner of the tomahawked gator.

Steve Spurrier "is a role model," said Mrs. Fleece, the Gator fan.

The game, and the strain, will be over soon. But the jokes will last all year.

A man walks into a store and says, "I want an orange hat, blue pants, orange shirt and blue shoes."

The clerk says, "You must be a Gator man."

"How did you guess?" the man asks. "By the colors?"

"No," the clerk says, "this is a hardware store."

George Corley Wallace

He took giant steps through history but was careless where he trod.

Emotional March Gains a Repentant Wallace

New York Times, March 11, 1995

DATELINE: Montgomery, Ala., March 10

The marchers swarmed around the old man in the wheelchair, some to tell him he was forgiven, some to whisper that he could never be forgiven, not today, not a million years from now. Yet to all of the people who retraced the steps of the Selma-to-Montgomery civil rights march 30 years ago, George C. Wallace offered an apology for a doomed ideal.

The former Alabama Governor, whose name became shorthand for much of the worst of white Southern opposition to the civil rights movement, held hands with men and women he had once held down with the power of his office. To one aging civil rights war horse, he mumbled, "I love you."

Three decades ago, he was preaching the evil of integration and found approval, even adoration, in the eyes of many white Alabamians. There was the legendary stand in the schoolhouse door, to keep blacks from registering at the University of Alabama. It was his state troopers who used billy clubs and tear gas to control and intimidate marchers in Selma. Then, he took his message nationwide in a run for President in 1968.

A would-be assassin's bullet in a Maryland shopping center in 1972 made him a cripple, but his old words and views echo today on the lips of conservative politicians and others, even though the man people here just call "Th' Guv'na'" has long since capitulated, apologized and begged for forgiveness.

Now 75, in a wheelchair for a third of his life, he was too old and sick to make a speech to the 200 marchers, mostly black, who gathered at the St. Jude School in Montgomery, as they did on this day three decades ago. Instead, an aide read his remarks as Mr. Wallace, who is almost completely deaf, sat in silence.

"My friends," the aide read, "I have been watching your progress this week as you retrace your footsteps of 30 years ago and cannot help but reflect on those days that remain so vivid in my memory. Those were different days and we all in our own ways were different people. We have learned hard and important lessons in the 30 years that have passed between us since the days surrounding your first walk along Highway 80."

A woman in a brown beret quietly said, "Amen."

"Those days were filled with passionate convictions and a magnified sense of purpose that imposed a feeling on us all that events of the day were bigger than any one individual," the speech continued in its borrowed voice. "Much has transpired since those days. A great deal has been lost and a great deal has been gained, and here we are. My message to you today is, Welcome to Montgomery.

"May your message be heard. May your lessons never be forgotten. May our history be always remembered."

The marchers applauded. For 10 years now, Mr. Wallace has admitted the wrongness of his deeds 30 years ago. Still, to many of the people who suffered at the hands of the law-enforcement officers he commanded, it was important that he said it on this symbolic day.

But 30 yards away, 58-year-old Rufus Vanable sat in the shade of a tall pine tree and refused to hear.

"I ain't even interested in what he's saying," said Mr. Vanable, a retired construction worker who was part of the march that was bloodied on the Edmund Pettus Bridge in Selma. "If you lived through it, you wouldn't be either. If he thinks this will ease his mind in some way, let him do it. I'm not interested in looking at his face. It brings back too many memories.

"Seeing him say that he's sorry ain't gonna do me no good at all."

Like many others in the crowd, he said Mr. Wallace, a religious man, was trying more to clear a path to heaven than to soothe the painful memories of others. He said that he held no malice for Mr. Wallace and that he even believed the former Governor had changed, "but it means a hell of a lot more to him than it does to me."

"He's trying to get right with his maker, that's what he's doing," Mr. Vanable said. "It was hell. Any man who'd sic dogs on a child. He ain't made up for it."

As the marchers sang "We Shall Overcome," Mr. Vanable sat under his tree and sang to himself. Mr. Wallace, lost in the crowd, never saw him, either.

Others were more forgiving.

"Thank you, for coming out of your sickness to meet us," said Joseph E. Lowery, the president of the Southern Christian Leadership Conference and an organizer of that first march. "You are a different George Wallace today. We both serve a God who can make the desert bloom. We ask God's blessing on you."

The politics and economics of race are more complicated now, and the marchers, including the old survivors of meaner days, worry that the nation is going backward in its racial tolerance. They hear modern-day leaders blame blacks, because of crime and welfare, for what is wrong with America.

The marchers said they hoped those leaders were watching as George Wallace joined hands with them and bowed his head with them. It might be only symbolism, they said, but it was the right kind of symbolism.

"It's very important, in this day and time," said Gerri Perry, the principal at St. Jude. "It is important for people to see him, saying this.

"Back then, 30 years ago, I didn't think I would ever see anything like this."

What she saw was an old man wanting to set things right, for whatever reasons. The marchers did not ask him to be there. He asked them if they would give him a few minutes of their time.

He might be the only Alabama Governor to meet them. As of Friday afternoon, the marchers and Gov. Fob James, a Republican who ran on a conservative platform, had still not agreed to meet.

Instead, the marchers gathered around the man they had once hated. That old Wallace, the fiery judge who stood on the back of trucks and shouted, "Segregation now, segregation tomorrow, segregation forever," was nowhere around.

"He's been about to die for the last 10 years, and he's still living," Mr. Vanable said. "God's gonna make him pay."

A Symbol of Alabama's Past,
Indelible to Black and White

New York Times, September 15, 1998

DATELINE: Birmingham, Ala.

For 65-year-old James Harper, sitting on his tiny front porch in West Anniston with the day still brand new, the news that George C. Wallace was dead caused him to lower his eyes and catch his breath for a second, as if some last, dying chorus of "Dixie" had lodged in his throat.

"I didn't know," he said. "You here to talk about him? Sit down. I voted for him. Every time. I liked him standing up there in that school door, by God," he said, referring to Governor Wallace's positioning himself at the entrance to the University of Alabama on June 11, 1963, to prevent integration there.

"And the Federals had to move him," said Mr. Harper, who is white, and then he grinned.

"He was a man, by God. He wasn't no boy."

But when he was asked if he still respected the former Governor after a would-be-assassin's bullet crippled him in 1972, after old age and history mellowed him and even made him say he was sorry, Mr. Harper seemed not to hear.

"I loved that man," he said.

To many in the state of Alabama, the people who hated, feared or loved him, that frail, apologetic old man who died on Sunday night in Montgomery failed to register in their memories as vividly as the young, fiery one with slicked-back hair and rigid finger stabbing the air, the one who promised "segregation forever." A lot of people said they could forgive him, and would even pray for him, but many of them said they just wish he could have learned he was wrong a lot sooner, and led his state out of racial hatred, instead of into it.

"Anybody can have my forgiveness if they ask the Lord to forgive them," said 87-year-old John Lilley, making his way slowly down Birmingham's 20th Street with the help of a cane.

"He did what he did to stay on the good side of the white people. He did it to keep his job. But I forgive him."

Mr. Lilley, who is black, smiled a little when he was asked if the pain-racked, paralyzed man had found peace in death. "I don't know if George Wallace is in heaven," Mr. Lilley said, walking away. "The only thing I know is he's been in hell long enough."

Young people, white and black, know only the historical Mr. Wallace, and spoke of him the way they would have spoken of a Confederate statue on the courthouse lawn. But across the state, people who are old enough to remember a time before his wheelchair, who heard his voice before it was slurred, talked as if he had not been some distant politician in Montgomery, but someone who protected them, or threatened them. They take him personally.

"I remember being at ball games and having my parents come and get us because they had heard the Klan was coming," said Ernestine Abraham, a black woman who grew up in Birmingham in the 1960's. "He could have changed that. He had the power, and could have turned that tide. He didn't," said Ms. Abraham, now 44 and an office manager at a Birmingham bank.

"If he had not been hurt, he never would have changed," she said. And by then, it was too late, she said. Too many people had been hurt in the era of racism that he had prospered in, she said.

"The man in the chair didn't matter," she said. "The young man who stood in the schoolhouse door mattered."

"I guess," she said, "he didn't have the courage to do it, then."

As she talked, the first of the rush-hour traffic was beginning to creep through downtown Birmingham, past Kelly Ingram Park, where marchers were torn by police dogs and blown along sidewalks by powerful fire hoses as if they were so many leaves.

Mr. Wallace is very personal here.

"I grew up here when you couldn't sit here, and you couldn't eat there, and you had to sit in the last row," said Rita Kendrick, a 50-year-old black woman who works for Alabama Power in downtown Birmingham. "He tried to keep it that way."

But she believes he was sorry, that it was not just politics when he begged for forgiveness later in his life.

"You have to have a big heart to forgive him," she said. "I can, but it's hard."

But the people who gave him his power, families who voted for him by generation and wept when he lay bleeding on the asphalt of a Maryland shopping center, loved him then and now.

They loved him when he was unrepentant, because he told them to stand up and be proud.

For many of the people in his power base, the poor farmers and factory workers who had always lived beneath the disdain of the aristocrats, his message was stronger than moonshine.

"When you'd hear him talk, you knew he was for you and for Alabama," said Gary Heathcock, a 46-year-old white steelworker who lives in Alexandria. "My daddy always voted for him," he said, and once the family even voted for his wife, Lurleen. It was really a vote for George.

Some of them had never been told that they were even good enough for their place in Southern society, let alone better than anyone, and now there was this man moving from town to town on the campaign trail preaching to the crowded auditoriums and county fairs that they were superior to a whole race of people.

"I drove trucks for 30 years, and I worked in the pipe shop," Mr. Harper said. "Every time I wrote him a letter, he wrote me back."

It was not, said some of his older white supporters, that they always agreed with him.

Sometimes, said 76-year-old Ed Mullinax of Anniston, "I had to vote for him because he was the only one running."

"He was a fairly good fellow who had his faults," said Mr. Mullinax, a retired millwright who is white. "It was a different world."

Blacks voted for him, as early as 1958, because they saw him as a lesser evil. Cicero Bynum, a retired black steelworker from Gadsden, remembers meeting Mr. Wallace during the 1958 campaign.

"I did vote for him in 1958 because I couldn't vote for John Patterson," said Mr. Bynum, 69. "He was more evil than Wallace at that particular time.

"We met with him when he was trying to drum up support. They brought him in the back door of the building so the white folks wouldn't see him coming in."

Mr. Wallace would repay them by claiming he lost because he was too soft on segregation — and would vow never to let it happen again.

But in a way, said Mr. Bynum, Mr. Wallace's defiance served them.

"If he hadn't made that stand in the schoolhouse door, we wouldn't have come as far as we've come," he said. "Our problems wouldn't have been shown around the world."

Around the country, aging warriors in that struggle for civil rights graciously spoke of George Wallace as a changed man, as a sort of tragic figure who was swallowed in a whirlwind of his own creation. Historians said he was the perfect enemy, who gave the people who believed in change someone to hate.

If that is true, then they needed each other.

"All throughout history, if you have an ugly enemy, if your enemy is cruel and monstrous or you can paint him as a monster," the battle over people's conscience can be won, said the Rev. Joseph E. Lowery, the former president of the Southern Christian Leadership Council and one of the Rev. Martin Luther King's chief aides in the 1960's.

"We didn't need to do that. We just had to reveal him," he said. "He did reveal himself, for that matter."

"So he will wear that," said Mr. Lowery. "Although I'm sure that there are some people who will remember that, like the prodigal son, he came to himself."

He points out that Mr. Wallace had once been a politician in the mold of Jim Folsom, the more moderate former Governor. And as he became older and admitted his mistakes, he seemed to try to return to that.

"The beginning was like the end," Mr. Lowery said.

Many, especially young people, will remember only the one in the middle, the demagogue.

Cedrick Rembert, a black junior at the University of Alabama, knows only that legacy of division. "I don't hate him," he said, but "I have never heard anything positive about him."

Some will not remember him at all.

"I really don't think he's going to have a legacy," said Angela Davis, a black sophomore at the University of South Alabama in Mobile. "There are a lot of people on campus who don't even know who he is."

Mr. Harper knows.

His Mr. Wallace never got old, never capitulated. His Mr. Wallace was almost President.

And while Mr. Wallace may have apologized for what he did, Mr. Harper will not apologize for the pride he once felt at being part of his climb, his legend.

"I worshiped the ground he walked on," he said.

Wallace Remembered, for Who
He Was and Who He Became

New York Times, September 17, 1998

The coffin, draped in the blood-red "X" on pure white that is Alabama's state flag, seemed almost too heavy to carry. Eight young, strong-looking Alabama state troopers bore the coffin foot by foot down the massive marble steps of the State Capitol, some of them having to place two hands on the rails of the coffin to steady it between them.

It was not the weight of it — George C. Wallace was just a small man, withered by paralysis and age — but the distance. The troopers carried his coffin some 100 steps, from the rotunda where thousands had viewed his body, down the steep walkway from the Capitol he had once used as a war room to preserve segregation, and off into history. It was eerily quiet, just footsteps on stone.

Just minutes before the troopers carried the coffin to Mr. Wallace's funeral and burial here in Montgomery, Janel Bell, a 32-year-old black woman, spoke of the man who had once been shorthand for racism in America, and then, after begging for forgiveness, had won the black vote in his final campaign for governor.

"A servant of the people," Ms. Bell said.

A populist, if there has ever been one, he mirrored the will of the people no matter if it was cruel or compassionate, and won an unprecedented four terms as governor from 1962 to 1986. But it was what he would call his greatest mistake — his defense of segregation — for which he will live on, in the history books.

"He was the mouthpiece for what a lot of people thought," said Ms. Bell, a public relations director for the Montgomery Museum of Fine Arts, mirroring them at their worst, and when their hearts began to soften.

It was what people said over and over here as Mr. Wallace, who had died Sunday night at the age of 79 from a heart attack after years of close calls, finally succumbed to time and the sickness and pain that had been his constant companions.

Mr. Wallace, people here said, did not lead Alabama anywhere it did not want to go. He was leading others in the United States there, too, before Arthur Bremer's five bullets left him crippled and in agony in 1972.

The Rev. Cal Merrell, 50, drove from Atlanta, and had his picture made with the coffin in the background.

"I heard him talk in Valdosta, Ga., when he was running for president," Mr. Merrell said, remembering that he was chilled.

"How can he have my future in his hands," he recalled thinking then.

Decades later, Mr. Wallace shook his hand and called him his brother.

"I cried, when I went up there," Mr. Merrell said.

Older white people mixed with older blacks in a steady but never overwhelming stream past the coffin, near a bust of Mr. Wallace's first wife, Lurleen, who was also elected governor but died of cancer in her first and only term in the late 1960's. People said she ran so that Mr. Wallace could continue to run Alabama and build his power base, but she received more votes than he ever did. Alabamians loved Lurleen, and some of them said with a smile as they filed inside that now, at last, the two were together.

"I think he's at peace now — you can see it in his face," said Ruby Shirley Noonan, who used to run errands for the Wallaces when she was 15 years old. "The pain is gone now."

One of those who came to say goodbye was James Hood, who was one of the black students whom the governor had tried to turn away from the University of Alabama when he stood in the door in 1963, blocking their way.

Like a lot of black people who lived through the civil rights movement, Mr. Hood said he believed that Mr. Wallace was sincere when he said he was sorry, though he could understand why some would doubt him.

"I think he made peace with God," said Mr. Hood, now 56. He was 19 the day Mr. Wallace, surrounded by a sea of state troopers, blocked the door.

Decades later, he met with a different Mr. Wallace.

"Whom the gods would destroy, they first make mad with power," Mr. Wallace told him, Mr. Hood recalled.

"If any man understands the true meaning of pain and suffering, it is George Wallace," said Mr. Hood, who found himself again surrounded by state troopers, but this time some of them had skin the color of his own.

It was not just the physical pain that Mr. Wallace endured, but the knowledge, he said, that no matter how many times he said he was sorry, there would always be those who would not believe, or accept.

"The fact the people could not forgive him" haunted Mr. Wallace, said Mr. Hood, who made a career in education administration and now lives in Madison, Wis.

Dorethea Knight, 35, from Alexander City, was just a baby when Mr. Wallace left many black people terrified.

"When you're scarred, you're always scarred," she said, and Mr. Wallace and the people he tried to suppress have that in common now. "Is he at peace, truly? You have to wonder about that."

As she stood over the coffin, one word crept into her mind: "Why?"

"You forgive," she said. "You don't forget."

As the last of the mourners and just curious trickled out, the honor guard of state troopers lifted the coffin and made its way, at least one on unsteady legs, down that tortuous stairway to the hearse.

At the foot of the hill, 68-year-old John Watkins waited on the hot asphalt. Like a lot of older black people, he compared Mr. Wallace to David of the Bible.

"God forgave him, in the 51st psalm," Mr. Watkins said. "There's no reason he can't do it for the Governor."

As the funeral procession wove through Montgomery, high school students and black people from a housing project lined the streets, not a big crowd, but enough to show that someone important had passed their way.

At his funeral, ministers emphasized that Mr. Wallace had found peace in his faith, and painted a picture of a very human husband and father, not the demagogue who put civil rights advocates at great risk with his fiery speeches that, some of those advocates have said, were like gasoline on a brush fire.

Dr. Lester H. Spencer, the senior minister at the elegant First United Methodist Church, described how Mr. Wallace, who would be married three times in his life, reacted to the death of Lurleen.

"He gently rubbed his fingers through her hair," Mr. Spencer said and recalled Mr. Wallace's words: "Oh, how much we loved you. Goodbye, sweetheart."

The legacy of George Wallace, the ministers at his funeral said, should be that he had the courage to admit he was wrong.

The crowds were smaller than those for Lurleen Wallace, after she died of cancer in 1968, and smaller than those who gathered to pray for Mr. Wallace when he was shot.

The crowd was much smaller than those for beloved University of Alabama football coach Paul "Bear" Bryant, when people lined overpasses to catch a glimpse of his hearse after his death in January 1983.

But older people at today's funeral said there was a reason for that. Mr. Wallace outlived his cronies, and many of the people who put him in office.

"God gave George Wallace a new heart," said Mr. Spencer, the minister. "The legacy of George Wallace is not the schoolhouse door. The legacy of George Wallace is one of God and change."

Monuments

I like graveyards and museums. They prop up our memories.

In New Orleans, a Day for Visiting the Dead

New York Times, November 2, 1998

In a graveyard where rows of crosses lean left and right, where one-inch-thin headstones bow to the dirt or tilt toward the sky and misspelled missives to the dead are inked onto rotted plywood markers, Cleveland Cobb spent a long time making sure he got the flowers just right.

Mr. Cobb, 75, first pounded the dirt of the family plot as smooth as he could with the flat of his shovel, then, with his hands, scooped a hollow place just big enough to root a small clutch of white flowers.

"My mother," he said, in explanation. "Mary. I like to see her grave looking good. Nothing else I can do for her."

Her headstone bears other names. Here, in this obscure cemetery in a city that lists its graveyards in tourist guidebooks because of their beauty and history, the dead are housed not in ornate crypts but buried in the soil, the bones of generations — six, eight, more — mingling in a single hole.

"I got a daughter in here, too," Mr. Cobb said. "She was 12, no, she was 7. Got hit by a car." He poured some water on the flowers, perfectly straight, and after a little while he looked up, embarrassed.

"Now," he said, "why can't I recall that child's name?"

Then, as if in penance, he went back to his knees and fussed some more with the little rectangle of dirt in Holt Cemetery, where his family, too many to recall, sleep.

Today is All Saints' Day, a day to honor the dead, and in New Orleans this Roman Catholic holiday is embraced by Protestants, Jews, everyone, it seems. People bring food, sit in the shade and visit in the long, granite rows of old and new crypts, what people here call cities of the dead. Because the water table is only a few feet beneath the surface, it is necessary to inter most people above ground — everyone except the poor, who must rest in the muck.

Marble and granite are expensive, but dirt is just dirt. Here in Holt Cemetery, established as a boneyard for paupers in 1879, people like Mr. Cobb cannot change the fact that, in death as in life, people with money can sleep easier. But all around this ragged place on this day for the dead are signs of love, honor and respect, signs that rival anything the richer people do in their manicured cities of fresh-cut flowers on polished stone.

If richer, older cemeteries are a record of New Orleans society, Holt Cemetery is a symbol of its potholed streets, its peeling shotgun houses, its un-air-conditioned churches, bingo halls, blue-collar social clubs and beer joints.

Just a few steps from where Mr. Cobb, a retired truck driver, knelt by his mother and daughter, 75-year-old Luella Marshall limped slowly away from a small but brand-new brass headstone inscribed with her husband's name. A young man, one of her great-nephews, held her hand, steadying her.

"If my husband was the one living, I know he'd be out here today, seeing about me," said Mrs. Marshall, whose husband died last year from a blood clot.

The gleaming headstone — "Edward Marshall, U.S. Army, World War II, Born Oct. 7, 1927, Died June 27, 1997" — tells only a little about him. In the hot sun of the afternoon — the only shade here is from a few oaks, gnarled with age, shrouded in Spanish moss — she told the things about him that mattered.

"He was a beautiful man," Mrs. Marshall said. "He treated me like a baby. If we was ever in the house, we was in the same room, always together. If I washed the clothes, he'd put them on the line. If we cooked, he'd cook one thing and I'd cook another thing, just so we could be in the kitchen."

Her arthritis is so bad now, she said, it is hard to tend the graves right, to make this annual trek to pull weeds and smooth the ground over her husband and other people she loves.

But Mrs. Marshall, who spent her lifetime caring for other people's children and ailing loved ones as what she calls "a sitter," swears she will find a way to care a little while longer for the man who made life sweet.

"As long as I can put one foot down in front of the other, I will be out here to visit my husband," she said.

Her husband's marker was designed to be laid flat on the ground, but she has it propped up, so people can see it better.

New Orleans, as poets and other intellectuals have often written, has seen more death than most other American cities, perhaps because it predates them, because disease, floods, storms and war have ravaged the city since its beginning, in the early 1700's.

Holt is a relatively new cemetery, having been built in the late part of the 19th century, but there are thousands of graves and uncounted bodies buried one atop the other. People tending the graves said a family has to wait at least two years before burying someone in the same plot in the city-owned graveyard.

"You can put them in, as their bones decay," Sidney Scott said as he painstakingly used gold paint and a tiny brush to trace the names of a faded, weather-worn headstone. "Some people call it a potter's field, but that's not what it is." That would mean the people buried here were unwanted, forgotten, and that would be wrong, said Mr. Scott, a maintenance man at a church.

"Momma and Daddy taught me to love," he said when asked why he came out each year on All Saints' Day to make these graves look nice, to make them look remembered.

Harry Scott, his father, died in 1958. Since then, Mr. Scott's father has been joined in that grave by a grandmother, two brothers and a niece. Because almost every inch of ground is used, only the people whose families are buried here can bury others here.

"I think they like it," Mr. Scott said as he finished painting in the names. He was referring to the dead. "At least, no one's come back and told me they didn't." He smiled at that.

People used to do more, on All Saints' Day and the days leading up to it, said Lillie Lewis, 72, and her sister, Ara R. Dozier, 74. They came to tend the grave that holds their mother, two grandmothers, a brother, another brother's first wife and "two babies."

"The Lord took them," Ms. Dozier said.

She promised her mother, before her death, she would tend the graves on All Saints' Day.

"Momma used to drive us here, and we'd have a picnic and stay all day," Ms. Dozier said.

The cemetery would be crowded with people, eating, talking, enjoying life as they remembered the lives of the dead.

People still do, but not as much. "They come but they don't stay," Ms. Dozier said.

She remembered a sweet potato vine that used to grow here. She wondered if it was still there.

Like many people here, there seemed no sadness in them. Mourning is not what All Saints' Day is for, people said, certainly not here, where people leave behind a favorite food and even a loved one's favorite beer — emptied, of course — on the graves.

As the two elderly sisters walked to their cars, they joked like children.

"She," Mrs. Lewis said of her sister, "is an old maid schoolteacher."

"She," Ms. Dozier said of her sister, "is not right, and has been that way all her life."

Because the burials here have far outnumbered the changes to the headstones, because it is impossible to tell where one grave ends and another begins, there is no telling how many people have been put here and forgotten. Once, the people say, stillborn babies and even body parts from surgeries were buried here, a less than dignified place, some people might believe, for a loved one.

But in this place where bones and memories mingle, where people work so hard to smooth the dirt and get flowers to grow straight and sometimes just remember a forgotten name, the dignity is in not letting the weeds and complacency claim the simple plots.

"It's one thing," said Cleveland Cobb, "I look forward to."

A Coach's Shrine, the Fátima of Alabama Football

New York Times, June 16, 1998

The bronze bust of Paul William (Bear) Bryant that glares from the museum's entrance is about five times life-size, and still might not be quite big enough.

If the sculptor had carved that craggy face on a mountain, a very big mountain, maybe the likeness of the former University of Alabama football coach might then be big enough to match the legend, might satisfy the fans who name children for him 15 years after his death.

"He was," said Emily Hornsby, who went to school at Alabama in 1938 and 1939, "wonderful."

The man that generations of fans just called Bear has his own museum here at this green and pretty university in western Alabama, a place where the coach's legacy is kept dust-free inside glass trophy cases and on videotape. On a hot June afternoon, the faithful — old women, teen-agers and grown men who see him as something more than mortal — filed past long-flat footballs and frayed jerseys and ancient cleats, just remembering.

"I was there, in Memphis. I've never been so cold," said the white-haired Mrs. Hornsby, staring up at a black-and-white photograph of Coach Bryant, his deeply lined face peering from a fur-trimmed hood, at the Liberty Bowl game, his last before retiring after the 1982 season as the winningest coach in Division I-A football. He died just a few weeks later, on Jan. 26, 1983.

For a lot of people here in Alabama, it has been cold ever since.

It is more than football idolatry that this museum holds. For 25 years, the coach, who got his nickname by wrestling a carnival bear when he was a boy, gave Alabamians something to be proud of in a time when the word "Alabama" drew scorn and jokes. Coach Bryant won three national championships in the 1960's — and six in all — and made the name "Alabama" stand for something good. Alabama was synonymous with George Wallace — and racism — then.

Mr. Bryant, though he also was criticized for being too slow to integrate his team, "gave us something positive to think about, about ourselves, in a bad time," said Kenneth Gaddy, the museum's director, who grew up listening to Alabama football games on the radio.

Ray Davis, a teen-ager in the 1960's in Opp, Ala., idolized Mr. Bryant. When he went to war in Vietnam, Mr. Davis walked with pride among other soldiers because Paul (Bear) Bryant and Alabama football gave him a status that others envied.

"You could be proud of being from here, no matter where you went," said Mr. Davis, who brought his teen-age son, Josh, to the museum. "Alabama did us proud, and it all came from him."

In his 25 years here as coach, 350 children have been named for him — Pauls and Paulas, Williams, Bryants, even a few Bears — according to a museum database. "That's just the ones we know about," said Mr. Gaddy, the director.

His players built their own legends. Kenny Stabler and Joe Namath threw touchdown passes for him before pro football made them heroes on Sunday afternoons.

Mr. Namath, under the stern coach, was just another schoolboy.

"My son-in-law was with Joe Namath that night," Mrs. Hornsby said.

"That night" was in 1963, when Mr. Namath broke team rules by going to a bar and was suspended for the last two games of the season, including the Sugar Bowl game against Mississippi on New Year's Day 1964.

"I'm sure they were drinking beer and singing," she said, "in a bar."

The museum chronicles the numbers — including his 323 career victories and a then-record 15 victories in bowl games — but the people who come here already know the numbers.

They come to gaze at the fuzzy houndstooth hat, now under glass, that was his trademark on the sidelines and to smile at the hideous black-and-white plaid couch that once sat in his office.

There is even a Waterford crystal copy of the hat, which glitters in one case like a massive jewel.

It seems a little fancy for a man who was born in Kingsland, Ark., on Sept. 11, 1913, and who rode to the University of Alabama in the rumble seat of a Model T in 1933, lettered in football then returned there to coach in 1958. Mr. Bryant, when asked about his success, would sometimes just mumble that he was proud not to be plowing.

The museum, like the legend it contains, shows no warts. There are no exhibits to the common knowledge that the man liked his whiskey, no reference to an accusation that he once conspired with a University of Georgia coach to fix a game. People here will not even entertain that talk. One does not spit in church.

A common refrain here is "Things ain't the same, since the Bear died." On Interstate 59, heading in to Tuscaloosa, a billboard for the Bryant museum promises otherwise.

"The Paul William Bryant Museum," it reads. "Where the Season Never Ends."

A Balladeer of Bluegrass Is Now Gone Yet Lives On

New York Times, November 4, 1996

DATELINE: Rosine, Ky., Nov. 1

The dirt has music in it.

Stand here amid the rain-streaked headstones in the Rosine cemetery, as dusk steals through the hills and hollows of western Kentucky and turns the steel towers of draglines into the skeletons of dinosaurs and the strip-mined coal fields into moonscapes, and listen to the dark.

For years, people have passed this way and sworn that they could hear the faint sound of a single fiddle drifting over from Jerusalem Ridge. Or was it Hell's Neck or Doodlepuss Hollow? It is just Uncle Pendleton Vandiver, on his way to another barn dance, fiddling on muleback as he rides and rides and rides.

Never mind that there is a headstone with his name on it, sunk in this ground.

He is the fiddler made famous in the song by Bill Monroe, his legendary nephew. Mr. Monroe, a mandolin picker and mule skinner, went on to become founder and ambassador of bluegrass music with tunes like "Uncle Pen," a tribute to the man who helped raise him and taught him to play. The lyrics are carved into Mr. Vandiver's headstone.

> Late in the evening
> About sundown
> High on the hill
> And above the town
> Uncle Pen played the fiddle, Lord
> How it would ring
> You could hear it talk
> You could hear it sing

Now, when the faint fiddling drifts through the night, some swear that they can hear the sweet, distant sound of a mandolin, joining in. It has been almost two months since Mr. Monroe's death, since he joined his uncle in the ground here in Rosine's cemetery and, if you believe such things, since his spirit joined his uncle's in the cool, crisp mountain air.

"People say that," said Mr. Monroe's niece, 66-year-old Rosetta Monroe Kiper, and she smiles at the notion. "People say a lot of things."

If ghosts of bluegrass do walk the night on earth, it must be here. Just as surely as the blues was born in the Mississippi Delta and a smoke-filled room in New Orleans gave birth to jazz, Rosine (pronounced RO-zeen) is the mother of bluegrass.

The scenery of this tiny hamlet in Ohio County is in virtually every song her uncle wrote, as is the character of the people, Mrs. Kiper said. She was still a child when Uncle Pen died but she remembers being laid in the bed with him when she was just a toddler. The old folks and babies went to bed early, and the grandparents and great-aunts and great-uncles would tell them stories until they went to sleep, as was the custom in that time and place.

"When I was a baby I had a lot of hair, and it was black — black and curly," said Mrs. Kiper, a strong-looking woman who used to beat the boys at baseball. "They would lay me in the bed with him and he would stroke my hair."

You can see the hardness and gentleness of her people in Mr. Monroe's music, she said. The men made their living strapped behind a mule or cutting timber. In some ways, the music softened them.

"Everybody played," said Mrs. Kiper, whose father, Speed, was Mr. Monroe's older brother. "People worked hard and they had to have their entertainment."

Rosine represents the Bill Monroe before the sold-out shows at the Grand Ole Opry. To many, the only Bill Monroe they have ever seen is the scowling, white-maned old man in a business suit and a cowboy hat, singing in his high lonesome tenor on the Nashville Network or Country Music Television.

Now Rosine, with help from the outsiders who love his music, plans to honor him with a theater, monument and museum. But in a way, these hills are already his theater, the tiny white-washed buildings his museum. This entire hamlet — estimates of the population range from 20 to 2,000 — is Mr. Monroe's monument, said Aaron J. Hutchings, who is a leader in the effort to keep alive Mr. Monroe's music and memory.

Mr. Hutchings, who is helping to rebuild the music barn in this unincorporated community, is the executive producer at Louisville's public television station, WKPC. His grandparents are Rosine natives, and his father met his mother here in a game of "Spin the Bottle."

Almost every day, visitors come through Rosine wanting to see Mr. Monroe's grave, see the places he sang about. Mr. Hutchings, or whoever is around, takes them to the cemetery, so they can grieve, and listen to the music on the wind.

It is fun to believe that the spirit of bluegrass legends wafts through here, he said, but what people may be hearing on the night wind is merely the legacy that people like Mr. Monroe and Uncle Pen left for flesh-and-blood pickers and fiddlers.

"There is something about this place that will make you hear the fiddle," Mr. Hutchings said in the graveyard. "Everybody around here plays." (They play on porches and on living room couches and the sound does drift, but it is no phantom.) "What you're hearing is the great tradition of this place."

What Mr. Hutchings cannot understand is why, every time he comes to either Uncle Pen Vandiver's headstone or Mr. Monroe's grave — his headstone is still unfinished but flowers cover it — there appears a snow-white cat with piercing blue eyes.

The cat came on Thursday night, Halloween, and pawed at his legs before leaping onto Mr. Vandiver's headstone and posing there, seeming to be a part of the design.

"That cat comes every time," Mr. Hutchings said. He is sure it is just a neighbor's cat, looking for affection. But it is funny how it only seems to appear at those headstones, he said.

Mr. Hutchings is one of the people pushing hard to bring the museum, theater and monument to Rosine. Larger places have been host to the big bluegrass shows — Uncle Pen's cabin was even carted off to Bean Blossom, Ind., as an attraction for big bluegrass concerts — but in Rosine the music is still played with the front-porch feel with which Mr. Vandiver and Mr. Monroe played it. Every Friday night, young and old gather in a barn-like building for a jam session of bluegrass. There is no plan to it. If you want to play, you play. If you want to sing, you sing.

"This man is exactly where he would have wanted to be," Mr. Hutchings said of Mr. Monroe's burial place. Mr. Monroe left here when he was 16, and died, at 84, south of here in Springfield, Tenn.

They had his funeral in the Rosine Methodist Church, which he sang about in "Little Community Church." In life he had always passed out quarters to all the children he saw. As he lay in the open coffin, mourners — the grown-up children he had been kind to — walked past one by one and laid quarters inside, Mrs. Kiper said.

Now and then someone puts one on his grave. "That and picks — mandolin and guitar picks," she said.

Mr. Monroe's most famous song, one that even Elvis recorded, was "Blue Moon of Kentucky," about loss and heartache. But in it, he wrote his own epitaph.

> Blue moon of Kentucky keep on
>   shinin'
> Shine on the one who's gone and
>   left me blue

Bourbon and Bayous

I should have been a Cajun. But I can't dance a lick.

French Quarter's Black Tapping Feet

New York Times, February 14, 1998

DATELINE: New Orleans, Feb. 13

The beer-bottle caps tacked to the bottoms of her sneakers collide with the brick sidewalk with a sharp clickety-clack, and the daytime drunks on Bourbon Street wobble their heads to stare at the child who dances to a song only she can hear.

> Hambone, Hambone, have you heard
> Momma gonna buy me a mockingbird
> If that mockingbird don't sing
> Momma gonna buy me a diamond ring

Rose Preston does not sing it, she merely plays it inside her head to keep time, her feet flying like she has just stepped in a bed of red ants. Miss Preston, whose nickname is Sweet Pea, is 14 but looks younger, an important thing in the city's French Quarter. In New Orleans, cuteness is a currency like anything else.

The youngest, cutest children make a little more money as they tap dance for tourists outside the two-drink-minimum bars, the lethargic striptease acts and the walk-up daiquiri stands. Most weekends, there are at least a dozen dancers here in the Quarter, all children, all performing beside a crumpled cardboard box.

The box is important. It needs to be big enough to catch the pocket change and wadded up $1 bills that the passersby throw at them with varying degrees of sobriety and skill. Miss Preston's box says "Zapps Potato Chips" along one side and contains just five quarters, a dime and a penny.

"Sometimes," she said the other night of her patrons, "they're grouchy."

The dancers are a tradition as old as this very old Mississippi River city. Generations of them have come and gone, all of them black, all from the poor neighborhoods that lie just out of sight and mind of the city's tourism epicenter. They form their own subculture, a community of children who dance for reasons innocent, and sometimes ominous.

Some do it because they like it, and others, like Miss Preston, do it to make money for their families. And a few dance because someone makes them. A small boy just outside the famous Cafe du Monde in Jackson Square, tiredly shuffles his legs in a sad pantomime of a dance as an older boy looks on, waiting to pocket any folding money the tourists drop.

But mostly, say sociologists and others who have watched this uniquely New Orleans tradition, the children who tap dance on the streets of the French Quarter do so because they have found a way to snatch at least a tiny scrap of the city's rich musical tradition, and make it pay.

Miss Preston was 5 years old when she started. She had seen little boys dancing in the French Quarter, and she mimicked them at home.

"My momma said, 'What you doing?'" Miss Preston said. "And I said, 'Tapping,'" "So momma brought me here," to Bourbon Street.

The logic was, if she was going to dance, she might as well get paid for it, Miss Preston said. When she is asked if she is any good at it, she grins and breaks into a blistering tap step that, at night, would strike sparks on the dirty sidewalk.

> If that diamond ring don't shine
> Momma gonna buy me a bottle of wine
> If that bottle of wine don't taste
> Momma gonna take me to the lake

Sometimes people pass by and wonder if they should feel sad about it, if the boys and girls perpetuate some racial stereotype. Miss Preston does not worry if her tap dancing is anything to be ashamed of. She only knows that it is necessary.

"I can make $20 or $30 a day," she said, and beamed.

Like a lot of children here, she gives the money to her family. And, like a lot of them, it is the only income they have outside of a government check.

While she likes the dancing, it is the money that has kept her here, on weekends and after school on weekdays, when the weather is good. No one makes her come. Nothing pushes her here, except, perhaps, her conscience. Her family can have more things if she dances.

"Food and stuff," she said. "Me and my family's trying to find a better place to stay."

She will never forget the day a black limousine pulled up to the curb and a well-dressed man stepped out, describing it this way:

"He gave me $50, and I said, 'Do you know what you give me,' and he said, 'Yes,' and I said, 'The Lord blessed me good.' I never stopped talking about that."

> If that water splash on me
> Momma gonna whip my b-u-t

She has three brothers and two sisters. They do not tap in the Quarter. "I won't let them," she said. Though she emphasizes that she is unashamed of what she does, she says, "I don't want them turning out like me." She sounds very old.

> If my b-u-t turn black
> Momma gonna buy me a Cadillac

"These are kids who are holding down jobs," said Joel Devine, a professor and chairman of the Department of Sociology at Tulane University here, "and making a very appreciable difference in a household income that is close to nonexistent.

"The sad thing is that it's not just a hobby. These are kids with very few alternatives. They go out and do put food on the table. That's the sadness. That there is a need for them to do it."

Not all the dancers bring money to their families. Some do it for candy money. Although a few, like Miss Preston, are teen-agers, most are younger than 8 or 9.

The new star of Bourbon Street dances at the corner of Bienville Street. His name is Raymond Keelen Jr., he is 5 years old, and he is cuter than a speckled puppy. His box is filled with money.

His father looks on and beams as coins tinkle into the box.

"He likes it," said the father, Raymond Keelen Sr. "Everybody in the French Quarter has a picture of him."

"It makes my legs big," Raymond Jr. said of his dancing. As he taps, he presses a hand to one ear.

"It hurts," he said, of the ringing from the bottle caps on his shoes.

A few blocks away, another little boy dances under the watchful eyes of a hard-faced teen-ager. Unlike Miss Preston and Raymond, he does not dance, he merely moves his legs back and forth, back and forth. He seems to be marching without getting anywhere. There are only coins in his box.

Sometimes, in this community of dancing children, Professor Devine said, "there is some real exploitation there."

He remembered the first time he saw the tap dancers, more than 18 years ago. "I had the liberal, northern, knee-jerk reaction" to black children tap dancing for nickels, he said, "but that was because I did not have the context of the city to put it in."

New Orleans has one of the poorest black communities in the nation, but in it are riches, the professor said, "of music and dance tradition, actively played out in the community."

And New Orleans has never worried much about being politically correct, say people who live there.

"For me it's just part of a New Orleans tradition, and I did not find it personally offensive," said Barbara Guillory Thompson, a professor of sociology and chairwoman of the division of social sciences at Dillard University here. "For me, it's perfectly good and honorable and honest."

Professor Thompson, an expert on the dynamics of black families, said that in the harsh realities in which the children live, "it's better than stealing."

Miss Preston's mother is out of work. Her father, the one who nicknamed her Sweet Pea because of her 40-watt smile, is dead.

She talks about a man from Alabama who will someday come and take care of her and her family, to be their new daddy. She talks about him the way other children would talk about a gleaming knight on a white horse.

Until then, the sound of her dance, the constant tap tap tap, will echo along Bourbon Street.

> And if that Cadillac don't work
> Momma gonna bring me back to Bourbon.

In a Louisiana Bayou Town, "Uncle Pat" Is the Law

New York Times, April 19, 1995

DATELINE: Jean Lafitte, La.

This town, surrounded by swamps, has one road in, one road out. If Police Chief Clarence (Uncle Pat) Matherne parks his police cruiser sideways across it, it is a dragnet.

Crime fighting is not much more complicated than that in Jean Lafitte, a town of about 2,000 people — including a considerable number of first and second cousins — just 30 minutes south of New Orleans. The Chief cannot remember the last time this town had a killing. And armed robberies, drive-by shootings and other ugly things happen to other people, not to his people.

That does not mean there is no crime here. The other day, when the Chief was getting ready to go fishing, the police dispatcher ruined what was shaping up to be a good day.

"Chief, you better get on down here," the dispatcher said. "It's them Vinnetts. They got into a fight at their momma's funeral, and now they're going to settle it with shotguns in the graveyard."

That was quickly followed by a call from the town's undertaker, who confirmed the dispatcher's fears. "Pat, I think there's liable to be gunplay," he said.

Chief Matherne, a rail-thin, 59-year-old man with a thick Cajun accent and long gray sideburns, handled it the way he handles most crime.

"I talked nice to de boys," he said, and defused the situation. "Uncle Pat," as some residents and even some criminals call the Chief, is more than the law in Jean Lafitte. He is also its conscience.

Suspected thieves, after a visit and talking to from the Chief, have been known to bring stolen merchandise and leave it at the Town Hall, which houses the two-room Police Department. Then they wait outside with their chins on their chests, morose, until he decides whether to send them to jail.

And it is not unusual for him to find a stolen outboard motor in the driveway.

"You see, babe (the Chief calls everybody babe), it's like this," he said. "I feel that if I just talk to de boys — and they're not bad boys — it's better than just banging them against the wall."

It is an often-misused cliché, when people talk about small towns, to say that everybody knows everybody else. But in Jean Lafitte it is more likely to be true. Dry ground is at a premium here in a town that is seven miles long but only a few hundred feet wide, so people know one another, and see one another up close.

Uncle Pat, who lives on Matherne Street and ran a propeller shop for 30 years, knows almost everyone. He has only been the Chief for four years, but he has been an observer of his community all his life. When there is a small breakdown in its character, he knows which tiny shack or mobile home to call on.

His style is a mixture of familial kindness and no-nonsense authority. He has never had to draw his shiny .38-caliber revolver, and has never even had to get rough with a man. But he is capable of it. He swung a 10-pound hammer much of his life, battering ship propellers into shape.

The Chief's biggest weapon is trust. Thieves know he will treat them like misguided children. He may file charges — often, he does not — but he will not talk down to them.

"We've had people who say, 'I'll turn myself in, but I ain't going to talk to nobody but Uncle Pat,'" said Sgt. Mary Jo Hargis, the other half of the town's two-member department.

The most startling example of the Chief's insights and influence came earlier this year, when a woman reported that thieves were stripping aluminum siding off her boathouse.

"She was riding down the road one day and saw this truck go by, and said, 'That looks like my damn aluminum!'" the Chief said.

He had a pretty good idea who one of the thieves was, he said, and he went by to have a talk.

The man confessed, and said he had accomplices. The Chief ordered him to round up the accomplices and appear at his Town Hall office at 2 o'clock the next afternoon.

At precisely 2 P.M. the next day, six men arrived and turned themselves in. Over the next few days, a total of 13 men confessed to the thefts.

"They may lie to me for a little while, but not for long," Chief Matherne said.

It seems like effortless police work, but it broke his heart a little, too. Some of the men brought their families with them, to wait in the Town Hall lobby. The sight of children always bothers him, he said.

"They say, 'Uncle Pat, I had to do it because my babies was hungry.' I say, 'You don't like to work too damn much, that's why you did it.'"

The bayou is not a rich place, populated mostly by fishermen and workers in what is left of the oil industry. Stealing has been a part of the culture for more than 200 years, but it was once done on a much grander scale.

This town, on the edge of Bayou Barataria, is named for the French pirate Jean Lafitte, who helped Andrew Jackson and his army of sharpshooters defeat the British in the Battle of New Orleans in 1815. Now the stealing involves mostly outboard motors and fishing boats.

"You steal something like that, you take away a man's living," the Chief said. "What does he tell his wife?"

Chief Matherne takes theft seriously, but he seems to despise drug dealers. If he suspects someone of dealing drugs, he parks his cruiser in their driveway at night and just sits there.

"They move on out," he said, sooner or later.

He became Chief because friends encouraged him, he said, and because he had always wanted to try it. He does not mind that some days his department does not even get a call. And when it does it may only be about another alligator that is stuck in a culvert outside the car wash, and that has to be lured out with catfish entrails.

"If I had been a younger man when I got started, I would have liked to have been a detective," he said, looking almost wistful.

Friends and other law-enforcement officers in the bayou country say he is a detective.

His dedication is unquestioned. He cannot remember his last day off. "I can't even go fishing," he said.

He never knows when violence will erupt at another graveside service.

In Louisiana, Card Game Reveals the Cajun Spirit

New York Times, February 18, 1996

DATELINE: Marksville, La., Feb. 15

The 68-year-old man in the robin's-egg-blue three-piece suit eased a long, thin cigar out of his wrinkled face and reflected on the best hand of bourré he had ever played. It was not in Acadian Louisiana, where the card game was born on the bank of the bayou, but in an officer's club at a United States Air Force base in chilly Newfoundland.

It was the 1950's, and Roy J. Nickens was still a young man, a kind of traveling salesman for a company that did business with the military base. He had a few hours to kill, and he asked the officers if they would like to join him in a hand of bourré (pronounced BOO-ray), a game similar in mechanics to hearts but like poker in its spirit and drama.

The Cajuns play it best, since they are the only ones who play it at all.

But how, he was asked, did he find enough Louisiana boys in ice-bound Newfoundland to get up a game?

"That was the beautiful part," he said. "They wasn't from Louisiana, them boys."

So how, he was asked again, did they know how to play?

"I showed them," he said, and grinned like a shark.

He won $7,000 playing dollar-ante bourré, and he caught the first plane out. "I did the boys a favor," he said. "If I'd of played poker, I'd of got all their money."

Bourré is a derivative of a card game that came to the lower half of Louisiana from France in the early 1800's, and has been a part of the culture here ever since, said Mr. Nickens, who lives in Melville, La., and learned to play by betting marbles and match sticks as a boy.

When the Grand Casino announced that it would be the host of the first-ever World Championship of Bourré Tournament here in the Parish of Avoyelles, Mr. Nickens came not to play but to insure that it would be played right. He has written what might be the only book on bourré, which players here say means "to trounce," and helped preside when hundreds of players converged this week on this tiny parish town of Marksville to see who is best.

To call it a "world championship" is perfectly legitimate, said the players, since the world of bourré only reaches from Lafayette over to New Iberia, to up around Cottonport, and down to Houma, none more than a few hours' drive from the other.

The rules in the game vary from parish to parish and sometimes from house to house, where grandmothers play marathon three-day games at kitchen tables littered with gumbo bowls and quarters, and oil derrick workers play for paychecks and wedding rings in no-name bars, drinking bronze whisky and looking mean.

Nicky Bordelon, the mortician in Mansura, put himself through college one semester at Louisiana State University playing bourré. "I lived like a king," he said. He even put off dabbling in the mysteries of love, for bourré. "I didn't date in high school," he said, "because on

Friday night and on Saturday night and on Sunday afternoon, I was playing bourré with elderly men."

Vella Normand, 71, played it for decades, but never with her husband. "It's best not to play with your husband," she said. "You don't have no friends when you play bourré."

It makes sense that the world championship of a game from Louisiana's past would be staged in the parking lot of its future, at the giant casino here, built on land owned by the Tunica-Biloxi Indians. Since the age of the cotton boats and beaver hats, there has been gambling in Louisiana.

There has always been bourré, and while it has never been legal, it has seldom been legislated. It was never a back-room game, really, because the sheriffs accepted it as a part of life in French-speaking Louisiana, like accordion music and turtle soup.

It is an odd sight, to pass through the clinking, clanging casino, with its small army of people mechanically jerking the levers of the slot machines with all the apparent joy of milking a metallic cow, into a tent filled with bourré players studying the cards as if there was some secret message between the rows of spades and diamonds.

Here, was Freddy Francois, 81, a retired cotton farmer, who came two hours early because he wanted to stake out his lucky table. He has played this game since he was a young man, and thought he might have a chance at the $25,000 prize. "I'd give it to my children," he said.

"I'd get drunk," said Charles Morton, 61, a retired factory worker who lives not far from Alexandria.

Bourré's closest ancestor is an obsolete 19th century card game, rams, played in France. Unlike bridge and other similar games, bourré is always played for money. For the Cajuns, a card game without stakes is like gumbo without okra.

It is a trump game, with rules about following suit, trumping, passing. You ante before the cards are dealt, which is a little like jumping off a diving board with a sack over the head.

The world championship tournament, which drew 700 players in one early round this week, costs $25 to enter. The players were divided into groups of seven, with each given $500 in chips. When a player ran out of chips, he or she was out of the game, and the tournament. The players who win their tables advance and get their $25 back.

Earl J. Barbry, the chairman of the Tunica-Biloxi Indians, said the casino wanted to hold the tournament to give the best players a chance to show their skills, and to draw people to the casino.

The people here learned the game in barber shops, in bars and at the knees of mommas and papas. It is a social game, mostly, played at a more congenial pace than poker, yet nobody plays bourré to lose. The old days, when men played with hole cards in their trouser cuffs and pistols in their sock, are gone, say the modern-day players, and most games between friends are quarter-ante, maybe dollar ante.

Mrs. Normand, who is one of the contestants, and her friends put a $50 limit on the evening's play. They call it "poverty bourré."

Every October in the flat land around Avoyelles Parish, the men of the small towns and back roads load up their .22 rifles and disappear for days. It is the start of squirrel season, but that does not mean squirrels are in danger, said Nicky Bordelon. "Because the men are really just sitting around, playing bourré."

At the same time, the women are inviting friends over to supper and playing marathon, sleep-over bourré. They are content, men and women, with this arrangement. "People play it because it's fun," said Mr. Bordelon, the undertaker. He learned to play from the elderly men in his parish, and put many of them to rest, respectfully.

But like any form of gambling, it can leave a man or woman with empty pockets, and worse. Throughout this part of central Louisiana, the players tell of high stakes games where people even lost houses.

Linda Bordelon, who is no relation to Nicky Bordelon (in Avoyelles Parish it is impossible to swing a dead cat without hitting a Bordelon), remembers the time her father gave her a diamond ring he won at the card table. Like many other men here, he played not for the money but for the sport of it.

Steve Polozola, 69, played it for a living for 30 years. He has seen men play it until they pass out at the table. "I used to go sleep on the pool table," he said, "and come back and play some more."

Cajun Christmas Tradition Refuses to Die Down

New York Times, December 24, 1995

DATELINE: Paulina, La., Dec. 22

Some things, you do just because your daddy did.

In Paulina, in Gramercy, in Lutcher and in a dozen other little towns that line the banks of the Mississippi River, much of life is not learned in school or even in the Catholic and Baptist churches that seem to appear every other mile along the River Road. Some things, say the people who live here, you know from the cradle and act accordingly.

You know that if the automatic barricade swings down at the railroad crossing outside the sugar refinery, that does not mean, absolutely, that a train is coming anytime soon. So it is considered good manners if someone just gets out of a car and holds the bar up until another 5, 10 or 15 cars proceed across before the rusty freight train lumbers anywhere close.

You know that just because the sign outside LeBlanc's store in Paulina says he sells "HOT BOUDIN," that does not mean there is actually any sausage inside. It sells out by 4 P.M. You know that the advertised "HOGSHEAD CHEESE" has nothing to do with cheddar, but is a congealed pork product made from unspeakable parts.

And even as a child you know that Papa Noel, whom some people call Santa Claus, cannot possibly find his way into this dark, swampy pocket of Earth unless you light a big fire, many big fires, to help him find his way.

In a time when Cajun accents seem to grow fainter with every generation, when the French and German that forebears spoke is all but forgotten, Christmas Eve bonfires are still burning bright in the River Parishes, a string of small towns and wide places in the road between New Orleans and Baton Rouge. It is a tradition older than the community itself, believed to have been carried here by settlers more than 200 years ago.

There is some disagreement between people here as to whether it began as a beacon for Papa Noel or just to light the way for travelers on the river going to midnight Mass, but over the years the lore has made it either or both, and the argument is unimportant. What is important is that it survived, aged and young people alike said.

"We just grew up doing it," said 15-year-old Mike Minvielle, as he and a friend, 16-year-old Heath LeBlanc, labored in a cold wind to finish one of many bonfires on the levee in Paulina. "This one is 20 feet. We used to build 'em 40 feet, but one fell on somebody so now we can only build 'em 20 feet."

It is one of the more unusual and, in some ways, puzzling of America's Christmas traditions. These bonfires are not just piles of refuse and splinters that someone sets ablaze, but rather carefully constructed teepee-shaped towers, built around a frame of willow and covered with cane reed. It takes as long as a month to do it right, and most families begin work on Thanksgiving.

Then, about 7 P.M. on Christmas Eve, when it is good and dark in the low country, the families will douse the towers with diesel fuel, toss in matches and, for miles and miles, light up the riverfront with the glow of 100, maybe even 200, bonfires.

The tankers and river boats glide between rows of orange and yellow flame. There are so many in some places that the glow is seen for miles.

When the fire gets going, the cane reed will begin to pop and shoot sparks into the air, "like shooting stars," said Guy Poche, whose family has been building them for all of his 60-some-odd years, and for generations before that.

"It is a sight to see," he said.

But people do not just sit around and watch them burn. They dish up steaming bowls of gumbo and plates of jambalaya, and wander from fire to fire and house to house, being neighborly. Sometimes, if they are not too close to a church, they pop the top on beers and toast everyone from Papa Noel to Huey Long.

Grandmothers tell children the story of "the gator that stole Christmas," and someone always sings "Silent Night."

The fires will burn until midnight, plenty of time, the older folks here say, for Papa Noel to locate the chimneys of their grandchildren.

Then, when the bonfires are down to embers, thousands of people will break away for midnight Mass.

"The old people just get older, that's a fact," Mr. Poche said. "But it doesn't have to end with us. The young people save it."

Mr. LeBlanc and Mr. Minvielle, the teen-agers, remember walking into the woods with their fathers and uncles when they were toddlers, armed with hatchets. It never occurred to either of them to question the logic of giving up so much of their free time to build a structure and then just burn it down.

"People enjoy themselves that night," Mr. LeBlanc said. It is an unspoken understanding that the young men of the community do most of the hard work in building them, and the sometimes dangerous work of climbing and nailing the last and highest pieces.

To not be involved would be, well, unmanly.

This is not, over all, a rich community. The jobs the people hold at the sugar refinery, chemical plants and aluminum plant have made it possible for many people here to build themselves a one-story brick house and a decent life, but there are still many tumbledown shotgun shacks on the flat, narrow streets.

But the week before Christmas, as the builders put the finishing touches on their bonfires, the entire community seems drawn to the levees. All kinds of people with all kinds of character get involved. In Paulina, a Confederate battle flag waved from the top of one bonfire just a few hundred yards from where a black family raised their own tower.

There is a community contest, much like a county fair. Glenn Madere, a 41-year-old chemical plant worker, said with pride that one of his family's bonfire's had once taken third place.

Although many people in these towns — the combined population is less than 10,000 — still consider this a celebration of family and community, it has drawn thousands of tourists over the years.

Herman Bourgeois, the Mayor of Gramercy, said that as many as 25,000 tourists were expected this year. Their cars will line the narrow roads, and they will sit on their hoods for hours sometimes, just watching.

The big river boats will glide up the river from New Orleans, weighted down with tourists, timing their arrival with the lighting of the fires. Their calliopes play Christmas music, adding to the spectacle.

The people of the River Parishes welcome the strangers into their homes, feed them and explain for the thousandth time the lore behind the fires.

"I had 120 people stop by house last Christmas Eve, and I didn't even know a lot of them," said Mr. Poche, the retired Mayor of Lutcher. "There was a busload of German tourists came in one year, and last year they came back. Must of liked the gumbo."

Although some people grumble about government involvement in the sizing of the things — an accident several years ago really did restrict the height — they agree that some of the changes over the years have been good ones.

The bonfire builders once burned old tractor and truck tires and creosote-soaked railroad ties to add a little chemical oomph to their fires, but had to stop when it was discovered that the River Parishes had more than their share of lung ailments.

Now only wood and some paper is used, just like in the earliest days of the tradition. Inside the neat towers, driftwood and other trash wood is concealed by the neat horizontal walls of the structure.

"We call it gut," Mr. LeBlanc said. When asked why, he just patted his stomach. "'Cause it's inside."

Over the years, Mr. LeBlanc and Mr. Minvielle said, bonfires have been built in the shape of river boats and airplanes and once, several years ago, in the shape of the state capitol in Baton Rouge.

There is, of course, the chance that a spark from a bonfire might set off another blaze, but that is remote in a place where catfish swim over much of the surrounding real estate.

Plus, Mr. Madere said, if the wind is blowing toward town, "the Fire Department won't let us light them."

Colors

I keep thinking that someday I will not have to write about race,
about hatred. I keep thinking that.

To Bind Up a Nation's Wound with Celluloid

New York Times, June 16, 1996

DATELINE: Jackson, Miss.

As soon as I heard wheels I knowed who was coming. That was him and bound to
be him. It was the right nigger heading in a new white car up his driveway towards
his garage with the light shining, but stopping before he got there, maybe not to
wake them. That was him. I knowed it when he put out the car lights and put his
foot out and I knowed him standing dark against the light. I knowed him then like
I know me now. I knowed him even by his still, listening back. . . .

He had to be the one. He stood right still and waited against the light, his back
was fixed, fixed on me like a preacher's eyeballs when he's yelling, "Are you saved?"
He's the one.

I'd already brought up my rifle, I'd already taken my sights. And I'd already got
him . . .

"Where Is the Voice Coming From?" by Eudora Welty

The killer was free again on the streets of Jackson. Or at least, for a span
of seconds, that was how it seemed. A loudly pontificating, feebly swag-
gering old man, too similar to Byron De La Beckwith to be anybody else,
paraded along the sidewalk to the Hinds County Courthouse. Reporters
chased him, clamoring for a word or two from the man who had hidden
in the honeysuckle more than 30 years ago and, aiming a high-powered
rifle, murdered a civil rights organizer named Medgar Evers.

One reporter asked him how he felt about going to trial for the third time in the same killing, a crime that shamed many Mississippians for three decades.

"I feel like an Indian let loose in a brewery," he said, proud.

Another reporter asked him if a pin on the lapel of his natty gray suit was a Confederate flag.

"Son," he said, "if you don't recognize the Confederate flag when you see one, you're doomed to go to hell in Africa." Then he marched on, as if he had a destination more pressing than a dark corner of history.

It was not really him, of course, not the real Mr. Beckwith. A few seconds later, the director, Rob Reiner, yelled "Cut!" and in the place of a killer there was only the actor James Woods. But when the cameras were rolling he was remarkably like Mr. Beckwith, not just in his haughty manner or his voice or his unapologetic defense of all things white, but something more, something that made people who knew this character in real life shake their heads in wonder or disgust.

"It's spooky," said Willie Morris, the Mississippian and Southern writer who serves as historical consultant for the movie, which is still untitled. It was Mr. Morris who encouraged Frederick Zollo, who is producing it with Mr. Reiner, to make the film in the first place. This movie tells a story about justice, about good triumphing over evil, Mr. Zollo said.

The film, a Castle Rock production that also stars Alec Baldwin and Whoopi Goldberg, is not just the story of the killing of a civil rights hero but of the man who brought the killer to justice 30 years later. At the time of the first two trials, which had ended in hung juries, no white man had ever been convicted of killing a black man in Mississippi. Bobby DeLaughter, an assistant district attorney who ignored advice to let the crime go unpunished, convicted Mr. Beckwith in 1994, but at great personal and professional cost.

The first third of the picture — for which filming will be completed in Los Angeles next month — is about Mr. Evers's life and death. But most of the rest of it revolves around the more modern-day story of Mr. DeLaughter's attempt to put the aging Mr. Beckwith in jail. Mr. Zollo views this film as a catharsis not only for Mississippi, which he sees as years ahead of other states in dealing with, living with, race, but also for the nation.

"Look at Boston, at New York, at Los Angeles," Mr. Zollo said. In a time of retro-racism, he continued, the movie proves, "It is never too late to do the right thing. This is an example of a state cleansing its past."

Mr. Baldwin plays Mr. DeLaughter. Ms. Goldberg plays Myrlie Evers-Williams, the widow of Medgar Evers, who has since remarried. Both of them, like Mr. Woods, say the movie is more than just another acting job, because the story they tell is true and the issue it examines is not dusty with age, pulled from graveyards and history books.

Mr. Beckwith's cell is within feet of where the cast and crew filmed parts of the movie in the old Hinds County Courthouse.

"He's right there," said Mr. Reiner, jabbing a finger at a blank wall of the courthouse. On the other side of that wall, Mr. Beckwith, who was 73 before he was finally convicted, spends his days pacing and writing racist literature. The state pays the postage and handling.

"You kill a man, you shouldn't be able to do that," Ms. Goldberg said between filming scenes on the courthouse's first floor. As she speaks, Mr. Woods, in full Beckwith makeup, walks up, takes her hand and waltzes her through the main lobby.

"I swear," Mr. Woods says in his Beckwith voice, "if I'd met a woman like this in my prime, I'd of changed my views on segregation."

It is too surreal for words, even for Hollywood.

In Jackson, people have different reactions to the film. Some say let the past die. Some say tell it, and let people know that Mississippi had the courage to do the right thing.

"It needs to be told," said Eddie Lee Cook, 62, who runs a luggage repair shop. "But tell it right."

During a break in shooting one day, Mr. Baldwin played basketball in a Jackson gym. One of the other players, a local man, asked him what he was doing in town.

"You're not going to make us look bad, are you?" the man asked.

"No," Mr. Baldwin said, "we're going to make you look real good."

GHOSTS AND ACTORS

Midnight, like the glass or two of whisky that had ushered it in, was just a memory. Patsy Cline was singing like an angel on the stereo, and Willie Morris, the author of "North Toward Home" and other critically acclaimed books, was sitting deep in an easy chair in his living room in Jackson, staring deep into his coffee cup, thinking about ghosts.

"It's a story about ghosts," he said of the movie that he had watched being filmed in Jackson the day before. "It's a story about redemption, really."

Mr. Morris, the former editor-in-chief of Harper's magazine, believes it will be a historically sound movie, and a good one. But the story of Mr. Evers and Mr. Beckwith is almost too profound to be real, as if it were pulled straight from Eudora Welty's short stories instead of being the inspiration for one of them, "Where Is the Voice Coming From?"

The killing came in June 1963, but the hatred that caused it had incubated over lifetimes. A fertilizer salesman and World War II hero whom friends just called Delay, Mr. Beckwith came home from combat in the Pacific to a new war. For most of his adult life he had been talking loud and mean, to anyone who would listen, about the inferiority of the black race.

The scion of a family whose old money had vanished long ago, Mr. Beckwith wore cream-colored suits and liked to pretend he was more than he was. His mother was a Yerger, and a Yerger had been wounded riding with the Confederate General Nathan Bedford Forrest. The one thing Mr. Beckwith was really good at, said people who knew him, was marksmanship.

"For the next 15 years, we here in Mississippi are going to have to do a lot of shooting to protect our wives and children from bad niggers," Mr. Beckwith wrote in a letter to the National Rifle Association in January 1963.

Five months later, Mr. Beckwith became a man of action. On June 22, he drove to the neighborhood where Mr. Evers lived, asking for directions to the Evers house, at 2332 Guynes Street. Then he hid in the sweet gum trees and honeysuckle across from the house and waited.

Medgar Evers, field secretary for the National Association for the Advancement of Colored People and one of the most visible and respected activists of the time in Mississippi, came home late from a rally, just after midnight. He got out of his car and was walking to his door when Mr. Beckwith shot him in the back, from 200 feet. The police, who found a vintage 1917 Enfield rifle in the weeds, later surmised that the killer had to have been an excellent shot.

Mr. Evers did not die immediately. He tried to crawl, and died in his wife's arms, his three children screaming, "Daddy, get up!"

Despite witnesses, despite the fact that a fingerprint of Mr. Beckwith's was found on the murder weapon, two all-white panels ended in hung juries. To show his contempt for the court, Mr. Beckwith would slip cigars into the pocket of the prosecutor.

It seemed that Mr. Beckwith would go free. He began introducing himself as "the man they say shot Medgar Evers." But in 1973, police in New Orleans stopped his car on Interstate 10 and found a time bomb and a city map marked with the address of an Anti-Defamation League leader. He did five years in a Louisiana prison.

Back in Mississippi, justice was only on hold.

A HERO TO RELATE TO

Rob Reiner was 16 when Medgar Evers was shot. His family (Carl Reiner, the writer-director-performer, is his father) was politically aware and supportive of the civil rights movement. "I always wanted to do a civil rights movie, but I didn't know my way in," he said.

He did not think he was qualified, did not want to presume that he understood what black Americans of that time had gone through. But the Evers-Beckwith case offered a story he could develop and a hero he could relate to, he said.

"I can make my way into the story with Bobby DeLaughter," Mr. Reiner said, referring to the young assistant district attorney who decided to give the case one last try.

Mr. Delaughter found the crowbar he needed to reopen the case on Oct. 1, 1989, in a newspaper story by Jerry Mitchell of The Clarion-Ledger of Jackson. Mr. Mitchell reported that files from the Sovereignty Commission, a state organization formed to aid the cause of segregation, had played a role in prescreening prospective jurors in the first Beckwith mistrial.

The racial climate changed in 30 years, but change was an imperfect process. Mr. DeLaughter knew he risked ruining his political career — he wanted to be a judge — but the evil of the crime, of one man lurking in the bushes to shoot another in the back, pushed him to pursue it, he said.

"This was something that ought to offend every decent human being, no matter what your race," Mr. DeLaughter said.

One scene in the movie illustrates that sentiment. Mr. Baldwin, as Mr. DeLaughter, receives a bomb threat at his home in the middle of the night, and he sends his children to a hotel where they will be safe. Racked with doubt over what he is doing and guilt over what it could cost his family, he goes for a drive and winds up in front of the Evers house. In his mind, he sees Mr. Evers's murder, hears the shot, feels the terror of Myrlie Evers and the children as they find him on the ground in a pool of blood. He starts to cry.

It did not really happen that way, Mr. DeLaughter said, but it was close.

"They've got an awful lot to condense and put into a period of two hours," he said. The scene in the movie is a composite of several events.

"I went out there to the house many times, throughout this whole ordeal," he said. He did weep.

Last month, he went back to the house to watch the filming of that scene. "I was amazed at what Hollywood can do to make things appear authentic. I had provided them with copies of the crime-scene photographs, and even the autos parked in the driveways seemed right. I was used to seeing it all in black-and-white. It was the scene that haunted me for years.

"After it was done, all I could do was sit there and stare at the monitor. Mr. Reiner turned and asked me, 'What do you think?' I told him that if feeling heartsick and angry all over again is a sign that this is a good shot, then it's a good shot."

Mr. DeLaughter did eventually run for a local judgeship. He was defeated, soundly, in part because of lingering resentment over the Beckwith case. While many Mississippians did feel proud that their state did the right thing, others refused to reward the man who was most responsible for bringing Mr. Beckwith to justice.

"He was hoping it would be just another case," Mr. Baldwin said. "He's kind of this classic American. He just believes that the right thing is going to happen. But he suffered."

FACE OF EVIL

Mr. Beckwith considers himself a political prisoner, a victim of a conspiracy between the black race and the liberal news media to control America. Mr. Beckwith has not talked about the movie, but Mr. DeLaughter said he would not be surprised if it gave him even more incentive "to proceed with his mission," to spread his hate mail.

Mr. DeLaughter was out of town the week most of the movie involving Mr. Beckwith's character was being filmed. "When I came home I was flipping through the papers," he said, "and I had to do a double take. It was his face." But it was really only Mr. Woods in makeup.

Mr. Reiner and Mr. Zollo wanted an older man to play Mr. Beckwith, but when Mr. Woods heard about the role at a Hollywood party, he practically begged for it. He read the script, then studied Mr. Beckwith's mannerisms.

"I can make you believe it," he said in his meeting with Mr. Reiner and Mr. Zollo. Then, according to Mr. Zollo, he became Mr. Beckwith.

Mr. Woods seems to have an odd love-hate relationship with the man. He loves the challenge of the character, but he loathes what he stood for.

He has no desire to meet him.

"Let him sit there and stew and be ignored," Mr. Woods said.

Just a Grave for a Baby, but Anguish for a Town

New York Times, March 31, 1996

DATELINE: Thomasville, Ga., March 30

The integration of the Barnetts Creek Baptist Church cemetery is done. A mixed-race baby, the most recent burial here in the cemetery's serene patch of stained granite and plastic flowers, can rest peacefully now. So, finally, can her family.

Church deacons, who had asked the relatives of the child, Whitney Elaine Johnson, to exhume her tiny body because they wanted to keep their graveyard exclusively white, have apologized for trying to persuade them to do the unthinkable.

"I got what I wanted. Whitney can rest," said the child's mother, 18-year-old Jaime L. Wireman, after the church's head deacon told her on Friday that he was sorry for asking her to move her baby to another cemetery.

"We admit our mistake," Logan Lewis, the deacon, told Ms. Wireman and the baby's father, 25-year-old Jeffrey Johnson. But while Ms. Wireman, who is white, and Mr. Johnson, who is black, welcomed an end to an ordeal that has drawn nationwide attention, they and other members of the family say it will be a long, long time before the hurt fades.

"What they did to us exposed something ugly," Sylvia K. Leverett, the child's maternal grandmother, said of the deacons' request that the family dig up the infant and move her to a graveyard that accepted blacks. The request rocked both locals and outsiders in its callousness.

To Mrs. Leverett and the rest of the family, it went beyond racism. It was inhuman.

"When I first heard what they wanted me to do with my baby, I thought I was dreaming," Ms. Wireman said.

In Thomasville, just minutes from the Florida line in the pine barrens of southwest Georgia, people seemed genuinely relieved that the dark cloud that has hovered over them has begun to lift.

"That baby did nothing to deserve this," said Angie Graham, a clerk in Thomasville. To her, and others on the streets of Thomasville, it was just one more example of how it colors them all as racists when a few people in a small Southern town act rashly.

Even people who believe that the mixing of the races has gone quite far enough were surprised, and dismayed, at what the deacons did. Members of the deacons' own congregation condemned them. An official with the Southern Baptist Convention called it an embarrassment to the gospel of Christ.

"This isn't the 1950's," said Mrs. Leverett, the baby's grandmother. But for several long, painful days, she said, it felt like it.

Thomasville is like a lot of other Southern towns. Its stately white houses and picturesque main street are ringed by wider streets of ugly strip malls and fast food joints. People who live here say race relations are no worse and no better than in other places where whites and blacks share schools, sidewalks and stores, but seldom neighborhoods and bedrooms.

Churches and cemeteries remain bastions of segregation in the Deep South and elsewhere. In Thomasville, cemeteries have been segregated for as long as anyone can remember. Unlike schools and lunch counters, it was just one of those invisible lines in Southern life that no one seemed to care to cross, for as long as people here can recall.

It seemed unimportant to most people, until the birth of the baby, Whitney.

Whitney's mother and father have been living together in a mobile home just outside Thomasville for more than two years. They do not own a phone, car or television. He works construction jobs to pay the rent and the light bill.

The sight of a biracial couple seems to draw out the worst of the racism that is here, Ms. Wireman said. When she and Mr. Johnson walk along Thomasville's street, people occasionally shout "nigger lover" at her from passing cars. They have ignored it. "We were in love," she said.

Last year, they applied separately for jobs at a sewing plant. They were hired, but they were laid off a week later when their boss saw them sitting together at lunch, Ms. Wireman said. The boss told them it was not personal, just a lean time for the company, she said.

Then, in the summer of 1995, she found out that they were going to have a baby. Whitney was born at 10 A.M. on March 19, incomplete. Her skull was not fully formed, and she lived just 19 hours.

"We named her after Whitney Houston, the singer," Ms. Wireman said. "They took her down to the big hospital in Tallahassee, but there wasn't anything they could do. God let her live long enough so that I could hold her. I wouldn't take a million dollars for that time."

Ms. Wireman wanted the baby to be buried beside her grandfather so Whitney would have company. The sound of the dirt dropping on her casket began a process of healing, but it was interrupted just days later.

"There was no peace in it," Ms. Wireman said. "It was bad enough that the Lord decided to take my baby. But then they wouldn't let her rest."

The deacons had apparently not known that the child being buried in their cemetery had a black father. Their tradition was in pieces, and there was only one way to repair it, they decided. The board of deacons voted three days after the funeral to ask the family to take the tiny coffin from the cemetery's ground.

"It wasn't all the people in the church," Ms. Wireman said. "I know there are some very, very good people there. But the deacons are the most powerful men in town. I used to look up them."

The deacons felt they had plenty of authority to make such a request, she said. But she wonders how they sleep at night.

"How do you do this to a child?" she said.

Only after reactions to the request rained down on them — bringing a flash flood of television cameras and reporters — did the deacons relent. First, the deacons told the family earlier this week that Whitney could remain in Barnetts Baptist Church's cemetery. Then, in a meeting at the baby's great-grandmother's house on Friday afternoon, the deacons asked for forgiveness.

"Our church family humbly asks you to accept our apology," said Mr. Lewis, a white-haired man who has done the talking for the deacon board.

But Mrs. Leverett, a strong-willed woman who has worked a big part of her life in law enforcement, said the deacons did not want to make a clear apology at first, and she had to goad them into it. "I wanted them to admit to what they did and say they were sorry for it," she said.

Mr. Johnson said he could live with the apology, as Ms. Wireman will live with it. The town will live with it for a long time to come.

"I can't go to town now without someone coming up to hug me and tell me how sorry they are that this all happened," Mrs. Leverett said. If anything good can possibly come out of the death of the child and the agony over her burial, Mrs. Leverett said, it is in knowing that people here could be hurt by it and that they refused to accept it as just the way things are.

"I believe people are sorry," she said. "She was just a baby."

Racism Wins in Small Town in Texas

St. Petersburg Times, August 15, 1993

DATELINE: Vidor, Texas

The last black man sits in the hot dark with his back to the wall, waiting for the rednecks to come. Somewhere in the dim living room a radio is playing Ray Charles soft and rich, the volume turned low so Bill Simpson can hear the rumble of a pickup or the thud of cowboy boots on concrete.

The only black man in Vidor knows they will come sooner or later, the same way he knows summer in East Texas is hell, dark is safe and Ray is blind. Vidor has 10,000 white people, and now and then one of the mean ones will shout: "Hey boy, I'm gonna come to your house tonight and bring me a rope."

Simpson, a 7-foot, 300-pound man with a high tolerance for fear, has been threatened and cursed by racists here for so long he cannot stand it anymore. The last survivor of a court-ordered integration of Vidor's one housing project, he is leaving for a place where people don't call him nigger to his face.

Only a few weeks ago he was swearing that no redneck peckerwood would run him away, but tense night after tense night peeled away his courage. Simpson has nothing but his own backbone to lean on, that and a police force made up of the kin and friends of the same people who tell him to leave Vidor or die here.

Racism has won in this little town in Texas. The KKK, its sympathizers and people who looked the other way made it happen, and let it happen.

"I know there's racism no matter where you go, but here it's meaner, it's more concentrated," Simpson said. "Here, if the racists threaten you, you can't ignore it. Because you know a lot of people stand behind them."

He used to have company here. There was an older black man and two younger women with small children, all lured by the housing authority's promise of dirt-cheap housing made possible when a federal judge ordered an end to whites only in the project.

But one by one they ran, chased off by racists both inside and outside a chain-link fence that corrals the poorest of Vidor's poor.

To Simpson, the saddest thing is that the whites and a handful of blacks were fighting for possession of rock bottom, the last and lowest place that people would want to live short of being homeless. The white people in town would not allow them even that.

In nearby Beaumont, an oil refinery city with a large black population, blacks say they won't turn off Interstate 10 into Vidor even if their tire blows.

"I'd just ride the rim to Louisiana," said Joseph Walker, who lives in a black neighborhood in Beaumont. "Them are some very, very bad folks. I can't believe the government would bring four families, drop them there and expect them to survive.

"Didn't they know what Vidor, Texas, stands for?"

The housing project is like any other place that catches people on the way down, the yard cluttered with Big Wheels and headless dolls. An old woman stands with her face pressed to a screen door, like she expects someone, anyone, to notice her and say hello.

A wounded Pontiac leans against one curb, hood up, tires flat. It looks like it would moan if someone turned the key.

It was never much, but it was home.

Back in Simpson's apartment, an ancient fan flutters feebly in the dark. He would like to sit outside like he used to, but that would make him a target.

It would be hard to miss a man as big as a Frigidaire.

"Is that what it's going to take? Does there have to be a killing out here . . . to make these people open their eyes?

"I feel defeated," he said. "And I feel disgusted."

"TALKING STUFF TO SCARE EACH OTHER"
The moist heat hovers at 92 as late as 8:30 P.M. and red and yellow flames from the refineries lick up into the evening sky. This is mean

heat, the kind that makes a man drink too hard and look for somebody to blame for his failed life.

One in 10 people in Vidor are out of work, which means there are 1,000 people with little to do except think too much. The Klan has blamed black people for white unemployment, and warned them that continued exposure to blacks will infect Vidor with prostitution and drugs.

In some towns, that would sound frayed and tired. Here, it sounded warm and comfortable.

"If I thought they (blacks) could live here in peace and harmony then I would be for them coming," said 28-year-old Gerri Henson, who runs a small store in Vidor.

"But I don't think they can. I want to believe in my heart that we are all good people here, but I know in my heart those black people would have been hurt if they had stayed. The Klan would have turned loose — people would have been killed."

Once, some 70 years ago, Vidor had black people. But blacks who left the town long ago for the safety of Beaumont tell horror stories of Klan nightriders who drove them out with whippings and beatings and murders still unsolved.

Bloody Vidor, as it was once called, would build on its image. In 1968, a mob beat two black truck drivers at the Spindletop truck stop cafe. A white man in pointy-toed cowboy boots kicked out the eye of one man. The attack was apparently started when a white man in the cafe said he couldn't eat "with a nigger."

Elex Brydson, who lives in a Beaumont neighborhood named The Peach Orchard, has lived his life within 5 miles of Vidor, but visited there just once. The waitress in one restaurant refused to serve him and three men chased him out of town.

"It's not just talk, people talking stuff to scare each other," he said. "Somebody put Vidor in a time warp. And if you live there baby, you live in danger."

There is not a lot to Vidor, only two interstate ramps, a few fast-food stands, strip malls and 50 churches. Vidor is dry but has four beer stores just across the city limit sign. It has a good catfish joint, a bingo hall and a shop where you can get a $5 haircut.

The Klan, which used to train here, seemed to weaken over the years in a town where the ideal society already had been established.

Then, a year ago, the town announced it would move blacks into a federally funded housing project. It wouldn't be many, just a few, enough to satisfy the federal government, but not enough to establish a real enclave of black citizens.

"Vidor is a unique animal," said Tom Oxford, a lawyer with East Texas Legal Services, which represented two black tenants forced to abandon Vidor. "It's the way most of the country was in the pre-1950s. . . . A place proud of its reputation as a white enclave, a Klan town. Because of that, over years, they drew a lot of extra nuts.

"And that is why it is overly represented by nuts: One kind that enjoys the Klan environment, and another, more benign racist that wants to live in communities where you don't have to see blacks and kids don't have to go to school with blacks."

The Orange County Housing Authority had to find people who wanted a home of their own so badly they would come here.

THE SWEET DEAL

The housing authority found Bill Simpson living on the street, relying on a new-found faith in God and the kindness of strangers.

It lured 58-year-old John DecQuir, who was living with family in Beaumont, with the promise of a home of his own.

It offered Brenda Lanus and Alexis Selders, mothers of small children, a haven from crime. It also offered used furniture, a U-Haul and cable television.

It seemed like a sweet deal. A still unformed, distant threat of racial violence could be weighed against the very real joy of a roof that didn't leak, a bed of their own and a rent that left money for little things like a night out at Pizza Hut.

A diabetic with painful and crippling arthritis in both knees, Simpson was sick of limping through his life without roots. This offered him a chance to straighten out his life, find a job, and maybe even do the unthinkable — rent a real house, with a yard, maybe even a dog.

He would trade the occasional racist slur for that dream, as long as it didn't get too bad.

"I needed this place," he said.

DecQuir was first, in January, and the others followed. They were Vidor's first black residents in more than 50 years.

After the initial shock, it looked as if an uneasy peace really had come to Vidor. Church leaders prayed for restraint to a crowd of 2,000 in the Wal-Mart parking lot. One woman, known as a hard-line segregationist, sent food to John DecQuir.

The Houston Chronicle did a big story about changing racial attitudes. The photographer took a picture of Simpson with little white children crawling on his lap. The children loved Simpson. He learned all their names, and even the tiniest ones would run laughing to swing on his baggy pants leg, yelling out: "Big Bill!"

Although the die-hard racists were still talking loud, the Klan's work to find new recruits seemed to be sputtering. The outspokenly liberal president of the project's tenants association, Ross Dennis, lauded the blacks as good neighbors.

Simpson and DecQuir were elected officers, and the first-ever black/white coalition of tenants started to work out a plan to rid the little project of drugs. Being all-white, apparently, had not spared their project from a drug problem.

Three candidates for mayor in the last election refused Klan support. The winner, Ruth Woods, said it was time Vidor lived down its past and became an example to the rest of Texas. Soon, the more open-minded people were patting themselves on the back. It all seemed too good to be true. A handful of blacks had healed Vidor's history.

But whatever disease of spirit Vidor contracted in the 1920s was only in remission.

OUTSIDE

No one will ever know what would have happened if Vidor's new black citizens had only stayed inside the fence.

DecQuir and Simpson didn't get out much and didn't attract much attention. The two young women did. They went to apply for jobs soon after getting here in July, and the misery started. Men called them bitches and whores, shouted threats about what they would do to them if they ever caught them outside in the dark.

Their children, just toddlers, heard it all.

The women were turned down for work at every place they tried and made the trip home under a fresh barrage of insults.

People in Vidor are quick to blame the Klan for its racism, but this time it was unlikely. To the women it seemed like the whole town was lining up to spit on them, and a few weeks was all they could stand. Within a month they were gone, afraid to tell anyone where.

"They shouldn't have been brought here because they were never going to be allowed to work," said Gerald Guilbeaux, who lives in the project.

Vidor's facade of racial moderation melted. Simpson and DecQuir received death threats. The town received threats that the housing project would be fire-bombed and the mayor killed if the black men didn't leave.

It was too much for DecQuir. He started making plans to leave in late July. That left Simpson, who felt he had a moral obligation to stay. But things just got worse.

Two children started wearing hoods and white robes around the project. Simpson and Ross Dennis, the head of the housing authority who supported Vidor's integration, were threatened. Vidor police started covering the project even tighter and the FBI moved in to investigate the threats, but Simpson never felt safe again.

"I got called nigger I don't know how many times," he said. "One time is enough."

He started staying inside. The children would come to his door now and then, but he couldn't come out to play.

"Children don't see color," he said. "Children just want to love and to be loved. But these children are going to grow up thinking that hatred is okay.

"I'm going to miss them."

In Vidor, people blamed the Klan. They did the best they could, they said, but the Klan would have burned the place down and hurt who knows how many if the blacks had stayed. It is better for everyone, Vidor's citizens agreed, that they're all going to be safely away.

"I have a 5-year-old child," said Gerri Henson. "I don't want my child to grow up hating people because they are black. But I don't want my child hurt if the KKK gets turned loose in Vidor."

FIGHTING FOR THE BOTTOM

Phil Williams is a college-educated engineer. He talks about the federal government's decision to artificially install blacks in Vidor with calm and reason — at first. But the more he talks the angrier he gets, until he uses the word "nig . . . well hell, I almost said it."

He calls the people in the project white trash and black trash. If a black person is going to move to Vidor, he says, let it be someone with a job who can pay his own way.

But Simpson believes that is impossible. He believes Vidor tolerated them for a while only because they were tucked away with the rest of the poor and unwanted. And even that, they were denied.

Even at rock bottom, people were afraid they would drive down the neighborhood.

"I'm not sure how much indignation I could stand, in order to live in a housing project," said Sam Bean, president of the Beaumont NAACP. "Not much, though."

Simpson decides it's time to go to bed. He sticks his head out the half-open door for just a second, to check the street, and a little girl comes running from next door.

"Big Bill!" she screams, her arms outstretched.

"Hey JoJo," Simpson says, but he can't step outside to pick her up. The little girl is still standing in the yard, waiting, when he closes the door.

Fort Bragg Area Is Haunted by Ghost and Two New Deaths

New York Times, December 11, 1995

DATELINE: Fayetteville, N.C., Dec. 10

The Rev. C. R. Edwards had hoped such crimes were locked away in the basement of time.

He is 70, a survivor of long, cold civil rights confrontations and a leader in the reconciliation of the city's races. He wanted to live out his days without hearing another story of white men who bolster their courage and prejudice with too many beers, then go looking for black people to harass, curse, kill.

"I never thought I'd see it again; I never thought we had that kind of hatred still in our midst," said Mr. Edwards, referring to the killings of a black woman and man last week in Fayetteville, an Army town near Fort Bragg. Two young soldiers who read racist literature, spoke of hate and disdain of blacks, have been charged with murder.

The killings have raised questions of extremism at military installations and prompted a Government investigation into racist activity at Fort Bragg. In Fayetteville, a town that fought its battles over race and moved on, that handled integration easier than other Southern towns, relatives of the victims are angry and puzzled that the two soldiers' racist views went unpunished, apparently unnoticed by superiors.

The circumstances surrounding the killings of Jackie Burden, 27, and Michael James, 36, seem more at place in a dusty history of the

South, said members of the victims' families. The Fayetteville police said the two soldiers spent an evening drinking, working themselves up with racial slurs, before going out looking for black people to harass.

The soldiers, James Norman Burmeister II, 20, and Malcolm Wright, 21, picked Ms. Burden and Mr. James at random, the police say. They spotted them as they walked along a sandy street in a mostly black neighborhood just after midnight, argued, then shot them both in the head with a semiautomatic handgun, the police say.

Whites and blacks in this city of 300,000 just shake their heads at what they see as an isolated incident, a senseless, stupid act and not a sign of any significant racial division.

But mostly, for the ones old enough to remember, it has brought a sharp and sudden chill that has nothing to do with the shifting season.

They have a term for it here, and in other places in the South. They call it "feelin' like somebody just stepped over your grave."

"I didn't want to believe that evil was still alive, not in this community," Mr. Edwards said.

Mr. James's mother, 71-year-old Lillie G. Smith, said, "I thought it was over." Today, her birthday, she sat in a favorite chair in her living room and wearily tried to make sense of it. That her son is dead because of the color of his skin is hard to accept in her city, in 1995.

A third soldier, Randy Lee Meadows, 21, is charged with conspiracy. He drove the car, the police said, but was apparently just along for the ride and did not share the racist views of the other two men. "I'm sorry," he said when he was led to jail in handcuffs.

The other two soldiers showed no such remorse in court hearings or questioning, the police said. All three men are paratroopers with the 82nd Airborne Division. As thousands of Fort Bragg soldiers mobilized today for duty in Bosnia, the three men sat in bright orange inmate uniforms at the Cumberland County Jail. They are being held without bond.

"We're praying for them," said Karon Knox, Mr. James's sister. "If they have so much darkness in them, they need God."

Mr. Burmeister, of Thompson, Pa., apparently made no secret of his racist views. He had a Nazi flag above his bed in the barracks, dressed as a skinhead and talked openly with Mr. Wright and other soldiers about what he called the inferiority of blacks and other minorities, said the police and soldiers who know the paratrooper.

A search of a room he rented in a Fayetteville mobile home, from a couple who shared his theories on race, produced white supremacist literature, a bomb-making manual, pamphlets on Hitler and Nazi Germany and magazines favored by survivalists and militias.

While Army officials said they knew of no secret cells of white supremacists at Fort Bragg, a group that calls itself the Special Forces Underground publishes a clandestine newsletter called The Resister, which supports individual rights and "republicanism" and denounces "liberalism, tribalism, internationalism."

One Fort Bragg soldier, who asked not to be identified because he fears reprisals from superiors and other soldiers for "speaking out of turn," said there were a few soldiers at the fort who flaunted their racism, but he believes their numbers are tiny. Until the killings, they had been dismissed as "nuts."

The police said there is little doubt that racial hatred is behind the killings of Ms. Burden and Mr. James, whom they described as acquaintances.

While less is known about Mr. Wright, of Lexington, Ky., than Mr. Burmeister, he shared the views of his friend and reportedly was heard speaking disparagingly of blacks.

This past Wednesday night, the two men had met to drink and talk, and later hooked up with Mr. Meadows, of Mulkeytown, Ill. He was known on the base as a tag-along, and a friend of Mr. Burmeister's.

The police said the soldiers cruised the streets in Fayetteville's predominantly black areas, looking for someone, anyone, to confront. They wound up at the corner of Hall Street and Campbell Avenue, a neighborhood of modest wood houses.

There, purely by chance, they saw Ms. Burden and Mr. James. Both of them, family members said, had made mistakes in their lives linked to drugs, but both had buried those problems in their past. They were only out for a walk, the police said.

Mr. Burmeister and Mr. Wright got out of the car. The police said the four got into an altercation that ended with one of the soldiers — they have not identified the shooter — firing into the heads of both victims. When he heard the shots, Mr. Meadows ran from the car and found the bodies. He was still standing there when the police arrived a few minutes later. Mr. Burmeister and Mr. Wright fled and were later arrested at the room Mr. Burmeister rented in the mobile home park, the authorities said.

There seemed to be nothing in their pasts to account for their hatred. Mr. Burmeister, the son of a mechanic, grew up in rural northeastern Pennsylvania and had little or no interaction with people of another color. Mr. Wright, a high school dropout, grew up in poor sections of Louisville and Lexington. The Army knew nothing of any racial activities in which the men had been involved, one officer said.

That infuriates relatives of Mr. James. As they gathered at Mrs. Smith's home for her birthday, they tried hard to be gracious and forgiving. But the notion that the Army allowed such people, with such views, to go among them made one of Mr. James's sisters break down.

"They should have known," said Sharon Smith, his older sister. She knows that the Army brings all manner of people to their city, and that some of those people will be bad.

"But did they have to shoot him down?" she said. "Is the color of a person's skin enough reason for you to take that person's life?" She fell into the arms of her sister.

Even if Army officials had known of the racist views, they are limited in how much they can control the private lives of soldiers. The discovery of a Nazi flag, for instance, might prompt an investigation into a soldier's views, but would not in itself be a reason for punishment.

Mrs. Smith does not want vengeance so much as answers. She would like to be able to look into the soldiers' faces and ask them, Why? What happened to them in their lives to make them hate enough to kill her son, an anonymous man to them?

"I put myself in their mothers' place, and wonder how I would feel now," she said.

People in Fayetteville, particularly the families of the victims, know that racism is alive, that blacks and whites wage war in bigger cities and still live in cold dislike in many smaller ones.

Fayetteville seemed to be beyond it. "This was just meanness and prejudice," said S. S. Williams, a Cumberland County deputy. But it took two men, and not a city, to bring that meanness to life, said white and black residents of Fayetteville.

But civic leaders said it might be time to begin the old communications again between blacks and whites, just in case, just to make sure that something old and ugly is not shaking itself awake again.

"How are we going to get along in heaven," said Mrs. Knox, "if we can't along down here?"

Unfathomable Crime, Unlikely Figure

New York Times, June 17, 1998

DATELINE: Jasper, Tex., June 16

The people who know Shawn Allen Berry, some who killed time with him, drinking beer and watching the insects whirl around the street lights, some who frequently waited in vain for him to show up for work at the town tire store, often feared that he was just one more drunken joy ride away from another trip to prison.

But they figured it would be something dumb, something little, not something mean. They never dreamed he would be charged, along with two other white men, with dragging a black man to death behind Mr. Berry's primer-gray pickup, a crime so cruel it sickened people across the country.

"Maybe," said a former employer, Bill Snelson, "he just got mixed up in the wrong crowd."

That is what Mr. Berry and his court-appointed lawyer maintain: that he was an unwilling accomplice to the June 7 murder of James Byrd Jr., 49. Those who know Mr. Berry, a 23-year-old part-time mechanic, theater manager and failed burglar, want to believe him, because they do not want to think that so evil a crime has a familiar face.

In Jasper, where almost half the population is black and memories are long, people understand prejudice. But few of them, black or white, understand what could happen in a life that would make a man hate with such intensity. As they look back on the lives of the three accused, they find clues, but not answers.

In a statement given to investigators, Mr. Berry has implicated the two other suspects, both friends: John William King, 23, a onetime schoolmate here in Jasper who became his partner in the bungled burglary that landed both in a prison boot camp in 1992, and Lawrence R. Brewer, 31, a day laborer from the Sulphur Springs area who had just completed a seven-year prison term for cocaine peddling when Mr. Byrd was murdered.

By the account of Mr. Berry, who had given Mr. Byrd a lift, Mr. King forced him to accompany the two other men on the ride of death and dismemberment after they had chained the victim to the rear bumper. Mr. Brewer and Mr. King, both linked to prison hate gangs, say they did not murder anyone.

People who know the three suspects, either here in Jasper or in Cooper, Mr. Brewer's tiny hometown, describe them alternately as good boys and small-time criminals. Mr. King often used racial slurs, but that did not set him apart here.

All three men were born in East Texas, where racism can be almost a recreation — in 1993, white supremacists in Vidor, some 50 miles from Jasper, succeeded in driving out of town the several blacks who lived there — but Jasper had not seen such meanness in decades, people here say. The mayor, the hospital administrator, the superintendent of education and other political and civic leaders are black. The country club has black members.

"Things have changed a lot in the past 20, 30 years," said District Attorney Guy James Gray, who has lived here for 48 years. Certainly, blacks and whites alike say, racism is alive in Jasper, but it is a thing of lingering resentment and hurtful words, not threats or violence.

A lot of people here believe that the suspects' time in prison, where inmates tend to split off into gangs by color for their own protection, intensified racial prejudice that had been part of their culture, and set the stage for an abomination. State prison officials say that Mr. King and Mr. Brewer were both members of the Confederate Knights of America, a racist group linked to the Ku Klux Klan, and that both have tattoos that mark them as white supremacists.

But this crime was so evil, so widely denounced, that Texas klaverns of the Klan have denounced it, too. A small group of Klansmen, 10 to 20, have applied for a permit to march here this weekend or the next, not in support of the suspects but to disavow any connection with them.

In any case, friends of Mr. Berry say they are certain that when he offered Mr. Byrd a ride that fateful night, he did so as a kindness.

Mr. Snelson, who owns Jasper Tire, where Mr. Berry worked off and on for about three years, said Mr. Berry's mentor there was an old black man who was dying of cancer.

"Shawn went with me to the funeral," Mr. Snelson said. "He was crying like a baby."

Dustin Wood, 21, a worker on offshore oil rigs who has known Mr. Berry for years, echoes what many say about him: People liked to like him. He made dumb mistakes, but he did not seem to have a mean streak.

"I never heard Shawn say anything racist," Mr. Wood said. "I have a lot of black friends. He has a lot of black friends. All this news has just shocked me and everyone he knows."

Mr. Berry drank beer, mostly on the weekends; shot pool, and got tattoos, "but there's nothing racist about tattoos," Mr. Wood said. "He had a Playboy bunny, a Grim Reaper and a cow skull, if I remember right."

He also had a child by a young woman in Jasper and, friends say, was planning to marry her.

"For the circumstances he was raised in," Mr. Snelson said, "he was a good kid."

His father died when he was a teen-ager, and he quit school in the eighth grade. "He never did talk much about his mother," said Mr. Wood, one of a number of acquaintances who say Mr. Berry and his mother were never close.

"He was raised on the street," Mr. Snelson said. "I tried to help the kid because I felt sorry for him," although ultimately "I had to let him go because he was not dependable."

In 1992, Mr. Berry and Mr. King, his friend from school, committed a burglary in Jasper and were sent to the boot camp, a detention center where guards used military-like discipline to try to turn around the lives of young offenders. It seemed to work for Mr. Berry, who came home and got a job at the movie theater. (The night of the killing, he had just finished showing "Godzilla.")

But for Mr. King, boot camp proved to be only preparation for two more years in custody. He violated parole so often that the state sent him to Beto One, a tough prison in the town of Tennessee Colony. He came out a much different person, by the account of friends and relatives, who say prison taught him to hate.

Unlike Mr. Berry, of whom people speak well even as they shake their heads, Mr. King seems abandoned by Jasper. Even his father, Ronald King, has conceded his guilt, in a letter to reporters. "It hurts me deeply," the elder Mr. King wrote.

While people here acknowledge knowing John King, they refuse to have their names attached to any recollection about him, if they talk about him at all.

They remember a mannerly boy, quiet around grown-ups. His family was blue-collar Baptist. The only vice he had as a boy was snuff.

He dropped out of school in 10th grade and did manual labor. Like Mr. Berry, he was just one of the sunburned young men who cruised town in ragged pickups, a six-pack from trouble. If he was overtly racist then, the people who remember him say they do not recall.

But in Beto One, he met Mr. Brewer, who had been in and out of jail for drug and burglary convictions much of his adult life. Like Mr. King, the new acquaintance came from a solid, hard-working Texas family, "real respected people," said Mr. Brewer's hometown sheriff, Benny Fisher.

"Everybody liked him," said Mr. Brewer's grandfather, Morris Gillham, 76, a retired electrician. "I don't know what to say. He didn't have that makeup," as a boy, to do the things the prosecutors say he did to Mr. Byrd.

Relatives say Mr. Brewer too learned to hate in prison. Both he and Mr. King joined the Confederate Knights of America, a loosely organized prison gang for white supremacists, although his lawyer, Bill Morian Jr., says Mr. Brewer joined the gang for protection.

"If you don't join," Mr. Morian said, "you become someone's wife."

Texas prisons have powerful black and Hispanic gangs, in particular one called the Mexican Mafia. They, and their white counterparts, espouse racial hatred.

"The level of racism in prison is very high," said Mark Potok, a spokesman for the Southern Poverty Law Center. "The truth is, you may go in completely unracist and emerge ready to kill people who don't look like you."

For Jasper, Just What It Didn't Want

New York Times, June 27, 1998

DATELINE: Jasper, Tex., June 26

Terrya Mitchell, who is black, is taking her 16-year-old daughter to Houston early Saturday morning, to go skating. Steve Seale, who is white, is leaving town before dawn, to go fishing.

In fact, many people in this little East Texas town say that they will not be here by Saturday afternoon, that they will not take part then, even as spectators, as the Ku Klux Klan, the New Black Panthers and the Black Muslims use Jasper's recent tragedy as a platform of their own at a Klan assembly. The town, most here say, simply does not need the divisiveness.

"I'll be fishing in Sabine Lake," said Mr. Seale, a lawyer who was born and brought up here.

Jasper, a racially mixed town of 8,000 people, has drawn praise around the country for keeping calm in the three weeks since a 49-year-old disabled black man, James Byrd Jr., was chained by his ankles to the rear bumper of a pickup truck and dragged to his death in what prosecutors are calling a hate crime.

Instead of living in simmering bitterness, instead of erupting in racial conflict, blacks and whites have joined in prayer vigils, rallies and sometimes just one-on-one discussions over chicken-fried steak, all intended to bind up the wounds caused by that crime and to show the outside world that what happened here hurt and outraged all the town's people, not just its blacks.

But the gruesome nature of Mr. Byrd's death — some parts of his dismembered body were found miles from others — has drawn worldwide media attention, and that focus has in turn drawn extremists who, people here say, want to capitalize selfishly, no matter how much that hurts Jasper.

The Klan initially said it was coming here only to disavow any connection to the three murder suspects, two of whom are said to have Klan affiliations from their days in prison together, but leaders of the KKK now concede that they will also talk about "white pride" and use the press attention to explain their platform.

"It's the outside coming in and disrupting a community that has been dealing very conscientiously with this situation," said Walter Diggles, director of the Deep East Texas Council of Government, a Jasper planning organization formed to help local governments. Mr. Diggles, who is black, plans to stay away.

"It's a distraction," he said.

It will be almost a blessing, residents say, if that is all it turns out to be.

The Klan assembly is set for the courthouse square between noon and 2 P.M., and the New Black Panthers of Dallas plan to attend. So does a group of Black Muslims, mostly from Houston, that has already marched here once, armed with rifles and shotguns. Residents fear a confrontation in which bystanders might be hurt.

"They're not from here and have no relatives here," said Ms. Mitchell, an office worker at the Mount Olive Baptist Church. Neither side has any stake in the community, and yet both feel free to use it as their battleground, she said, adding, "It's a bad situation."

President Clinton and Gov. George W. Bush have asked the groups not to assemble here, to let the town alone, but have been ignored. So more than 200 Federal, state, county and city law-enforcement officers are to be on hand to keep the peace.

It is still unclear how many people will attend, but at least 20 Klansmen and an equal number, or more, from the two black groups are expected.

No one in the Klan assembly — made up of klaverns from Vidor and Waco, along with some members from Georgia — will be armed, its leaders say. But some individual Klansmen are making no such promise. And on Thursday the Panthers issued a statement urging black residents of Jasper to "load your guns, stand on your porches" and protect themselves and their homes. It is legal in Texas to carry a loaded weapon, even at an assembly like the Klan is planning.

Of the crime from which Saturday's gathering sprang, Michael Lowe, a leader from the Waco klavern, said, "A lot of blame has been put on Klansmen."

Three men — John William King and Shawn Allen Berry, both 23 and both of Jasper, and another East Texan, Lawrence Russell Brewer, 31 — are charged with the killing. As prison inmates several years ago, Mr. Brewer and Mr. King joined the Confederate Knights of America, a loosely defined prison gang for white supremacists that has ties to the Klan. Mr. King was disciplined in prison in 1995 for a racial disturbance between white and Hispanic inmates.

But Mr. Lowe said neither Mr. Brewer nor Mr. King were Klansmen. "I do not know a Klansman," he said, "who would condone such a murder."

While gruesome killings may be every bit as much a part of the Klan's identity as is racial hatred, Mr. Lowe said that was the old Klan. His Klan, the one assembling in Jasper, is a Klan with a national platform.

"We believe that all immigration should be stopped in America for 10 years," he said, "until there are enough jobs to support our working force in America. We do not believe in spending billions of dollars overseas to nations who do not care for us in the first place. We could be spending it on our inner cities. We do not believe that anyone should just be allowed to move plants" out of the country. Overseas expansion by companies is fine, he said, but "they should not be allowed to just shut their doors here, putting Americans out of a job."

"The Klan is not just racial," Mr. Lowe went on, but he said that whites in Jasper had been smeared by the crime and that the Klan rally was also in support of them.

Mark Potok, who tracks Klan activity for the Southern Poverty Law Center, called the Klan's presence in Jasper "completely opportunistic."

"Their assertion that they are coming to instill white pride in Jasper is a ludicrous concept," Mr. Potok said. "This is not a crime that can be blamed on the white community in Jasper. Why would they need white pride?"

As the town steels itself for Saturday's assembly, Jasper County officials have cleared the way for prosecutors to seek executions in the case. The officials said this week that they would try to obtain a capital murder indictment of at least two of the three suspects — presumably Mr. Brewer and Mr. King, although the officials would not say — when a grand jury is impaneled here on July 6. To gain a capital murder conviction, the prosecutors must prove that the killing occurred in tandem with another serious crime, like kidnapping.

While prosecutors have declined to speak publicly about a possible deal for testimony, only one of the accused, Mr. Berry, has so far cooperated with investigators.

Bombs

I have seen a lot of cowards in my life.
The bomber is the greatest coward of all.

In Shock, Loathing, Denial:
"This Doesn't Happen Here"

New York Times, April 20, 1995

DATELINE: Oklahoma City, April 19

Before the dust and the rage had a chance to settle, a chilly rain started to fall on the blasted-out wreck of what had once been an office building, and on the shoulders of the small army of police, firefighters and medical technicians that surrounded it.

They were not used to this, if anyone is. On any other day, they would have answered calls to kitchen fires, domestic disputes, or even a cat up a tree. Oklahoma City is still, in some ways, a small town, said the people who live here.

This morning, as the blast trembled the morning coffee in cups miles away, the outside world came crashing hard onto Oklahoma City.

"I just took part in a surgery where a little boy had part of his brain hanging out of his head," said Terry Jones, a medical technician, as he searched in his pocket for a cigarette. Behind him, firefighters picked carefully through the skeleton of the building, still searching for the living and the dead.

"You tell me," he said, "how can anyone have so little respect for human life."

The shock of what the rescuers found in the rubble had long since worn off, replaced with a loathing for the people who had planted the bomb that killed their friends, neighbors and children.

One by one they said the same thing: this does not happen here. It happens in countries so far away, so different, they might as well be on the dark side of the moon. It happens in New York. It happens in Europe.

It does not happen in a place where, debarking at the airport, passengers see a woman holding a sign that welcomes them to the Lieutenant Governor's annual turkey shoot.

It does not happen in a city that has a sign just outside the city limits, "Oklahoma City, Home of Vince Gill," the country singer.

"We're just a little old cowtown," said Bill Finn, a grime-covered firefighter who propped himself wearily up against a brick wall as the rain turned the dust to mud on his face. "You can't get no more Middle America than Oklahoma City. You don't have terrorism in Middle America."

But it did happen here, in such a loathsome way.

Whatever kind of bomb it was — a crater just outside the building suggests a car bomb — it was intended to murder on a grand scale: women, children, old people coming to complain about their Social Security checks.

The destruction was almost concave in nature, shattering the building from the center, almost front to back, the blast apparently weakening as it spread to both sides of the structure. Blood-stained glass littered the inside. So complete was the destruction that panels and signs from offices several stories up were shattered on the ground floor.

People could not stop looking at it, particularly the second floor, where a child care center had been.

"A whole floor," said Randy Woods, a firefighter with Engine No. 7. "A whole floor of innocents. Grown-ups, you know, they deserve a lot of the stuff they get. But why the children? What did the children ever do to anybody?"

Everywhere observers looked, there were the discarded gloves, some blood-stained, of the medical workers.

There seemed to be very little whole inside the lower floors of the building, only pieces — pieces of desks, desktop computers and in one place what appeared to be the pieces of plastic toy animals, perhaps from the child care center, perhaps just some of those goofy little things grown-ups keep on their desks.

Much of it was covered in a fine powder, almost like ash, from the concrete that was not just broken, but blasted into dust. One firefighter said he picked through the big and small pieces almost afraid to move them, afraid of what he would find underneath. Here and there, in a droplet or a smear, was blood.

One woman, one of many trapped by rubble, had to have her leg amputated before she could be freed. Earlier in the morning, firefighters had heard voices drifting out from behind concrete and twisted metal, people they could hear but could not get to.

A few blocks away, Jason Likens, a medical technician, wondered aloud how anyone could have walked away unhurt. "I didn't expect to find anybody living," he said.

He was sickened by what he saw, but did not know who to hate. "I would get mad, but I don't know who to get mad at," he said.

Next door, a group of grim-faced medical technicians, police and others gathered just outside the foyer of a church, not to pray, but to watch over the dead that had been temporarily laid inside in black body bags.

The stained-glass windows of the brick building had been partly blasted out, with a few scenes hanging in jagged pieces from the frames, but it was still the most peaceful place for blocks.

"I hope this opens people's eyes," Mr. Woods, the firefighter, said. What he meant was, it should show people everywhere that there really is no safe place, if a terrorist is fanatical enough.

Like others, he believes it was intended to send a message to the United States: not even your heartland is safe.

A few blocks away, two elderly women slowly made their way up the street, their faces and clothes bloody.

They are retirees, living in an apartment building next door to the office building that was the target of the explosion. Phyllis Graham and Allene Craig had felt safe there. But this morning, as the glass went flying through their home, life changed forever.

"It all just came apart," Ms. Craig said. It was not clear if she meant her building, or something else.

Tender Memories of Day-Care Center
Are All That Remain after the Bomb

New York Times, May 3, 1995

DATELINE: Oklahoma City, May 2

The babies used to try to grab the sunlight.

Their cribs, four of them, were always lined up next to the windows of the America's Kids day-care center on the second floor of the Federal Building, said Melva Noakes, the 42-year-old Sunday school teacher who owned the business.

"The sunlight was good for them," said Mrs. Noakes. "The infants loved to watch the clouds, to watch the cars, to watch the people pass by. I used to watch them reach out for the rays of sunlight — they thought they could touch them — and make little shadows with their hands. It was good for them."

For a few minutes she drifts through the everyday memories of the day-care center she opened just a little over a month ago, a place where teachers read stories to babies on their laps, and little boys would sneak away at nap time when the lights were dim, to sneak homemade cookies from a jar. Then the nice thoughts disappear in smoke and flames.

Of the 21 children who were inside the day-care center on the morning of April 19, the morning of the bombing, 15 are dead, including all four of the infants by the window. Five are hospitalized, burned and broken. Only one returned home, a little girl with a broken leg. All three teachers in the center were also killed.

The children in the America's Kids center have become the focus, the epicenter, of the nation's bereavement over the blast and its rage and loathing at the bomber. The emotions were born when the truck packed with thousands of pounds of explosives turned the nine-story office building into a tomb. The number of dead, children and adults, pulled from the ruin so far is at 141, and about 40 people are missing.

The oldest of the day-care center's children was 5 years old. The youngest was 6 months old. It was the possibility of finding more children alive — a possibility that died a little every day — that helped keep the searchers digging long after reason told them that they were surely dead.

Over and over again, in the days after the blast, people said the same thing: Surely the bombers did not know there was a child care center in the building. Surely they did not mean to kill the children.

"I don't want to believe that," said Faye DeBose, whose 4-year-old granddaughter, Nekia McCloud, was critically injured in the blast. She was in intensive care with a fractured skull, the most serious of her multiple injuries.

"I want to go to bed every night," she said, "and say, 'They didn't know,' I don't want to believe it, because I don't know if I could live knowing that they did mean to do it."

Mrs. Noakes believes that the bombers did know, that they did plan to kill the children. Common sense tells her that, because the babies were in plain view of anyone in front of the building.

"I feel sorry for the man," she said, referring to Timothy J. McVeigh, the main suspect. "Because he is so sick. No one in their right mind would pull their vehicle right under the window where the cribs were.

"You could see them there, in the windows. People always liked to walk by, on the sidewalk, and look at the babies there."

All three of the children who are still missing are infants, the ones who slept, played and cried in the sunshine by the second-floor windows, just a few feet from the origin of the explosion.

Rescue workers have promised not to quit until everyone is found, but they are afraid that there might be nothing left of the tiny bodies.

What they have found are mangled tricycles, shredded teddy bears, melted dolls and pieces of carriages, but no children in the past several days. There were story books in ashes, but no toy guns.

The teachers did not allow them. They said they wanted to protect the children from things that represented violence.

Mrs. Noakes said the children belonged to two-career families and single working mothers trying to scrape by, mostly office workers of various pay scales and promise. The parents worked close by and parents often came by to eat lunch with their children. Mothers would nurse babies on their coffee breaks.

"We named it America's Kids," said Mrs. Noakes, who has two teenage children of her own. She was not in the building on the morning of the bombing. She was working on a payroll at another child care center she operated in a nearby town, and planned to go to the Oklahoma City center later that day.

But she knows the routine. She has been running day-care centers for 11 years.

At 7 A.M., the first of the children would have arrived. Some of them would have cried a little as their parents left. At 8 A.M., they would gather for breakfast. By 8:10, the first milk would be spilled.

Just after 9 A.M., the time the truck loaded with explosives rolled up to the building, they would have all gathered around their teachers and sang a song, probably several songs. Like millions of other children in America, they had been singing the Barney song.

"The one that goes, 'I love you, you love me,'" said Mrs. Noakes.

If the unthinkable had not happened, they would have gone to play at about 9:30, or formed a circle and told something that happened in their lives to their classmates.

The babies would have been lifted from the buggies and taken for a ride. If the bomber had been just a little later, the infants would have been speeding down the hallways in buggies, away from the windows.

In the afternoon, about 2:30 P.M., would have been nap time. The toddlers and older children would have snuggled with bears and drifted off. P. J. Allen, 20 months old, would have either pretended to sleep or else awakened early, and would have sneaked into the director's office to search for cookies.

He is in critical condition with burns on 55 percent of his body.

At 3 P.M., it would have been snack time, with crackers, cookies and fruit, with milk. The rest of the afternoon would have been devoted to reading stories, playing with building blocks, maybe more singing.

Nekia and the other older children would have painted pictures. "Sometimes I couldn't tell what it was, when she brought it home," said Nekia's grandmother.

Someone would have had to have broken up a fight between 3-year-old Zackary T. Chavez and another child. Zackary died in the blast. The director, 24-year-old Dana Cooper, would have been surrounded by children, wanting a cookie, a story, a hug. "She was a pushover," and the children knew.

She and her 2-year-old son, Christopher, who was there with her, were both killed.

"Now her husband has a big empty house," Mrs. Noakes said.

Wanda Howell, a 34-year-old teacher, would have had a child on her lap, reading a story. Brenda Daniels, 42, was the strictest one. She wanted the children to finish what they started, even if it was just coloring books.

Teresa Brown, 19, called in sick that day, and lived.

Mrs. Noakes tries not to question why some people were at work that day and died, and others, like herself, were spared by pure chance.

But because of it, "I'll get to see my daughter graduate from high school in a few days," she said. "I'll get to raise my son."

As the search dragged on last week, she sat beside the mother of one of the children killed, Zackary, and held the young woman's hand as she waited for word on whether the boy was alive or dead.

"She just kept saying, 'I know he'll be fine,'" recalled Mrs. Noakes.

Mrs. Noakes was so shaken, so dismayed over what happened, that she wondered if she would ever be able to hold a child again.

A few nights ago, her sister-in-law brought her grandson over to Mrs. Noakes's house.

"I picked him up and held him," she said, and everything seemed better somehow.

Oklahoma Toll Is No Longer in Deaths, but in Shattered Lives

New York Times, April 19, 1996

DATELINE: Oklahoma City, April 18

The shark-nosed 1968 Plymouth Road Runner is alive again. Rick Tomlin, a middle-aged civil servant, had been working in his spare time to help his son restore it, but that project was cut short when a truck bomb tore through the Alfred P. Murrah Federal Building, killing Mr. Tomlin and 167 others one year ago.

Jeremy, his 22-year-old son, finished the work himself. Now and then he steers the old car out onto one of the thin black ribbons of tar and gravel that link the wide, windswept country around Piedmont, just 30 minutes outside Oklahoma City, for what begins as a slow Sunday drive.

Then he gets to thinking about his father, about their life together and the manner of his death, "and I just stomp it to the floor and let it run."

The car thunders down between the fields and cows and barns until the young man who looks a lot like his father is somehow satisfied, until he pushes the car over 110 m.p.h. and outruns the pain.

There is an anger in Jeremy Tomlin, his brother Richard, 25, and their mother, Tina, that sits like lead in their bellies. It is something that the passing months, with their countless memorials, tributes and newspaper and television interviews, have done little to change.

"People tell me, 'Take Rick's picture down, don't turn it into a shrine,'" said his wife, who has dreaded April 19, the anniversary of the bombing. "But that's what I have. I have a picture."

When you ask them — and others who either survived the bombing or lost someone to it — how this thing has changed their lives, they almost laugh. A few say they have moved on, have tried to put it behind them, but most are still trapped in the horror and sadness and cruelty of it. They live in a limbo of loathing for the two men charged in the bombing, and say they will never find peace as long as the men, Timothy McVeigh and Terry Nichols, are alive.

They have been asked to share their deepest feelings so many times by reporters and other total strangers that some of them answer with perfect television sound bites, or with long, eloquent passages that answer the most personal questions even before the reporters can ask them. There is nothing false in it; underlying the words is deep pain punctuated with tears. It is only that they are veterans at expressing their grief, anger and hatred. They are good at it.

"A year ago this week, Satan drove up Fifth Street in a Ryder truck," said Jannie Coverdale, whose two grandsons, Aaron, 5, and Elijah, 2, died in the blast were along with 19 other children. "He blew my babies up. He may have looked like a normal man, but he was Satan. And I have to wonder, 'Where was God at 9:02 A.M. on April 19?'"

She has done so many interviews she cannot remember them all. Others, like Mary Bolden in Newcastle, Ala., have been left mostly alone with their grief.

Mrs. Bolden, a 63-year-old retired cook, shuns interviews to talk about her daughter, Sgt. Lola Rene Bolden, an Army recruiter who was killed in the explosion. Far from the reporters' satellite trucks that prowl the streets of Oklahoma City, she watches her daytime dramas on television and wonders every now and then why her daughter had to die.

"The phone will ring and I'll forget and think it might be her," said Mrs. Bolden.

Others, like Gunnery Sgt. Paul Cooper, who was partially buried in the blast and is scarred forever, says he only wants to get on with his life. But the blast that damaged his face also closed his tear ducts, so that this tough, abrupt veteran soldier sometimes finds himself "crying all over myself" in a crowd.

And then there is Marilyn Travis, a 37-year-old Army recruiter whose body, career and future have been damaged beyond repair, who watched a 3-year-old child disappear in the rubble when the building blew apart, who hates to see or read news accounts about Mr. McVeigh because she is so afraid he will somehow get away with it.

"Somebody's got to pay for this," she said.

Here are five stories of lives changed forever by the explosive force of a terrorist attack on the U.S. Government, an attack that left much more than concrete and glass in pieces on the ground.

THE TOMLINS: DOING TIME, LEARNING TO HATE

The watch is mangled and twisted from the blast, the crystal cracked. Tina Tomlin keeps it under a plastic case. It is one of those watches that is powered by the wearer's movements, so that every time someone picks it up or shakes it it will run a second or two longer before the hands go motionless again.

It makes her angry when people tell her to get on with her life. She was married to one man for 25 years, and believed she would be married to him forever. In many ways, he was her life.

"Rick was a nice looking man. I don't ever see another nice looking man being interested in me, at my age," said Mrs. Tomlin, who is 43. Her sons are in college. "I see my life as being by myself."

Her husband had been an administrator in the Department of Transportation, a Vietnam veteran and a Republican who loved to work on classic cars — always Chryslers, Plymouths and Dodges — and drive them a little too fast.

She is certain he never knew Mr. McVeigh or anyone else linked to the bombing, but he is dead anyway. She was never the kind of person to hate, never believed much in capital punishment. But she has learned.

"I'm so tired of him, of his mouth, of him sitting there so smug," she said of Mr. McVeigh's courtroom appearances. Like most of the bereaved, she is sure he is guilty.

"I hear people say that this was something that 'just had to happen.' Why did it have to happen? You don't go out and kill innocent people, never mind what the cause is.

"I'd like to sit down with him and ask him what he was thinking. What was he striving for. I'd like to ask him what was so evil in his life that made him this way."

She wants him to die. She feels he has to, along with everyone else connected. There will be no peace until then, and she prays she can find it then.

Her son Richard said he could not say what he would like to see happen. "Justice won't permit it," he said.

For Mrs. Tomlin, the worst thing about it all is the change it has forced in her own personality. She used to be a trusting person, outgoing. Now she is suspicious of strangers, and carefully measures out her words.

It seems, some days, that she is in prison with Mr. McVeigh.

"How many years," she wonders, will she serve?

THE COVERDALES: TWO DEATHS, ONE LIFE ALTERED
The reporters come to her almost every week, because she lost so much. The little boys Aaron and Elijah, killed in the building's day-care

center, are enshrined in the small bedroom that they shared, their bicycles and toys neatly arranged. There is a pair of shoes for each on the well-made beds. They have been recently shined.

Mrs. Coverdale has dwelled so much on their deaths that it has become life itself for her. She was working two jobs to help support her grandsons, as a clerk and taking care of a shut-in elderly person, but since the bombing she stays at home with her son, Keith, the boys' father. She used to travel to court to sit during hearings and stare hard at Mr. McVeigh and Mr. Nichols.

In interviews her words roll out smooth, rich and descriptive. They sound almost rehearsed, but that is only because she has said them so often. Listen to her:

"I don't have any life. I live off anti-depressants and anxiety pills and cigarettes. It's one long night, waiting to wake up. We'll probably never wake up. We will live in this dark forever. Sometimes Keith comes home and sits in their room all evening.

"Aaron was just 5, but he was the man of house, he took care of me. In the mornings when we were getting ready, he would go get my glasses, put them in my purse, have the door keys ready. He tried to take care of Elijah, but that was an impossible job. He was smart, though, for five. It's too quiet in the evenings when we come home. I talk about them because I want everyone to know them, so that when McVeigh and the others go to trial, it's going to mean something.

"I've seen McVeigh five times in person. I saw a young-looking man who seemed like he was celebrating something, laughing, talking, passing notes, and every time I saw him I stared in wonder. I wished I could reach out with my mind and ask him what made him destroy so many lives. What could have happened to you? Terry Nichols looks sad.

"I have never been a person that believed in capital punishment, but now what am I supposed to do? I used to hear people scream about executing people, and I wondered how they could be like that, it won't bring back your loved ones. But I'm a different person now."

MARY BOLDEN: WONDERING HOW SHE GOT IN THE WAY

Mary Bolden is polite in the way people who have lived their lives in the Deep South are, the kind who will ask even the insurance salesman in for a glass of tea. Few reporters have reached as far as her Alabama home, so far from the site of the blast, to find reaction. She would rather not talk about it at all, because every word cuts her like a razor. She is just too nice to refuse.

"I had seven children, and I stayed at home until all of them was grown, then I went to work for 27 years," said Mrs. Bolden, who has lived most of her life in the town of Newcastle, about 30 minutes outside Birmingham. Her daughter, Sergeant Bolden, wanted something better, and joined the Army to get away. Now she is buried under the Alabama clay, and her mother wonders how any of it — the talk about militias and right-wingers and people mad at the Government — had anything to do with her, with her daughter. How did they get in the way of this awful thing?

"She wanted to get away and she never wanted to come back," said Mrs. Bolden. "I just wanted her to retire and be happy. Then she lost her life for nothing. I don't understand it."

"I don't know what he was thinking," she said, speaking of Mr. McVeigh. "I'm afraid to know. I don't think he was evil. I think his mind just snapped."

That does not mean she wants him to live. She wants him to die.

"I hate to say it, but I think he should be treated the same," she said. "Why do they keep holding it up? Go on and do it."

MARILYN TRAVIS: AFTER THE HEALING, TRAUMA REMAINS

Marilyn Travis, a sergeant with the Army recruiting office on the building's fourth floor, was passing a fresh sheet of coloring paper to a visiting child when the bomb exploded. The child, 3-year-old Kayla Titsworth, disappeared in a pile of rubble along with seven of Sergeant Travis's co-workers, including Sergeant Bolden.

Her face shredded by flying glass, her hair on fire, splintered bones showing through her dangling arm, Sergeant Travis thought she was dreaming as the child's mother began screaming for her daughter.

"I kept saying, 'No, she's here, she's right here somewhere,' but I couldn't find her," she said. "Then I started feeling faint and I thought it must be because I hadn't eaten breakfast that morning. A little later I heard someone yelling, 'It's a bomb, you can smell it,' and I started to realize that it wasn't a dream."

She carries the memories with her like the shards of glass still imbedded in her body. She goes to the doctor and hospitals four to five times a week and spends two hours a day in therapy. Her injuries included the near loss of one eye, a concussion, a badly broken arm and shoulder and thousands of glass cuts. Her face alone took more than 100 staples to close.

The wounds have ruined her once steady life. She said that the Army had not given her enough time to heal, and that she had been denied points toward promotion because of her time off. Under the military's system, she must make staff sergeant within 15 years after enlisting. She is in her 12th year, and has no chance of making that deadline.

"I can't work a full day, I can't take physical training tests, I can't do my job properly enough to gain promotion points," she said. Her superiors show little sympathy, she said.

Last week, after a dispute with a superior about the pace of her work, she finally broke down. She began screaming, threw papers, slammed a door and then began pounding it with her injured arm. She believes it was post-traumatic stress.

She hopes that someday she will see the accused bombers, especially Mr. McVeigh, suffer as much as she has. She said she saw him in the building two days before the explosion, in an elevator. Tired that day, she had "kind of collapsed against the elevator railing and he said, 'Are you having one of those days?'"

PAUL COOPER: SHOWING SADNESS IN SPITE OF HIMSELF

Gunnery Sgt. Paul Cooper of the Marines never heard the blast. One minute he was by his desk and the next he was buried under rubble, covered in blood, tendons cut in his left arm, trying to plug a nicked artery in his leg with his one good hand. He survived in part because of his training, because he never panicked. He is a lifer, a Marine through and through, and shrugs aside questions about his feelings, his recovery.

He mostly wants to forget it, to get on with his life, for things to be the same again for his wife and children. "A lot of people were hurt a lot worse than I was," he said.

He does not think much about the bombers. He said he would let the courts deal with them.

"But every morning I look in the mirror and I see the scars," and he is forced to remember for a little while. "It's the cards I was dealt," he said, but conceded that he was a little surprised that after serving all over the world, including the Gulf war, he was wounded at a desk job in Oklahoma City.

The embarrassing thing, for this tough man who answers questions in short, machine-gun bursts, is the damage to his eyes. The blast injured his tear ducts, so that there is nowhere for the tears to go except down his face. One of the few people marked by the bombing who does not feel compelled to cry looks like he cries all the time.

In Oklahoma City, Recovery a House at a Time

New York Times, June 8, 1997

DATELINE: Oklahoma City, June 7

Every day, people walk the chain-link fence and browse the notes and toys and trinkets hung there, heartbreak woven into wire. They circle the vacant space where the Alfred P. Murrah Federal Building stood, and they try to decipher the prayers and sentiments that the rains have turned to a blur.

There was a toy Elvis, a hubcap and a bouquet of yellow plastic roses. There was a small wooden cross blessed by Pope John Paul II, and a business card from Edward G. Schmidgall, Moose Lodge No. 1571, Farmington, Ill. There were 425 stuffed animals and a picture of a child who died here.

"I have been here for two days, and walked around the fence 20 times," one visitor wrote on a scrap of white cloth tied to the fence. "It never hurts any less."

The people who live here know that feeling, of great sadness circling around and around itself, all too well. Once, before the morning of April 19, 1995, Oklahoma City was known as the home of the Cowboy Museum, as a place to find oil and eat steaks. The blast changed its identity just as a sniper's bullets did Dallas, but here the victims were friends and neighbors, crushed, blown apart. It became a city of victims.

Now that Timothy J. McVeigh has been held accountable for the bombing of the Federal Building, which took 168 lives, people who were not hurt directly by the bomb, and a few who were, say it may finally be appropriate for the city to turn loose of its collective sadness, if it can.

The city's firefighters, among the first to enter the nightmare of the shattered building, "can now talk about the bombing in past tense," said Kenneth Bunch, the Assistant Fire Chief. But the scale of death and destruction was so great that it seems to reach everywhere.

A Methodist minister compared the bombing to rape, and like a rape, said others here, recovery will be complicated, tenuous, uneven.

There has never been a hurt this deep in an American city at the hands of terrorists. It goes well beyond the some 900 people who were injured, said those who have lived through it.

It is impossible to walk into a business, stroll a sidewalk, even fly on a plane in and out of Oklahoma City and not brush up against the sadness.

Julie Smith and her husband, Pat, own and operate the Goodyear tire store downtown, near the bombed property. They were not hurt.

But early on the morning of April 19, a man brought his car in to be worked on and asked for a ride to his job. One of their workers drove him there, to the Federal Building. That man died in the rubble.

It is a link, however insignificant, between the Smith family and the families of those who suffered.

The day of Mr. McVeigh's conviction, Julie Smith brought her five daughters to the chain-link fence around that vacant lot, because she believed she had to.

"I just think it's important for my kids to remember this," Mrs. Smith said. It is as if, by sharing in the misery that befell their neighbors, the pain was spread a little thinner.

The sadness even insinuated itself into wedding albums.

Dedra Hayes, 23, and her husband, Chad, 22, got married just two weeks after the bombing. "Only 35 people came to our wedding," she said, "because of course we couldn't send out all the invitations. But it was a really nice wedding."

She was on the second floor of the nearby Journal Record Building, working as a temporary accountant for the state. "I faced the blast," she said, and the concussion injured her eyes. She has to wear glasses now.

No one talks about forgetting. No one wants to forget. They just want to stop hurting.

"It's similar to being in a war," said the Rev. J. Harold Thompson, the pastor of Carter Park Baptist Church. "I don't know anyone who has put this behind them.

"Time lets you get on with your life," he added, but that cannot happen as long as the courts resurrect those awful memories. Even if the Federal jury in Denver decides that Mr. McVeigh should die, there is still the trial of his alleged co-conspirator, Terry L. Nichols. Even after that, the chief prosecutor in Oklahoma City wants to try Mr. McVeigh here on state charges.

Once all those trials and punishments are decided, it may take 5 years, maybe even as long as 10, before anything close to widespread recovery will be a fact of life here, Mr. Thompson and others said.

The Rev. Rick Marion, the pastor of Capitol Hill United Methodist Church, said his congregation was mostly spared, but the blast still caused distress. "That resurfaced, strongly, with the trial," he said.

"The city is healing," he said. "People are able to function. But that process will be slow. People are still working through their anger, and some people are even still working on acceptance. People feel like we've been raped. In Oklahoma City, you don't expect to be blown up."

Some thought it would be best to erect a modest memorial and build another high-rise on the building site, to start fresh, but that would have been like building in the middle of a cemetery for most people here. The site will be enshrined with a large permanent memorial, and the Journal Record Building, also wrecked, is to be renovated and turned into a museum, Gov. Frank Keating said.

"We will always have a sad memory in our past," Lieut. Gov. Mary Fallin said. "The guilty verdict will help close a chapter in the book" of this recovery.

Few people here would ever dare say that the grieving has lasted too long, certainly not to people who lost someone in the bombing, or who were maimed in it.

"If you can come up with a life that doesn't revolve around it, it's better," said Martin Cash, who lost an eye. But that is asking too much, for now.

"If I ever saw any of these people or their relatives on the street," he said of the people linked to the setting of the bomb, "I'd kill them with my bare hands."

The truth, people here say, is that there may not be any such thing as collective healing, as recovery of a city. That will come house by house.

"I have my life to deal with it," said Bud Welch, 57, who lost his daughter, Julie Marie, 23. What happens to Mr. McVeigh now will not affect that, he said.

Mr. Welch runs a gas station, but lately, he said, "I've been doing some farming, been plowing fields."

There may not be peace in it, maybe just distraction, but he likes how he feels doing it.

Tina Tomlin's life, in many ways, stopped after her husband, Rick, was killed in the blast. "I'm still not cooking, my house is atrocious — you should see my bedroom," she said. "It kills me, that I don't care. But I have no reason to. I kept it all up for Rick. Why bother now?"

But she knows that is giving up, giving in to Mr. McVeigh and those others who took part in the bombing.

"I can't let McVeigh ruin my life the way he ruined Rick's," Mrs. Tomlin said. "I can't let him take my life." She just has to figure out how to stop it. Recently, she dyed her hair. At least, it was a change.

Richard Williams is the buildings manager for Federal offices here, and he was in the Federal Building when the bomb went off. A rescue worker found him, took his pulse and found none, and left him for dead. But later, he was told, another rescuer heard him moaning and carried him out. His right hand was smashed and his right ear was left hanging by cartilage, among other injuries.

After months of physical therapy, he can pitch again for his traveling softball team of players older than 50, the Classics.

He will dedicate the rest of his life to the building and keeping of the memorial to honor those who died and those who suffered, but he will also make sure he keeps living. "Before this I wouldn't have taken time to go to a concert or a ball game," Mr. Williams said, "but now I realize it can all be over in a blink of an eye."

To many people, the chain-link fence is the memorial to the Oklahoma City bombing. Diann Cunningham, a receptionist at First American Title and Trust, three blocks north of the bomb site, drives past here on her way home from work.

"Rain, snow, wind," she said, "there is always someone here."

Someone from Magic City Sewer and Drain of Nashville wrote, "We have come a long way to see and remember, but I never imagined I would feel so close." The writer's name is not legible. There was one T-shirt signed by the Grambling State University track team, another from Boy Scout Troop 1988 in Houston.

The visitors come from across the nation, or just across town.

The picture of the dead baby, part of a homemade memorial, is signed: "I love you the most, always, Mama."

Altered by Bombing, but Not Bowed

New York Times, June 18, 1998

DATELINE: Birmingham, Ala.

The bombing at the abortion clinic here changed the face of Emily Lyons forever and left a co-worker dead, but its impact on the battle over abortion in Birmingham has faded since that Jan. 29 morning. The blast maimed and almost blinded Mrs. Lyons, a nurse and counselor, but while she can see only a little, she can see that little has changed.

In the parking lot of Milo's hamburger stand, a few blocks from where the bomb scorched the front of the New Woman All Women Health Care Center, a bumper sticker on a Buick warns, "Abortions Stop Heartbeats." At the center, the picket lines are made up of familiar faces — nurses at the clinic know protesters by name — who shout familiar warnings to pregnant women who keep coming.

All the bomber did was end one life and drastically alter another, Mrs. Lyons said, as this city — and both sides in a seething, long-running confrontation — went cautiously back to business as usual.

"What," Mrs. Lyons asks of the bomber, "were you thinking?"

A police officer, Robert Sanderson, who was trying to earn some side money as a security guard at the clinic, is dead. Mrs. Lyons, who often counseled patients to go home if she felt they were unsure about having an abortion, lost her left eye and is undergoing a series of surgeries to repair her right eye. She has had to learn to walk again on legs shattered by the bomb intended to kill and injure, not to topple walls or set fires.

"It doesn't affect anyone that much," said Mrs. Lyons, a 41-year-old mother of two daughters, 17 and 13 years old. "Nobody quit the clinic where I worked. They're all just stronger."

She believes that she is, too.

"I used to be a wallflower," Mrs. Lyons said. "But I'm not intimidated by anything any more. Now that I've made it through this, now that I've been blown up, I don't think there's anything that can."

"I may never be in a pair of heels again in my whole life," she said, referring to her badly injured legs. "But so be it. Yes, it's sad. But the options are worse. I could be six feet under."

She does not even believe that what happened at the clinic is the work of an anti-abortion zealot, she said. "The pro-life protesters we had, we all knew by name," she said. "I hate to say it, but you just kind of wrote them off as morons, some of them, and ignored them."

She does not want to waste on anger the energy she needs for rehabilitation, but it creeps into her voice when she talks about the explosion, which happened as she and Mr. Sanderson stood at the center's entrance. The bomb, a fragmentation device studded with nails, was set to go off as clinic employees arrived for work, investigators said.

Mrs. Lyons does not pretend to forgive the bomber, who the police say they believe is 31-year-old Eric Robert Rudolph, a fugitive who is being hunted nationwide. Mr. Rudolph was seen running from the area of the clinic minutes after the bombing.

Less than a week after the blast, still sightless, racked with pain and covered with fresh scars, Mrs. Lyons held a news conference from her wheelchair.

"I want to show the world the end effect of a senseless act," she said. She called on the bomber to turn himself in, to take responsibility for the act that she will live with for the rest of her life.

The bomber, she said, "was fanatical." If it is Mr. Rudolph, she said, she wants to see him brought in, "dead or alive."

"Alive would be pretty good," Mrs. Lyons said, "but it really doesn't matter. They could just tell me it was him in a coffin, though, and I'd be satisfied."

Investigators and others involved in the case have called Mrs. Lyons the flip side to the bomber's cowardice. The months since that blast have been a nightmare of operations and physical therapy, but she now believes that she will "soon be able to drive and read and jump, all that."

Bones in her shins were shattered and the skin on her legs shredded.

"I can walk," she said, "but I can't do it for very long, because of the swelling."

She is confident she will eventually see well enough to lead a normal life, although "normal" means different things now.

"I can't go back to the clinic," she said. "It's just too physically demanding. I just don't have the dexterity."

She would if she could. The bomber, she said, did not scare her away.

"I believed in what I did," said Mrs. Lyons, who has also worked with infants and the elderly in more than 20 years of delivering health care. "Some people questioned if I was ashamed of what I did, and the answer is 'no.' I wouldn't let somebody like him keep me away.

"I'm angry about the things I have to miss: my job, reading, driving. I'm angry about my limitations." For now, her 17-year-old daughter drives her around, which she concedes is a little frightening in itself. "At least she's in her own car," which she would be less prone to wreck, Mrs. Lyons said.

She said she thrived on the love and support of her husband, Jeff Lyons, who owns a computer business, and her daughters. She has been amazed at how many people have called or written to tell her how they have been affected by what happened to her. Most of those have been good, but someone wrote that she would die in a "lake of fire" because of her work at the clinic.

"I've already been in a lake of fire," Mrs. Lyons said.

Susan

The story of Susan Smith is one of such sadness that I try not to

think about it too much. When I do, it is like touching a cold current,

deep in a warm river. You jerk your foot back, instinctively.

An Agonizing Search for Two Boys

New York Times, October 28, 1994

DATELINE: Union, S.C., Oct. 27

Susan Smith said she stood in the middle of a dark, isolated road on Tuesday night and screamed, "I love y'all" as a carjacker disappeared in the distance with her two children in the back seat. So far, the people of this small textile town in northwestern South Carolina have been unable to pray Mrs. Smith's two little boys home again.

Hundreds of law enforcement officers and volunteers have been searching the highways and deep forests of this rural piece of the state, hoping the carjacker released 14-month-old Alexander and 3-year-old Michael. But as of this evening, investigators still had no solid leads, and the worst crime in recent memory in pastoral, peaceful Union County remained unsolved.

"I pray for him," said Sue Morris, Mrs. Smith's neighbor, of the carjacker who had become the focus of a frantic four-state search. "I pray for God to touch his heart and make him let those children go."

What has appeared to be the real-life manifestation of every parent's nightmare began about 9 P.M. on Tuesday when Mrs. Smith, her two children strapped into car seats in the back, stopped her car at a traffic signal in Monarch Mills, a few miles outside Union, the county seat.

Mrs. Smith said she was looking out the driver's-side window when a man with a gun jerked open the unlocked door on the passenger side of her burgundy 1990 Mazda and said, "Shut up and drive or I'll kill you."

Mrs. Smith, who works for a textile company, told Sheriff's Department investigators that she did not know the man and that he seemed out of breath, as though he had been running or was frightened. The man ordered her to drive northeast for about 10 miles, then told her to stop and get out.

She begged him to let her take the children with her, but the man told her: "I don't have time. I'll take care of them."

She said she watched in shock, standing in the middle of the road, as the man drove away with her children. Later, family members said Mrs. Smith was sick with grief, asking herself how she could have let the man drive away with her sons.

"She just thought, when she got out of the car, that he'd let her have them," said her cousin, Dennis Gregory, a woodworker who lives in Columbia, S.C. "This is a crazy thing. It doesn't happen here. People sleep with their doors open here."

Investigators have almost nothing that would lead them to the children. The crime scene vanished down the dark road.

"Very rarely do you have a crime and not have a crime scene to work," said Union County Sheriff Howard Wells. "I've been in law enforcement 20 years, and I've never had a case where there is so little to work on."

Sheriff Wells did not sound optimistic when asked about what could have been a sighting of the suspect north of Union, across the state line in North Carolina. A convenience store about 100 miles north of Union in Salisbury, N.C., was robbed on Wednesday by a man matching the description of the kidnapper. The robber was reported to have fled in a burgundy car, but none of the witnesses saw any children.

A composite drawing of the carjacker has been circulated in the South and several East Coast states, but it is vague and, according to volunteers who helped look for the children, could be anyone.

Mrs. Smith described the man as black, 20 to 30 years old, 5 feet 9 inches to 6 feet tall, and wearing a dark blue ski cap, blue jeans and a blue jacket.

"Me and my wife plea to you, please return our children to us," said their father, David Smith, hoping that the man would see his appeal on television or read it in a newspaper. Mr. Smith is an assistant manager at a Winn-Dixie grocery store.

Mr. and Mrs. Smith are separated and have filed for divorce, and Sheriff Wells, although he said investigators were approaching the case as a carjacking and kidnapping, has questioned the Smiths about the possibility of a custody dispute. But in a press conference today, he said investigators considered the man described by Mrs. Smith to be their suspect.

Mrs. Smith's stepfather, Bev Russell, said that although the Smiths were separated, "there has never been any disagreement between them over the children." The children live with their mother in a residential neighborhood in Union, a town of about 10,000.

The whole county, which is made up largely of Sumter National Forest, has just 30,000 people. Today, volunteers walked through the changing leaves calling the children's names. At the Sheriff's Office, where deputies and clerks have been working 48 hours without sleep, phones rang continually. Sometimes the caller would have a legitimate tip. Sometimes it would be, as Sheriff Wells put it, "some crackpot."

The department has had calls from psychics offering help in finding the children, and from people offering money for a reward.

So far there is no reward, because Sheriff Wells said he would rather have his investigators work solid leads from people whose motivation is common decency, not money. A reward might cause a flood of dubious leads, investigators said.

On the streets of Union, where the courthouse is still the biggest building in town, cars cruised past the Sheriff's Office with yellow ribbons tied to their antennas. Some overpasses on the major highways had huge ribbons draped over their sides. Some people said the man, if caught, should be hanged immediately. But many others said the suspect was unimportant. "I don't give a damn if we never catch that man," said Lieut. Jeff Lawson of the Sheriff's Department, "just so long as we get those kids back."

Mr. Russell said the two children were just normal, hard-playing, rambunctious little boys who broke a lot of toys. "They're just a great blessing," he said. He said he did not understand why the carjacker kept the children, why he did not just drop them off at a hospital or some other public place.

Others in this town echo him. They understand the man stealing the car, but to keep the children is a meanness, a callousness they just don't understand.

"None of it makes any sense to me," Mr. Russell said.

Mother of "Carjacked" Boys Held in Their Deaths

New York Times, November 4, 1994

DATELINE: Atlanta, Nov. 3

In a turn of events that some people in her town expected but few wanted to believe, a South Carolina woman who reported that her two little boys had been abducted by a carjacker was arrested and charged today with two counts of murder in their deaths.

According to the arrest warrant, 23-year-old Susan V. Smith confessed to the murders of her sons — 3-year-old Michael Smith and his 14-month-old brother, Alexander.

Mrs. Smith, of Union, S.C., had appealed over and over to God and to the people of her state to help return her children to her.

The prosecutor for the area that includes Union County, Thomas Pope, was quoted by The Associated Press as saying that Mrs. Smith was charged tonight. She will be arraigned on Friday in Union County instead of York County as originally planned.

Two decomposed bodies, believed to be those of the boys, were found today inside the mother's car, deep under the waters of John D. Long Lake. The lake is a popular spot for fishing and picnicking a few miles outside Union, a small mill town in northwestern South Carolina.

The boys, who were reported missing on Oct. 25, apparently drowned, the authorities said. The bodies were expected to be identified in autopsies today.

Sheriff Howard Wells of Union County announced Mrs. Smith's arrest at an early evening news conference outside the County Courthouse.

Sheriff Wells would not answer questions about motive or how such a hoax could have fooled investigators and others for more than a week.

A portion of the arrest warrant was read to The New York Times. The discovery of the bodies and the arrest of Mrs. Smith came a few hours after she had made the most recent in a string of tearful appeals in front of television cameras to have her children returned to her.

"I have prayed to the Lord every day," Mrs. Smith said. "It's just so sad that someone could take such beautiful children. I have put all my trust and faith in the Lord that He will bring them home to us."

Even as the news spread that Mrs. Smith was to be charged with murder, ministers in Union held a prayer vigil. Signs were taped to columns on the courthouse that said, "We love you, Michael and Alex, Susan and David." David Smith is the boys' father. Hundreds of volunteers have scoured this corner of the state, with the names of the two boys on the lips of almost everyone.

"No one here can believe it," Gene Gregory, who runs a restaurant in Union, said in a telephone interview. "People are sitting here crying, Dear Lord, how can this happen?"

Mrs. Smith had said that an armed man forced her out of her car at a crossroads stoplight a few miles outside Union and drove away with her children still strapped into the backseat, leaving her screaming in the middle of the road. As the man drove away, Mrs. Smith said, she yelled, "I love y'all!"

Mrs. Smith said that she had begged the man to let her have her children, but that he had refused, telling her he would "take care of them."

She described the carjacker as a black man between 20 and 30 years old. Based on her description, a vague sketch was produced and distributed widely by the authorities. Sheriff's deputies, Federal Bureau of Investigation agents and other law officers subsequently tracked down one dead-end lead after another, many of them tips from people across the country. On Wednesday, the police received a report that a boy who looked like Alex had been dropped off at a motel in Seattle by a car with South Carolina plates.

The unraveling of Mrs. Smith's story bears similarities to the 1989 Charles Stuart murder case in Boston, in which Mr. Stuart, a white man, told the police that a black man had fatally shot his pregnant wife, Carol. Mr. Stuart later leaped to his death from a bridge as investigators zeroed in on him as the killer.

Since last Thursday, John D. Long Lake was searched twice by divers, who found nothing. Sheriff Wells would not answer questions about why the car, a burgundy 1990 Mazda, was not found.

The lack of progress in the past few days led investigators and others in Union County to doubt Mrs. Smith's story, but over and over Mr. Wells seemed to deflect suspicion away from the mother.

Even when two lie detector tests showed that Mrs. Smith seemed to be trying to deceive the questioner, Mr. Wells said only that he had not dismissed her, or her estranged husband, as suspects. "The public is trying to make her the suspect," said Mr. Wells, who did say it would not be unusual for a mother scared over the abduction of her children to give conflicting statements.

Mrs. Smith, a secretary at a textile mill, has filed for a divorce, contending that her husband, the assistant manager at the Union Winn-Dixie grocery store, had committed adultery. But there has been no custody battle. Mrs. Smith was given full custody of the children, a ruling that Mr. Smith did not challenge.

In an interview today on the CBS News program "This Morning," Mrs. Smith said that she had agreed to let the authorities search her home on Wednesday but that she did not know what they were looking for.

With her husband by her side for the interview, she denied knowing anything about their sons' whereabouts.

"I did not have anything to do with the abduction of my children," Mrs. Smith said in the interview.

"I don't think that any parent could love my children more than I do, and I would never even think about doing anything that would harm them," she added. "It's really painful to have the finger pointed at you when it's your children involved."

Both white and black residents of Union said they were concerned as the investigation dragged on that Mrs. Smith had claimed that a black man had taken her children. The artists' rendering was taped to the windows of every store in Union.

John McCarroll, the branch president-elect of the National Association for the Advancement of Colored People in nearby West Spartanburg, said Mrs. Smith's decision to describe the carjacker as a black man showed "that there is still a lot of prejudice between the races here."

"We try to turn our back on it, hoping it will go away," he said, "but sometimes it just gets worse. Certainly, our main concern is with the death of these two little children. But this just points out to us how racism lingers."

For Union, a town of 10,000, a nationwide manhunt that brought international attention to the quiet, peaceful town, ended in the worst possible way.

Mr. Gregory, the restaurant owner, and others in Union were asking themselves why Mrs. Smith would want her children dead.

"I've seen her with those two babies," he said, breaking down into sobs. "She was a sweet girl. She came from a good family. I don't understand any of this."

In an interview on Thursday morning on the NBC program "Today," Mrs. Smith spoke in anguished tones about her missing children, ending with a message to them delivered through the television camera.

"I was thinking last night, as a mother, it's only a natural instinct to protect your children from any harm," she said in an interview. "And the hardest part of this whole ordeal is not knowing if your children are getting what they need to survive. And it hurts real bad to have that protection barrier broken between the parent and the child.

"But I have my put my faith in the Lord, and I really believe that He's taking care of them. And they're too beautiful and too precious that He's not going to let anything happen to them.

"And, Michael and Alex, I love you, and we're going to have the biggest celebration when you get home."

Sheriff Says Prayer and a Lie Led Susan Smith to Confess

New York Times, July 18, 1995

DATELINE: Union, S.C., July 17

Nine days after the big lie, the one that had people across the nation praying for the lives of her children, Susan Smith bowed her head in a church gymnasium, took the hands of the county sheriff and confessed to God and man.

The Union County Sheriff, Howard Wells, who held her and prayed with her that afternoon of Nov. 3, told a hushed courtroom today how he had tricked Mrs. Smith into a confession with a small lie of his own.

His testimony, before the judge ruled that Mrs. Smith's written confession in the drowning deaths of Michael, 3, and Alex, 14 months, was admissible, detailed how Mrs. Smith's story that the boys were taken by a carjacker came apart slowly and painfully.

That afternoon, as hope was running thin in the search for her sons and suspicion against her continued to build, Mr. Wells told her that he knew her claim that the children had been taken at an intersection outside the small town of Union was a lie because his deputies had been working a surveillance at that crossroads.

"This could not have happened as you said," he told her, sitting face to face with her in a small room in the gymnasium, where they had gone to get away from reporters. There had been, in truth, no such deputies at the intersection.

"I told her I would release it to the media" because her lie about a black carjacker was causing deep pain among blacks, and he said he owed it to the town to end the racial divisiveness it had caused.

"Susan broke at that time," he said, and she burst into tears, just short of hysteria. She asked him to pray with her, he said, and face to face, holding hands, they did.

"I'm so ashamed," she said to Mr. Wells, he testified. "She asked for my gun so that she could kill herself."

Mr. Wells said he asked her why she wanted to do that.

"You don't understand," she said, the Sheriff testified. "My children are not all right."

"I said, 'Susan, don't say anything else,'" Mr. Wells said, before going to the hallway for a Miranda form to read her her rights.

The 23-year-old mother gave both a spoken and written confession before she left the room, telling how she released the parking brake and allowed her Mazda to roll down a boat ramp and into a lake with her sons strapped inside.

Over objections from her lawyers, who said Mrs. Smith was tricked into the confession and coerced with prayer when she was out of her mind with grief, Judge William Howard of the state's Circuit Court ruled that the jury could hear the written confession and other statements.

The testimony by Mr. Wells and other investigators gave a preview of the capital murder trial, which is expected to begin with opening statements on Tuesday.

Judge Howard also removed a juror from the panel and put her in jail. Gayle Beam, the only black woman on the jury, was held in contempt and jailed because she did not disclose that she had recently pleaded guilty to credit card fraud.

She told the judge that she had not even looked at the questionnaire the court required all potential jurors to complete and that her daughter had completed it for her.

She could be fined $10,000 and sentenced to six months in jail. Judge Howard must now proceed with just one alternate juror. Only two were picked.

But it was the tale of Mrs. Smith's doomed deception that held many people in the courtroom spellbound.

As it unwound, Mrs. Smith, whom the state psychiatrist calls suicidal and who relies on the anti-depressant Prozac to make her more alert, sat quietly in the courtroom, not crying. She looked lost, out of touch with what was going on. Her body seemed to tremble, but it was because she was jiggling her leg absently, for minutes at a time.

Investigators testified that from the beginning they were suspicious of Mrs. Smith, who held to her lie for nine days, even pleading for the safe return of her sons from the fictional carjacker. They described a woman who cried without shedding any tears, who seemed more interested in how she looked on television than in getting her sons back and who spoke about going to the beach to get away from hounding reporters.

An agent with the State Law Enforcement Division said he had noticed inconsistencies in her story from the start and passed that information on to other agents.

"She started out extremely vague," said Roy Paschal, who helped Mrs. Smith with the composite drawing of the phantom suspect. She gave conflicting descriptions, saying once that the man had worn a baseball cap, then a knit cap.

David Espie, an agent with the Federal Bureau of Investigation, said she would make sobbing noises, "but when I would look at her eyes, no water, no tears."

James E. Harris, another state investigator, said Mrs. Smith had seemed strangely unconcerned about the children.

"She asked if I had seen her on CBS," he said. "She asked me how she looked. She said she wanted to get away from the media and go to the beach." He said she had asked him if he knew how to do a dance called the shag and said he could perhaps teach it to her.

Even though suspicion grew, Mrs. Smith was not arrested. Mr. Wells said that until the confession, he had not been certain of what had happened to the children.

Pete Logan, a former F.B.I. agent who now works for the state, was with Sheriff Wells on the day of the confession. When he walked into the room, after Mrs. Smith confessed, she was on her knees with her head in the chair, as if in prayer.

She was sobbing, said Mr. Logan, a white-haired man, whose coaxing of Mrs. Smith over the previous two or three days seemed to help bring on the confession. "No question, it was total remorse," he said. "I've been doing this 35 years, and I've never seen someone quite like that. Several times she said she wanted to kill herself."

She told Mr. Wells that she had gone to the lake to kill herself and her children, but found herself running away from the lake with her hands over her ears so she could not hear the car slide into the water.

Mrs. Smith has a long history of mental instability. Psychologists wanted to admit her to a psychiatric hospital when she was 13, but her mother and stepfather refused to cooperate. Her stepfather later molested her when she was 15.

Her lawyer, David Bruck, is expected to argue that she is either innocent by reason of insanity or guilty but mentally ill.

Mr. Wells seemed, from the beginning of the case, to be almost protective of her. She knew and trusted him, he said.

As they bowed their heads in prayer, he told her: "All things will be revealed to us in time."

Psychiatrist for Smith's Defense
Tells of a Woman Desperate to Be Liked

New York Times, July 22, 1995

DATELINE: Union, S.C., July 21

Before Susan Smith had taken more than a few steps up a boat ramp after rolling her car into the lake with her two children strapped inside, she was already wondering what people would think of her, already forming her alibi, a forensic psychiatrist hired by the defense testified today.

What would seem to be a sign of selfishness, of cold-blooded behavior, was instead a sign of the 23-year-old Mrs. Smith's desperate need to be liked, a need that manifested itself in the months before the killings in a series of sexual encounters with some of the most unlikely people, her lawyers tried to show today.

Seymour Halleck, a psychiatrist and law professor at the University of North Carolina, testified that Mrs. Smith, suffering from depression and suicidal thoughts in the months leading up to the Oct. 25 killings, fell into a destructive cycle of sexual relationships to ease her loneliness.

In August alone, she had sexual relations with her stepfather, Beverly Russell; Tom Findlay, the son of the owner of the mill where Mrs. Smith worked; with Mr. Findlay's father, J. Cary Findlay, and with her husband, David Smith, from whom she was separated at the time.

By having sex with four men in the late summer and early fall of 1994, she temporarily eased her depression, but the guilt ultimately deepened her depression, Dr. Halleck said.

He went down the list of her sexual partners in an effort to poke holes in the prosecution's theory that Mrs. Smith killed her children, Michael, 3, and Alex, 14 months, so she could rekindle her love affair with Tom Findlay. Mr. Findlay had said he did not want a relationship that included children.

Dr. Halleck said David Smith went to Mrs. Smith's house and asked for sex at least twice in August 1994, which she agreed to even though she told Dr. Halleck she did not enjoy it. He said he believed she agreed to have sex because she wanted to save her marriage.

Dr. Halleck said that she had sex with Tom Findlay, the 28-year-old textile heir, but that he was not the main focus of her life.

"A passing love affair," Dr. Halleck called it. "I found she had strong feelings for a lot of different men, and it was very unlikely that Tom Findlay was No. 1 on her list."

The idea that she would kill her children, the most important things in her life, to reclaim Mr. Findlay is "an absurd idea," Dr. Halleck said.

Mrs. Smith wrote in a letter to Mr. Findlay that she would never love anyone as much as him.

She had sex with his father, J. Cary Findlay, perhaps because she had developed, when she was molested by her stepfather, a need for the love and approval of an older man, Dr. Halleck said.

The afternoon before she killed her children, Mrs. Smith told Tom Findlay that she had slept with his father, then, that evening, told him she had not slept with him, that it was "a joke." Friends said it was because she wanted to hurt him, but lied about it later to try to salvage their relationship. He had already broken off his relationship with her at that point.

Dr. Halleck said Mrs. Smith slept with Beverly Russell, the stepfather who had molested her when she was 15, even though she told Dr. Halleck that "it made her skin crawl." He said that perhaps she did it for the same reasons she slept with others — to find love and win his approval. Mr. Russell, who mortgaged his house to pay Mrs. Smith's legal costs, was a respected leader of the Christian Coalition and active in the Republican Party.

Today's testimony was the most lurid so far in a trial that has at times seemed more soap opera than circuit court.

Dr. Halleck said that the affairs, bunched together in such a small time frame, showed how desperate and depressed Mrs. Smith became in the summer and fall leading up to the boys' deaths.

Dr. Halleck, who acknowledged to Tommy Pope, the chief prosecutor, that most of his information came from Mrs. Smith herself, said her constant need for affection was a symptom of "brief intermittent depressive disorder," in which Mrs. Smith was able, much of the time, to make co-workers and friends believe she was fine, even happy.

But he painted a dark, hopeless image of the months leading up to the killings. He said she began to drink heavily, was happy only when she was reinforced by the love of another and began to contemplate killing herself every day.

Dr. Halleck said she told him that on the night of the killings, she drove to a bridge over the Broad River and thought about taking her children in her arms and jumping. The sound of her sons crying made her get back in the car and drive away, she told him.

Then she drove to the boat ramp at John D. Long Lake. She told Dr. Halleck that she pulled near the end of the ramp and disengaged the gears, so the car would roll, and started it down the ramp. She jerked up the hand brake to stop it, let it roll a second time and jerked it up again.

Dr. Halleck said he believed that she intended to kill herself. But the next time she released the brake she ran from the car, "as some survival instinct" took over, he said.

He said she might have somehow blocked the presence of the two boys out of her memory, at the instant she released the brake.

As she ran through the forest, she began making up her story because she was so afraid of what others would think of her. Even after doing what she did, Mrs. Smith was still thinking about what others would think of her, he said.

The trial is expected to conclude in the next two days — court will continue this weekend — and then, after a 24-hour break, begin its penalty phase.

Mrs. Smith's lawyer, David Bruck, has rejected both technical defenses such as not guilty by reason of insanity and guilty but mentally ill. Mrs. Smith is not insane, Dr. Halleck said, but does suffer from mental disorders.

Mr. Bruck knows he cannot get an acquittal because Mrs. Smith has confessed, but he hopes the jury will see she did not maliciously kill her children and will decide not to give her the death penalty.

Mrs. Smith's lawyers are expected to save much of the more sympathetic testimony for the penalty phase of the trial. But several legal experts said they were surprised by how much information on her troubled life has already crept into the trial.

Through Dr. Halleck and other witnesses, Mr. Bruck has given the jurors a sad silhouette of Mrs. Smith without having to put her on the stand. That might not happen even in the penalty phase of the trial because, as even the state's own psychiatrist said, Mrs. Smith cannot be trusted to help herself on the stand.

She has said she wants to die and might sabotage her own case if allowed to testify.

Although Mr. Bruck has said that he will not try to make excuses for Mrs. Smith, and that she accepts responsibility for what she did, the past four days have featured one witness after another — even some for the prosecution — who made excuse after excuse for her, attributing the deaths to her depression.

Mr. Pope, the prosecutor, tried to counter that by asking Dr. Halleck whether Mrs. Smith knew she was committing a crime. Dr. Halleck said Mrs. Smith knew that what she was doing was legally wrong, but he hedged on whether she knew it was morally wrong. Dr. Halleck kept referring to the killings as part of a suicide attempt.

Mr. Pope said the youngsters had no decision in Mrs. Smith's actions. "She did know right from wrong, and had the ability to make a choice?" Mr. Pope asked the witness.

"Yes," Dr. Halleck replied.

Father Testifies in Penalty Part of Smith Trial

New York Times, July 26, 1995

DATELINE: Union, S.C., July 25

David Smith's hand trembled so much today that the photograph of his two little boys seemed to vibrate, inches from the faces of the jurors. Three jurors wept with him as he told them about his 3-year-old's terror of water.

"Michael didn't like water on his face," said Mr. Smith, who testified against his 23-year-old former wife, Susan Smith, in the penalty phase of her murder trial. "He would try to climb out of the bathtub" when water splashed onto his face. Mr. Smith would have to shield Michael's face with his hand, he said, when he rinsed his hair.

Across the courtroom, the woman who drowned Michael and his 14-month-old brother, Alex, lowered her face to the defense table, hugged herself and sobbed.

"All my hopes, all my dreams, everything that I had planned for the rest of my life — it ended that day," said Mr. Smith, whose sons died Oct. 25 when his estranged wife let loose the hand brake on her car and sent it rolling into John D. Long Lake. His sons were buckled in their safety seats.

"I didn't know what to do," he said, starting to cry. "Everything I had planned on, my life with my kids, was gone."

The judge, William Howard of State Circuit Court, called a recess as Mr. Smith wept. As Mrs. Smith passed by him on her way out of the courtroom, she said softly, "I'm sorry, David."

He did not look at her.

Mrs. Smith, found guilty of the double murder on Saturday, is now in the sentencing phase of her capital murder trial. The prosecution is trying to convince the same jury that her crime was so bad, so evil, that she should not be allowed to live. The verdict must be unanimous to put her to death. If one juror balks, she will receive a life sentence with the possibility of parole in 30 years.

The prosecution presented the heart of its case today, first with Mr. Smith, then with a videotaped re-enactment of Mrs. Smith's red Mazda rolling down the boat ramp and into the water. At one point, the rear of the car rose up as the car's nose dipped, which meant, said Keith Giese, the assistant prosecutor, that Michael and his brother would have faced the lake's water before it engulfed them.

But it was the boy's father who turned the courtroom into a place of mourning.

Mr. Smith, whose testimony was expected to be crucial in the state's efforts to put Mrs. Smith to death, left more than the three jurors in tears. Throughout the courtroom people cried as his tears dripped onto the pictures he held, photographs of his sons at play in the yard, on the sand at Myrtle Beach.

One network correspondent cried out loud. Mrs. Smith's lawyer, David Bruck, said he had shed a tear, too.

Mrs. Smith's side of the family seemed mostly unmoved. During the break after his testimony, several members of the family even smiled. They have been angry with Mr. Smith since he said he wanted his sons' mother to die. The courtroom is divided down the middle — his relatives and friends on one side, hers on the other.

Tommy Pope, the lead prosecutor, confronted a potentially damaging cross-examination of Mr. Smith by asking him about marital violence between the two and about a book deal in which Mr. Smith has pocketed some $20,000.

Once, Mr. Smith said, "she hit me upside the head" after he was sarcastic with her, then he chased her into the yard and tackled her.

Another time he dragged her out of the bed and onto the porch after an argument, but he did not hit her, he said.

But that testimony seemed forgiven in his grief over his sons.

"Everything I planned is gone, teaching them how to play ball, taking them fishing, teaching them how to ride a bike, watching them go to school on their first day," said Mr. Smith, who friends called a much better father to his sons than he had ever been a husband.

He often took them to play and loved being with them, friends said.

"All this has been ripped from me," he said between sobs, "and I don't know what I'm supposed to do."

The prosecution also questioned him about a book about his life with Mrs. Smith, released today, for which he reportedly received as much as $110,000. He said he kept only $20,000 to help pay his way through the trial — he has taken a leave from his job as a night manager at the Winn Dixie supermarket. He testified today that he had donated $200,000 to $300,000 to children's charities but did not say what the source of that money was.

Mr. Bruck, who has surprised several people throughout the trial by doing exactly the opposite of what legal experts predicted, had been expected to make Mr. Smith out to be a villain, one of the reasons for her sad life.

Instead, he told the judge he had no question for him.

"Thank you," said Mr. Smith, his eyes still wet, when he walked by Mr. Bruck.

After the trial, legal and psychiatric experts said he would have gained little with a tough cross-examination of Mr. Smith after the father had won the jury's heart.

Mr. Bruck seemed to agree.

"I don't think I have ever — no, I know I have never — been in a courtroom where such moving testimony was heard as that of David Smith," Mr. Bruck said.

But that statement came as part of an appeal to the judge to leave out the re-enactment of the car rolling down the ramp and slipping under the lake.

Mr. Smith stood by his estranged wife during the nine days she lied that a carjacker had taken the children, prompting a nationwide search and sympathy that disappeared into anger and resentment when she confessed on Nov. 3 that she had drowned the children. Prosecutors said she did it to reclaim a wealthy lover, Tom Findlay, who dumped her partly because she had children.

Mr. Smith told how he frantically drove to a house near the lake the night of Oct. 25, when Mrs. Smith first told her story of the carjacker.

As he drove Mrs. Smith to her mother's house, she made what he called an "inappropriate" statement, considering the fact that she had said her children had just been snatched away.

"She said, 'I hope you don't mind if Tom Findlay comes to see me at my mom's,'" Mr. Smith testified.

Carolina Jury Rejects Execution for Woman Who Drowned Sons

New York Times, July 29, 1995

DATELINE: Union, S.C., July 28

A jury today decided that Susan Smith should not be put to death for the drowning of her two young sons, and instead should spend the rest of her life in prison, to remember.

It took the jury two and one-half hours to reject the prosecution's request for the death penalty and settle on the life sentence. The jury's unanimous decision saved Mrs. Smith, 23, from death row, but left her alone in a tiny cell with the ghosts of her dead children, for at least the next 30 years, her lawyer said.

"This young woman is in a lake of fire," said the lawyer, David Bruck. "That's her punishment."

Mr. Bruck had argued that Mrs. Smith was so distraught over the deaths of her children, Michael, 3, and Alex, 14 months, that she did not want to live. But as the jury's verdict was read, she gasped, and slipped her arm around Mr. Bruck's waist to give him a quick, firm, hug.

Mrs. Smith, at the center of a murder case that first drew the sympathy and later the loathing of the nation, was convicted last Saturday of murder. To reclaim a lover who said he did not want a relationship with a woman who had children, the prosecutor contended, Mrs. Smith drove to a dark lake on the night of Oct. 25 and sent her car rolling into the water with the two little boys strapped inside in their car seats.

For nine days, Mrs. Smith looked into television cameras and mournfully begged a phantom carjacker, whom she described as a young black man with a gun, to bring her babies back.

Then, after thousands of volunteers had combed back roads, dredged lakes, passed out flyers and prayed for her sons' safety, she broke down after a prayer with a plain-spoken, methodical county sheriff and said the words that no one wanted to believe.

Now, after nine months of what residents here call a collective pain over these murders and the national attention — for all the wrong reasons — it has brought to this little mill town, it is over.

Almost on cue, as the county court clerk read off the verdicts in the courtroom, it started to rain hard, washing away for at least a little while a summer heat wave that has lasted throughout this trial.

"Poetic justice," said Andy Wallace, a state investigator, as he watched the rain run down the street.

Inside the courtroom, Mrs. Smith's family members clasped their hands and prayed as the verdict was read. Across the courtroom, the boys' father sat like a statue. David Smith had said he wanted his estranged wife to die for what she did.

It was a lifetime of deep depression, punctuated by destructive sexual affairs and suicide attempts, that caused Mrs. Smith to snap the night of the murders, and do what few human beings could ever do, her lawyers claimed.

That sickened Mr. Smith, who buried his children in the same coffin as Mrs. Smith sat in her prison cell.

"Me and my family are disappointed that the death penalty was not the verdict," he said, his lips quivering as he held back his tears. "But it wasn't our choice. They returned a verdict they thought was justice.

"I'll never forget what Susan has done to me, my family and her family. I can never forget Michael and Alex.

"But forgive? That's something I guess I'll have to deal with further down the road."

He said he would probably leave town. There are too many memories here, crowding in on him.

"There are a lot of things I would rather not look at for the rest of my life," he said.

The state's lead prosecutor, Tommy Pope, had tried to show that Mrs. Smith was fooling everyone with her claims of remorse, the way she fooled everyone for nine days in October and November.

"She may be sorry now," Mr. Pope said, his voice rising from a near whisper to a shout as he urged the jury for a death sentence in his closing argument. "But was she sorry when she dropped that hand brake down," and sent her children to their death.

He laid photographs of the two little boys on the rail of the jury box as he spoke of what the boys must have felt as the car slid under the lake at about 9 P.M., and how Mrs. Smith ran from the edge of the lake with her hands over her ears.

"When that car filled up with water they probably didn't see it," said Mr. Pope, because of the dark of the night. "But they felt that water in the darkness as it covered their faces."

His case against Mrs. Smith, and his refusal to accept a plea bargain for life in prison, caused the town to have to relive the worst thing that has ever happened here.

The prosecutor has been criticized, and accused by Mr. Bruck and others of using Mrs. Smith to build a reputation and future political career.

"I stand by it," Mr. Pope said of the decision, "and I always will. Even at the end of this road we've all been through, I'd say it was still worth it. It had to be done."

If he had not done what he did, Mr. Pope said, the horror of what she did would have slipped easily by, with the lives of the children.

Mr. Bruck said that would not have happened, because Mrs. Smith will pay every day for her crimes.

She is afraid, he said, because of her mental condition, to be alone, and her depression deepens every time she is left alone.

"Her life doesn't look too much different today than it did yesterday," Mr. Bruck said. "She is relieved for her family. She knew the people she loved could not bear her death."

But now Mrs. Smith will go back to a cell so small she can almost touch the walls from side to side when she stretches out her arms.

She will be permitted to have visitors, but she will spend most days alone, except for the guards.

"There is no good outcome in this case. This case was an awful case of tragedy from the beginning and still is," Mr. Bruck said. "It was such an awful thing, an unbearable thing."

Mr. Bruck countered Mr. Pope's appeal for an eye for an eye with his own scripture and verse.

Holding a Bible in his hand, he read the story from the Gospel of John about the woman who committed adultery, and was to be stoned.

"He that is without sin among you, let him cast the first stone," Mr. Bruck read, in his nondescript Yankee accent.

In South Carolina, state law requires a death penalty verdict to be unanimous. If one juror holds out, it is an automatic life sentence, with a chance of parole after 30 years.

The jurors refused to comment on the case today, so it was not clear why they decided to spare Mrs. Smith. But during jury selection, several of the jurors had talked of the enormity of the decision of life or death.

Guilt was always a foregone conclusion. Mrs. Smith confessed on Nov. 3, and her childrens' bodies were recovered later that day. Divers had missed the car in their first search of John D. Long Lake, a recreation area outside Union, because they did not search far enough into the lake.

The jury of three women and nine men, eight whites and four blacks, took the same amount of time to convict her — two and a half hours — as it did to reject the death penalty. In such a small place, picking a jury with no ties to her had been impossible. One of them, the wife of the police chief, had been Mrs. Smith's babysitter when she was a child, and others had friends or co-workers who saw members of her family almost every day, at the mill, at the Wal-Mart, at ball games.

"I think a part of each person in the courtroom was swayed by the nature of the crime, and the impact on its victims," said the Judge, William Howard, during the sentencing.

"I know your hearts have been torn, as everyone's hearts have been torn," he told the jury.

For black residents of Union, there was a special pain. Mrs. Smith chose a black man as a scapegoat, they believed, because it was more believable.

But everyone here was affected, one way or another, residents said. Beverly Russell, the stepfather who molested Mrs. Smith when she was a teen-ager, was once a big man in town, a respected political leader, church goer and businessman. Other secrets have been spilled.

Most are just glad it is done, and want life to resume some normalcy, if that is possible.

Others felt cheated, because they still are not sure which of the two Susan Smiths killed the boys that night.

"There are some things that are going to remain somewhat mysterious," said Mr. Bruck. "I wish it wasn't so."

One fact still haunts Mr. Pope. Mrs. Smith parked her car on a steep incline that night, in what her lawyers said was a failed suicide. She let go the hand brake, reconsidered and pulled it up again, then let it go and — in some instinct for survival — jumped from the car.

But Mr. Pope, and common sense, say that is impossible. She would have had to have flung herself as the car began to roll immediately, and would have certainly torn or dirtied her clothes. Her clothes were clean when she walked to a nearby house to tell her lie about the carjacker.

Mr. Pope, and common sense, say she must have stood outside the car, leaned in to let go the hand brake, and jumped back.

And how, many people here wonder, was that a suicide attempt?

A Killer's Only Confidant: The Man Who Caught Susan Smith

New York Times, August 4, 1995

DATELINE: Union, S.C., July 31

The case of a lifetime is closed for Howard Wells. The reporters and the well-wishers have begun to drift away, leaving the Union County Sheriff at peace. He will try to do a little fishing when the police radio is quiet, or just sit with his wife, Wanda, and talk of anything but the murderer Susan Smith.

It bothers him a little that he told a lie to catch her, but he can live with the way it all turned out. Mrs. Smith has been sentenced to life in prison.

Still, now and then his mind drifts back to nine days last autumn, and he thinks how it might have gone if he had been clumsy, if he had mishandled it. It leaves him a little cold.

For those nine days — from Mrs. Smith's drowning of her two little boys on Oct. 25 until she finally confessed on Nov. 3 — he handled her like a piece of glass, afraid her brittle psyche would shatter and leave him with the jagged edges of a case that might go unsolved for weeks, months or forever.

"Susan was all we had," Sheriff Wells said, sitting in his living room the other day with a sweating glass of ice tea in his hand. If he had lost her to suicide, or to madness, because he had pushed too hard, there would have been nowhere else to turn. There had been no accomplices, no confidants, no paper trails.

The manhunt for the fictitious young black man she had accused of taking her children in a carjacking would have continued. The bodies of the boys would have continued to rest at the bottom of nearby John D. Long Lake, under 18 feet of water. The people of the county would have been left to wonder, blame and hate, divided by race and opinion over what truly happened the night she gave her babies to the lake.

Even if the car had been found, it would have yielded no proof, no clues, that everything had not happened just as she said, Mr. Wells continued. He would have been left not only with the unsolved crime but also with the burden of having driven a distraught and — for all anyone would know — innocent woman to suicide at the age of 23.

Mr. Wells says he has no doubt that he and other investigators walked a tightrope with Mrs. Smith's mental state and that as the inquiry closed around her, she planned to kill herself. For nine days she lived in a hell of her own making, surrounded by weeping, doting relatives she had betrayed in the worst way. "She had no one to turn to," he said.

So although he was her hunter, he also became the person she could lean on, rely on, trust. But unlike Mrs. Smith, he had no way of knowing that the boys were already dead, had no way of knowing that they were not locked in a car or a closet, freezing, starving.

Someday the Smith case will be in law-enforcement textbooks. The Federal Bureau of Investigation has already asked Mr. Wells to put down in writing the procedures he used in the case, as well as any useful anecdotes from it.

But the story of how he, with the help of others, was able to bring the investigation to a close in little more than a week begins not with anything he did but with who he is.

Mr. Wells, 43, is the antithesis of the redneck Southern sheriff. He has deer heads mounted on his wall but finished at the top of his class in the F.B.I. Academy's training course. He collects guns but quotes Supreme Court decisions off the top of his head.

"I'm not a smart fellow," he said. But tell that to the people who work for him and around him, and they just roll their eyes. When the attention of the nation turned to Union in those nine days last fall, and in much of the nine months since, "we were lucky he was here," said Hugh Munn, a spokesman for the State Department of Law Enforcement.

People in the county say they like him because he is one of them. He knows what it feels like to work eight hours a day in the nerve-straining clatter and roar of the textile mills that dominate Union's economy: after high school, he worked blue-collar jobs until he was hired by the town's police force at the age of 23.

He went on to be a deputy in the county Sheriff's Department. Then, for several years, he stalked poachers and drug peddlers as an agent with the State Wildlife and Marine Resources Division.

When his brother-in-law quit as Sheriff in 1992, Mr. Wells himself ran, as a 10-to-1 underdog. He promised not to operate under a good ol' boy system of favors gained and owed, and white voters and black voters liked his plain-spokenness and the fact that he was neither back-slapper nor backscratcher.

He won, by just 10 votes.

His mother, Julia Mae, was then in the hospital dying of cancer. She had lain there unmoving for hours but opened her eyes when he walked in after the election.

"Who won?" she asked.

His father, John, has Lou Gehrig's disease, and every day Mr. Wells goes by to care for him. The Sheriff went without sleep when the Susan Smith saga began on Oct. 25 but did not skip his visits to his father.

The Wellses have no children. Wanda suffered a miscarriage a few years ago, so they have become godparents to children of friends and neighbors. The Smith case pitted a man who wants children against a woman who threw hers away.

His investigation had to take two tracks. One, using hundreds of volunteers and a national crime computer web, operated on the theory that Mrs. Smith was telling the truth. The other, the one that would build a bond between a weeping mother and a doubting sheriff, focused on her.

Mr. Wells says Mrs. Smith never imagined, would never have believed, that the disappearance of her children would bring in the F.B.I., the state police, national news organizations. He thinks that when she concocted her story, she believed that the loss of the boys would pass like any other local crime.

Like other investigators, he was suspicious of her early on. As he talked to her only minutes after she had reported her children missing, he asked her whether the carjacker had done anything to her sexually. She smiled.

It would be months before the comprehensive history of her troubled life, of suicide attempts, sexual molestation, deep depression and affairs with married men, including her own stepfather, became known. But as bits and pieces of it fell from her lips during questioning, and as cracks appeared in her already unstable mental state, Mr. Wells began to realize that Mrs. Smith, and the case, could come apart in his hands.

He had to hold her together even as he and other investigators picked her story apart, had to coax and soothe and even pray beside her, until he sensed that the time was right to confront her and try to trick her into confessing.

And he had to shield her from others, who might push too hard. Once, on Oct. 27, a state agent accused her outright. She cursed loudly and stormed away.

After that, the people who had contact with her were limited. With the assistance of Pete Logan, a warm, grandfatherly former F.B.I. agent now with the state police, Mr. Wells asked for her help in finding the boys, but did not accuse her.

The whole time, her family, her hometown and much of America were following her story, sharing her agony.

"She couldn't turn to her family, she couldn't ask for an attorney," said Mr. Wells. "She painted herself into a corner where no one could help her."

On Nov. 3, he told her, gently, that he knew she was lying, that by coincidence his own deputies had been undercover on a narcotics case at the same crossroad where she said her babies had been stolen, and at the same time, and that the officers had seen nothing. Actually there had been no such stakeout.

He prayed with her again, holding her hands, and she confessed. "I had a problem telling the lie," he said as his story unfolded in his living room the other day. "But if that's what it takes, I'd do it again."

After the confession was signed, as she sat slumped over in her chair, there was still one thing he had to know.

"Susan," he asked, "how would all this have played out?"

"I was going to write you a letter," she said, "and kill myself."

He feels sorry for her, and is disgusted by the men who used her and in their own ways contributed to the tragedy. But he is not surprised that a 23-year-old mill secretary could fool the whole nation, at least for a little while.

"Susan Smith is smart in every area," he said, "except life."

Schoolyards

For much of the school year in 1997–98, I rode airplanes from one little
town to another to write about children who had killed their classmates
for reasons as trivial as "they didn't like me." I thought,
until then, that I really had seen it all.

Arkansas Boys Held as Prosecutors Weigh Options

New York Times, March 26, 1998

DATELINE: Jonesboro, Ark., March 25

The two young boys used to tease 12-year-old Erica Swindle about her glasses. She thought they were mean.

On Tuesday, those same young boys, one 11 and one 13, were being held in juvenile detention at the Craighead County, Ark., jail, facing murder charges after bullets fired outside a middle school on Tuesday killed four girls and one teacher, wounded 10 other people and plunged this small city into despair.

For Erica, who stood unhurt as bullets flew around her and watched classmates fall in bloody heaps on a neat, white sidewalk, it unveiled a meanness that she, like others here, could not even imagine.

"They made fun of me all the time," Erica said. "I didn't like them much." She went back in her mind to a time when being cruel still meant mean words hurled at her by unruly boys on a school bus.

But as the apparent cold-blooded nature and awful scope of the crime continued to baffle law-enforcement officers and residents alike, prosecutors tried to find a way around a state law that, at least on its face, would require them to try the two boys under the lenient guidelines of juvenile court.

The very thing that made the crime so shocking — the ages of the two suspects — could result in sentences of just a few years in juvenile detention for Mitchell Johnson, 13, and Andrew Golden, 11, despite the ominous sounding charges of murder.

As prosecutors built their case, counselors and ministers sat with children and parents still shaking from the bullets that ripped apart much more than bodies. Grown men, including the Mayor, stood in parking lots and wept. White ribbons, to honor the dead, fluttered along the flat, gray landscape.

All around this part of Craighead County, people who had seen such violence interrupt the lives of others in usually quiet places — like West Paducah, Ky., and Pearl, Miss., where other students had died from gunfire — wondered if there was a place far enough in the pines to protect them from this kind of thing.

Judge Ralph Wilson of Juvenile Court ruled this afternoon that there was sufficient evidence to keep the boys in jail until a hearing on April 29. At the hearing, Brent Davis, the county prosecutor, said he would file charges of 5 counts of murder and 10 counts of battery — one for each of the wounded — against the boys.

But under Arkansas law, anyone under 14 must be tried as a juvenile and, if convicted, can only be held behind bars until his 18th birthday, unless he commits a crime while in juvenile detention that could prolong his sentence, prosecutors said. That would mean that, if convicted, the oldest boy could be free after five years.

"We're looking at all other options," including Federal charges against the two boys, Mr. Davis said. He would not say what those charges might include.

Law-enforcement officers said the two boys, dressed head to toe in camouflage and hidden in a grove of trees, opened fire on students outside Westside Middle School about lunchtime on Tuesday as the 11-, 12- and 13-year-olds filed outside the school on what they thought was a fire drill.

Investigators said a fire alarm — probably set off by one of the boys — lured the students outside, where the shooting began. In all, 27 shots bored into the bodies of the students and two teachers, one of whom — the one killed — sheltered students with her own body.

Investigators had at first wondered whether a third person was involved and had pulled the alarm, but students said they saw one of the boys inside the school do it.

Law-enforcement officers say the boys used several handguns and rifles — among them semiautomatic rifles with clips holding as many as 15 rounds and a high-powered .30-06 hunting rifle — to spray bullets into the crowd of students and teachers. A white van, reportedly belonging to Mitchell's stepfather, was parked nearby. It was apparently loaded with other guns and hundreds of rounds of ammunition.

Late today, Andrew Golden's grandfather, Doug Golden, tearfully told reporters that the boys had stolen some of the guns from him.

"They used my guns," Mr. Golden said, his lip trembling. His grandson, he said, had been tutored by his father in the use of guns.

Law-enforcement officials would not comment on most evidence in the case, leaving the hundreds of reporters who have swarmed into this city of almost 50,000 people to get most of their information from the youngest witnesses to the shooting.

It was they, the students who went to school with the boys, who first provided a motive: that Mitchell and Andrew had planned the shooting to get even with a girl whom Mitchell felt had spurned him, and that he had bragged to them, "I got a lot of killing to do."

Andrew, students said, was just mean-spirited. One parent, who knew him, would not let his children play with the boy.

At the detention hearing, the 13-year-old Mitchell sobbed and held his hands together as if praying. The 11-year-old Andrew seemed unfazed, and smiled at his parents at one point. The parents of both boys were in the courtroom. They refused to talk with journalists.

The crime the boys are accused of is off the scale of the experience of people in this city. Guns are a fact of life here — most of the boys go hunting for deer, birds and rabbits with their fathers when they are still in elementary school — but guns turned on people is still something they see on television and at the movies. The Mayor, Hubert Bordell, said two murders in a year was a violent year for Jonesboro, a college and farming city where teaching and blue-collar jobs put food on the table.

"I don't know," Mayor Bordell said, with tears in his eyes. "I don't know what to say."

The funerals are expected to begin later this week, and on Thursday students at the middle school are expected to go back to school, not for regular classes, but for counseling.

Teachers and principals said they hoped they could do something to make the images of that day lay quiet in the minds of the children.

But that might be impossible. Erica Swindle, the seventh grader whom the boys teased about her glasses, remembers every detail.

"We were inside and the fire alarm went off, and when we went outside we heard big old loud pops," Erica said. "The teacher who was with us yelled at us to run toward the gym. The girl standing next to me went down. I could have died just standing there.

"At first it was slow," she said of the gunfire. "Then it got faster. And there was screaming, and everybody was running, hugging and crying. We ran into the gym and they made us sit on the floor and the teacher said, 'Stay down.' Everybody was scared half to death and didn't know what to expect.

"We thought it was a prank, but when we saw the boys were crying, we knew it wasn't."

Five people would die, including the English teacher, Shannon Wright, who shielded at least one girl with her own body.

The rest of the dead, the four girls, were at the beginnings of their lives.

Natalie Brooks was 12, a softball player who shared the outfield with her friend, Britthney Varner, 11. They were often together. Bullets found both of them outside the school, and killed both of them.

Paige Ann Herring, 12, was known for her jump shot and her ponytail. Stephanie Johnson, 12, was quiet and kept to herself, but was almost painfully nice when people sought her out.

As the girls moved from the building with the sound of the fire alarm, Britthney, apparently a little frightened, held to the back of a friend's shirt. Her friend, Whitney Irving, led them from the building.

"I heard her say 'Whitney, Whitney,' and then let go," she said.

Of the wounded, Amanda Barnes, 13, was one of the most severely hurt. The Rev. Jonny Watkins, the minister of students at Nettleton Baptist Church, went to see her in the hospital, where she remained in critical condition with a chest wound and wounds to her knee and shoulder.

Amanda lay still as Mr. Watkins walked into the room. The pastor recalled, "I said, 'Open up those eyes,' and she smiled big."

It meant everything to him, he said, a flash of joy in the middle of a horrific afternoon.

Mr. Watkins was visiting another child when the first of the wounded were brought in, a boy who had his face kicked in by a group of boys at another school. The boys, made up of football players, had formed a gang.

The pastor had spoken earlier to the boy's mother, who told him: "Jonny, the next thing that's going to happen is there's going to be a shooting here."

It seems so out of place here. But as the residents of West Paducah, Ky., and Pearl, Miss., can attest, there is no really safe place.

Barbara Robbins, 39, works as a hotel maid. She has a son in junior high. They moved here from Memphis, she said, because they thought it would be safer for their children.

"Now, I'm just lost," Ms. Robbins said. "You can't run from it. I mean, you can't get smaller than Jonesboro. I can't understand how a child my son's age could have the state of mind to do that. He'd have to be dead inside."

Determined to Find Healing in a
Good and Decent Place

New York Times, March 27, 1998

DATELINE: Jonesboro, Ark., March 26

This is a place that has learned to cherish a slow day.

Most days, Dennis Woody and the other paramedics at Emerson Ambulance have a nice, long wait between calls, and sit talking on the soft, secondhand sofa, watching television, thinking about how they could throw darts at the dartboard, if they really wanted to.

On Tuesday, an afternoon that forever altered the lives of so many in this small city, Mr. Woody found himself on his knees in a blood-spattered schoolyard, trying in vain to make a young girl live again as her father stood over him and chanted, "Come on, come on, come on."

Most days, T. J. Kelley of radio station KFIN cracks jokes, reports on soybean futures and spins country music ballads for lovesick teenagers, helping to heal broken hearts that are never really broken all that much. This week, he tries to help young listeners who feel guilty for just being alive while their classmates and friends are dead from a hail of bullets, and pours words out onto the airwaves that remind this place how good and decent it was before this, and will be again.

Most days, Mitchell Faught, who has run the flower shop for 34 years, and Grover Cooper, longtime superintendent of schools, join other older men in the McDonald's to drink coffee, read newspapers and joke about Mr. Cooper's impending retirement.

This morning, as four of his students and a teacher lay in funeral homes and two young schoolmates sat in jail, charged in the killings, the talk was kinder than usual.

"How you doing, Grover?" Mr. Faught asked.

"I'm going to be fine," Mr. Cooper said.

Most people here say that. They will be fine, only different.

Jonesboro, which is expected to pass 50,000 in population by the next census, will always be known, at least partly, as the Arkansas city where two boys, ages 13 and 11 and dressed in camouflage as if they were going deer hunting, shot to death four of their classmates and an English teacher in a rain of bullets that also wounded nine other children and another teacher.

Before that, it was a place to live and work and raise children, where the worst thing that ever happened was a 1983 bus accident that killed eight people: a tragedy, but a thing that they could understand.

It was a place where only one store carries Playboy magazine and you have to ask for it "under the counter." There are no blinking beer signs or hotel happy hours because there is no booze — Craighead County is dry as old bones — and faith in God is a given. In a town dominated by the Church of Christ and Baptists, the Methodists are about the most liberal people in town.

Both of the two boys charged in the killings were given Bibles as they were locked away. One of them asked Sheriff Dale Haas whether he had "any Bible thoughts" that might help him through his ordeal.

John Deresbach, assistant minister of music at Central Baptist Church, said, "When you hear people say, 'It isn't supposed to happen here,' what they're saying is, 'This is not the atmosphere that breeds this sort of violence.'"

That is why people in this mostly white, largely blue-collar college town get angry when they hear psychiatrists talk on daytime television about how Southerners are just more prone to violence, or that a proliferation of guns — deer hunting is a rite of passage here — led to the slaughter at Westside Middle School.

What happened at Westside Middle School, these people say, was born in the disturbed minds of one of the two boys, perhaps both, and carried out in a freakish, unmentionable moment in time. It had nothing to do with them, people in Jonesboro say of themselves. They only have to dig the graves, and live with the memory of what happened here.

Mr. Deresbach has noticed one change in people.

"People are gentler," he said, in dealing with each other. They will help each other, feeding the need with food baskets prepared at churches and binding up their wounds with thousands of white ribbons, some on mailboxes, others on car antennas, all honoring the dead. Marquee signs that once advertised fried catfish promised prayer.

At Emerson Ambulance, the lobby was crowded with men who had worked to save the students who were shot down. They talked angrily about news accounts blaming breakdowns in society — their society — for what happened.

If that were true, these men wondered, why had they not seen this horror before now?

Most days at the ambulance service are "pretty much like recess," said Rickey Elder, a 42-year-old paramedic.

Charlie Ferguson, a 32-year-old paramedic, described a usual day: "We sit, we eat, we get fat."

Some days, they may answer two or three emergency calls. In 1996, there were two killings. In 1997, two again.

"This is a college town," Mr. Ferguson said, "and the wildest things that happen here are the parties. And, it's a dry county," so those parties are not often drunken brawls resulting in trauma.

The 911 calls changed all that.

They all scrambled to it, men like Mr. Woody, Mr. Ferguson and Toby Emerson, who is also the coroner. Mr. Woody, the first to arrive, described how he had knelt over the already dead child, at the feet of her frantic father, and could do nothing. Mr. Woody said he knew she was dead, but could not tell him.

But that was not the worst of it. "The thing I'm going to walk away with," Mr. Woody said, "is the memory of looking up and seeing another girl," in the arms of another rescuer, and how "her head fell back, and the blood coming out."

They did not question whether this would not have happened if guns were absent from the culture.

"You lay a gun on a table and a hundred years from now the gun will still be sitting there, unless someone touches it," reasoned Mr. Elder. Like the others, he wore a white ribbon across his badge.

At KFIN, T. J. Kelley is more accustomed to callers who want to hear the latest by Garth Brooks or dedicate a song to their boyfriends.

"It's not really small town," Mr. Kelley said of his city, which has an economy that mixes farming, factory work and teaching jobs at Arkansas State. "But it's hometown."

He used to be the late-night disk jockey, and he got to know a lot of 12-year-old boys and girls.

"You know when their boyfriends or girlfriends break up with them, know when they're acing a test or got special homework," he said. "They're good-natured Southern kids. You have some doing the nose ring thing, but they're good kids."

When he first heard the names of the dead and wounded, he said, he recognized some of them from those late-night calls. Now he reports on prayer vigils. He hears dedications to dead children.

But like the paramedics, Mr. Kelley cannot blame the world the children grew up in for this. If anything, he said, young people here know better than inner-city youths what a gun can do.

They do not carry guns in their waistbands, for the feel of it. They have seen bullets strike and kill animals, he said. If anything, he said, they have more respect for the gun.

What they are losing respect for, say many here, is the news media. The first mass invasion of news media here has been an ugly one for so many people. Two television camera people cursed each other outside the county jail because one had gotten in the way of the other's shot.

Today, Sheriff Haas told reporters, some from around the world, that his switchboard was flooded with complaints from people here. Television trucks block driveways and access roads. Some reporters have refused to leave doorsteps when people asked them to, or have been trespassing or offering money for stories.

"If it doesn't stop," the sheriff said, he will ask his deputies to start arresting people.

But mostly, people have gone about the necessary things in this bad time. Mr. Faught, the florist, usually does about 75 arrangements a day. Today, he and his workers did more than 200. The orders for the funerals are still coming in.

People here say the city is still small enough so names and faces are familiar, and history seems to circle around itself. In the bus accident of 1983, one passenger, a man named Terry Woodward, was credited with saving the lives of several students.

Mr. Woodward is the stepfather of 13-year-old Mitchell Johnson, one of the two boys sitting in jail, blamed for the killing of his classmates.

Past Victims Relive Pain As Tragedy Is Repeated

New York Times, May 25, 1998

Since the doors on the first yellow school bus swung open at the first morning stop last fall, at least a dozen students and two teachers have been slain by schoolmates around the country, in lunchrooms, in schoolyards, at morning prayers.

"It seems to have no end," said Roy Ballentine, the principal at Pearl High School, after hearing of the shootings at a school in Springfield, Ore., on Thursday morning. "Where is the end?"

Pearl is where the school year's killing began, on Oct. 1, when, prosecutors say, a 16-year-old boy stabbed his mother to death, then fatally shot his former girlfriend and another girl at the high school. Seven other students were wounded in the attack. Six boys, ages 16 to 18, were charged with conspiracy to commit murder, as part of what police have called a cult bent on assassinating its enemies within the school.

The shooting deaths here were followed by other killings elsewhere. In the towns that saw the worst of the violence — Pearl, West Paducah, Ky., and Jonesboro, Ark. — the news of the shootings in Oregon forced people there to re-live their own agonies. For many of them, it was not the first time.

In Pearl, a suburb of Jackson, the steady drumbeat of youthful murders has been like a bandage ripped over and over again from a wound that just won't heal.

"It gives me the same sickening feeling each time this has happened," Mr. Ballentine said. "It seems it's happening every month now, and the details are so similar."

Even as parents, teachers and students talk about making progress in moving on, it takes only one fleeting image on a television newscast of a place they've never heard of to bring the sadness back.

After Pearl came West Paducah, where a 14-year-old boy has been charged in the shooting deaths of three girls as they stood in a prayer circle in a hallway at Heath High School on Dec. 1. Five other students were wounded. More might have died if the leader of the prayer group, Ben Strong, had not confronted the shooter, telling him to stop.

And after West Paducah came Jonesboro. On March 24, the authorities say, an 11-year-old boy triggered a fire alarm to lure students at Westside Middle School outside, then opened fire with a 13-year-old friend from a nearby stand of trees. Four girls and a teacher were killed and nine other students and a teacher were wounded. The boys had bragged the day before that they were going to get even with enemies at the school.

"Jonesboro has put such a hurt in us," said Bobby Strong, a pastor in West Paducah and the father of Ben Strong, the student who was praised for his bravery. "We said then, 'not again,' and here it is again. Not again."

In Jonesboro, where the pain was freshest until Thursday morning, Suzanne Wilson, whose 11-year-old daughter, Britthney Varner, was among those killed, said that the way parents look at school has changed forever.

Ms. Wilson has a 14-year-old daughter. She said that Thursday, the start of summer break for the Westside school district, was the first day that she had not worried about her daughter's safety.

"Every day she goes to school I worry about her," Ms. Wilson said. "I know exactly what these parents are experiencing now, the devastation they are dealing with. Their world is never going to be as safe as it was. My 14-year-old daughter looks to me to give her reassurance now that school is a safe place. I can't do that."

HAVING NO ANSWER TO OFFER AS CONSOLATION
Shannon Wright, the 32-year-old Jonesboro teacher who died saving the life of a 12-year-old girl, left behind her husband, Mitchell, and a 3-year-old son, Zane.

Mr. Wright heard about the Oregon shooting after dropping Zane off at his mother-in-law's house Thursday morning. "At first I was in shock and disbelief, but then I always knew it was going to happen again," he said. "It's already sort of happened," he said, referring to shootings elsewhere around the country where a single student was killed each time. "I watched a little of it on TV last night, all the students injured, the media," he said. "I just can't watch it. It re-opens everything up."

He and his son are trying to get on with their lives, but even before the Oregon killings it had been hard.

"He'll go a couple of weeks without mentioning her and then he'll throw something in out of the blue," he said of his son. "Like Sunday night, we were going home and he asked, 'Is Momma going to be home when we get there?'"

"I know what those people are facing," he said of the families of the Oregon victims, "and it's going to be tough."

The Jonesboro killings, probably more than any of the episodes of school violence, have left the country scrambling for answers, for a way to stop what seems to be a new national trend. But there are no answers among the people hurt worst by it, just a greater desperation.

Ms. Wilson doesn't know where to lay blame: maybe on parenting skills, maybe violence on television, maybe violent lyrics in popular music. She just knows that the world she thought her children lived in is drastically out of kilter.

"We used to be able to warn our children about bad things, like getting in a car with a stranger and things like that," she said. "But now they have to worry about their peers, the person they think is their friend. I think the whole United States needs to take a look at this. These kids are at war with each other."

Lynette Thetford, a sixth-grade social studies teacher at Westside Middle School in Jonesboro, was shot in the lower abdomen. She will not return to school this year because she has to have physical therapy three days a week.

She heard about the Oregon shooting when a reporter called her home.

"I just started crying, uncontrolled crying," she said. "I feel so bad for them. I tried to call the Mayor there and tell him if there is anything I can do to call me and especially ask him to give my number to the parents of those students.

"One of the best things that helped me was a letter of a parent who lived in the Paducah area. Just letting me know she was thinking about me really meant a lot to me."

She does not have any answers either, except in her own faith.

"I immediately started praying for them and I've been praying for them all day long," she said. "I can't get it out of my mind."

A KENTUCKY GRADUATION FILLED WITH REMINDERS

Tonight was graduation night at Heath High School in West Paducah, where Michael Carneal, 14, has been charged with shooting to death three of his classmates. Reminders of the killing were everywhere.

"We have a student who is dead who is receiving her diploma," the school's principal, Bill Bond, said before the ceremony. "And the valedictorian of the class is the sister of the shooter, who transported him to school that day and believed just like the rest of us that he was carrying a science project." But what the boy really had in his backpack, the police say, was guns.

The news from Oregon was "just kind of an ongoing nightmare," he said. "In each case it's young males, 7th, 8th and 9th graders, not even high school age, and in each case their intent was to kill and they really didn't care who they killed as long as they killed."

It has changed the way Mr. Bond looks at the students in his charge.

"We're very helpless in stopping it," he said. "You don't want to look at kids as dangerous, but your thoughts change and you almost get paranoid. You look at kids with their hands in their backpacks now and you watch and you are relieved when they pull out a book and it's not a gun."

In some ways, Mr. Bond said, the media is to blame. "You have to understand how a troubled 14-year-old boy thinks," he said. "Attention is attention and this is the ultimate attention getting. I mean getting your picture on the cover of Time and Newsweek. *That* is going out in a blaze of glory. I used to be a troubled kid myself and I can tell you, you could love me or hate me but you were not going to ignore me. We have to understand that."

OFFICIAL SAYS CHILDREN DON'T SEE CONSEQUENCES

It has been almost eight months since the high school in Pearl endured what the other schools have gone through. Thursday was the last day of school, but because of the news from Oregon, the murders of two girls here were fresh in the minds of students and their teachers as they left for summer vacation.

In Pearl, the circumstances of the murders were more troubling than most this year in what the police have described as the motive.

Luke T. Woodham, 16, pulled the trigger that killed a 16-and a 17-year-old girl after he had stabbed his mother to death earlier that morning, the police said. But investigators here have said those killings are part of a more troubling situation. A group of teen-agers had planned a bizarre siege of the school in which selected enemies would be killed. Mr. Woodham, the investigators said, chose to go ahead with his assassination of a girl who had once dated him, and another girl.

The Oregon shootings resurrected memories of that incident. William Dodson, superintendent of the Pearl school district, said it is almost as if students can no longer discern the line between fact and fantasy.

"Students do not accept consequences for events anymore," he said. "It's like life is like watching a movie. At the end of the movie, everything is like it was before it started. Somehow we are not getting that across to young people, that life is not a movie. There are consequences.

"We've had a long year at Pearl," Mr. Dodson said.

Jonesboro Dazed by Its Darkest Day

New York Times, May 25, 1998

The white ribbons, symbolic of the city's grief, are beginning to fray. It has been almost a month since the schoolyard murders of four girls and a teacher, apparently by an 11-year-old boy and his 13-year-old buddy, and the shock and rage have given way to dull anger, a nagging, heartbreaking puzzlement.

The why of it, the explanation for the worst thing that has happened here, evades Jonesboro even as the new spring grass creeps across five fresh graves. People speak about moving on, but until there is an answer they wait, bogged down in their own uncertainty, like the farm machinery that sits idle in muddy fields around this city, waiting for clearer, warmer skies.

"If you had asked me to list the names of any student who might have done something like this, I don't know if I could list the name of one child," said Lynette Thetford, who taught sixth-grade social studies at Westside Middle School. She was shot in the schoolyard ambush on March 24 and is at home now, recovering.

There has been new information, wild opinions, but no explanation, and many of the excuses offered for the killings seem to defy common sense, said people who were touched by the killings or just deeply troubled by them. In Craighead County, Ark., that includes just about everybody.

The 13-year-old boy, Mitchell Johnson, was sexually abused, said one of his lawyers, declining to give specific information about where and when. The boy lied about being in a gang, apparently because he felt shunned by some of his peers. He talked about killing his ex-girlfriend because she had broken up with him. But not every boy who is abused or is not popular or is jilted becomes a cold-blooded killer, people here point out.

As for the 11-year-old, Andrew Golden, his history and character change from that of saint to demented child, depending on who is asked. He played trumpet in the school band and once bottle-fed a lamb. His grandfather said he was a fine marksman, and neighbors said he liked to wear a skinning knife strapped to his leg when he rode his bike. But guns and knives are almost playthings here for boys his age, no more ominous than other toys.

Beyond vague references to getting even with people who had been mean to him, he seemed to have no motive.

"I never even paddled him," said Ms. Thetford, who taught Andrew.

The answer is that there is no answer, at least none that makes sense, for why two young boys, apparently angry at things young boys get angry about, somehow made the leap from bombast about revenging petty disagreements with classmates to murder.

The inability of people to fully grasp what happened is apparent in Ms. Thetford's description of the minutes leading up to the shootings.

Heather Pate, a sixth grader, had left class to go to the bathroom and saw a boy dressed in camouflage pull the fire alarm. She returned to find Ms. Thetford readying the class to walk outside, in an orderly fashion.

"Ms. Thetford, it was Andrew who pulled that fire alarm," Heather told her teacher.

"Well, we have to respond anyway," Ms. Thetford said.

But as she directed her students outside, she thought, "He's really going to be in trouble for ringing that bell."

Seconds later, her students, lured outside by the phony alarm, started to fall in the path of bullets.

Mitchell and Andrew are charged with five counts of murder and 10 counts of battery. In Arkansas, those under age 14 cannot be tried as adults, no matter how heinous the crime, and the State Legislature cannot retroactively change the law. If found to be "delinquent" by the juvenile court judge, they can be held only until their 18th birthdays, then automatically set free. They could, under Arkansas law, walk to the nearest pawnshop or firearm store and buy a gun.

Excuses from the families of both boys have only angered people here. Friends and relatives of the boys say neither could have done this on his own, but people around Jonesboro say that does not make sense.

Common sense tells them that one young boy did not force another young boy to become a killer. Most children, they theorize, would have told their mommas or daddies if a friend had wanted them to murder their schoolmates.

Investigators found 22 spent shell casings in the copse of trees where the boys are believed to have ambushed the other children. Five casings were from a .30-06 rifle, which the police took from Mitchell. Fifteen were from a .30-caliber rifle they took from Andrew.

"It's just too sad to understand," said Pat Whitlock, who runs Whitlock's Country Music Store on Linwood Drive in nearby Paragould. Musicians and others gather here on Thursday nights to pick and sing and talk, and lately the talk has been about the killings.

"I don't think we'll ever really know why," Ms. Whitlock said. That has become almost the anthem of people here. Everybody wants an answer, but few people believe they will ever get one that satisfies them.

"Maybe," Ms. Whitlock said, "they just needed attention."

They have it now.

Several pieces of mail addressed to the boys are intercepted daily by the sheriff's department, which turns the letters over to the boys' lawyers and parents. Some of them are hate mail, including death threats, said Dale Haas, the Craighead County Sheriff.

Mitchell, in turn, wrote a letter that his father read aloud on television. He wrote, "My thoughts and prayers are with the people who were killed, or shot, and their families." He went on, "I really want people to know the real Mitchell someday."

Relatives, visiting the boys in detention, have said they sob and appear dehydrated and even unhealthy.

"He isn't holding up real good," said Doug Golden, Andrew's grandfather.

But a worker at the detention center who spoke on the condition of anonymity said the boys were well fed, that they watched cartoons on television and "never cry or show emotion except when they are with their families or lawyers."

[The case took a turn on Wednesday when a judge ordered Tom Furth, a lawyer for Mitchell, removed from the defense team. The judge said he feared Mr. Furth's conduct outside the courtroom was detrimental to Mitchell's interests and expressed particular concern that Mr. Furth was speaking too freely with reporters. Bill Howard, a public defender in Jonesboro, remains assigned to the case.]

Reporters and investigators have combed the boys' backgrounds, looking for the one thing that set off this irreversible act, but there are only pieces.

Of the two, Mitchell, from a broken home and with apparent problems of self-esteem, seems to have the most complicated background.

His childhood has been less than perfectly Middle American. His lawyer told the ABC News program "20/20" in an interview broadcast on April 6 that Mitchell had been sexually assaulted repeatedly when he visited Minnesota. The boy's father, Scott Johnson, said the abuse was "by a family member of the day care where he was placed," but offered no details.

Last summer, Mitchell was charged with molesting a female toddler in Minnesota. According to an incident report filed in Mower County, Minn., he was caught in a room with the girl, his pants down.

His mother and father divorced in 1994. His mother, Gretchen Woodward, moved her sons, Mitchell, and Monte, now 11, first to Kentucky, where she worked as a prison guard, and later to Arkansas, where she married a man who had served time in prison on felony drug and weapons charges.

On a return visit to see relatives in Minnesota, Mitchell told a good friend, 13-year-old Sarah Laack, that he did not like Arkansas, that other children were mean to him. He was slightly paunchy, and he confided to her "how people made fun of him," Sarah said.

"He wanted to be with his grandma and his dad," she said. "He missed them a lot."

To her, it seemed that Mitchell had tried to cultivate an image as a tough guy. "I just think Mitch wanted everybody to be scared of him, so they wouldn't mess with him," Sarah said. "I still can't believe he did it."

His Arkansas classmates said he had bragged about being in gangs, but even 12-year-olds knew that a white boy in Arkansas bragging about being a member of the Crips or Bloods, big-city street gangs mostly made up of black youths, was far-fetched.

So, when he and Andrew, a friend he knew mostly from the school bus, bragged that they were going to get even with other children, even killing them, no one took them seriously.

In particular, Mitchell was mad at 11-year-old Candace Porter. She had not been afraid of Mitchell when she told him she did not want to be his girlfriend anymore, because "boys don't hit girls," she explained in an article in The Jonesboro Sun.

Candace was his girlfriend for three days. She thought he was nice at first, but broke up with him several weeks before the shooting when Mitchell began acting strange, talking big about hurting other boys. "He was trouble," she told reporters recently.

But she, like all the other students, thought he was just talking big again when they heard he had put together a list of students he planned to kill. Two students said he told them he was going to shoot Candace first, then kill everyone else in the building. Again, they ignored him. Teachers at the school said they were never warned about the boys' threats.

Candace, a brown-haired, freckle-faced sixth grader, was shot in the back, but the bullet did not go in deep.

Andrew's parents have been mostly silent. The boy's grandfather, Doug Golden, is obviously heart-broken. Andrew stole his guns to use in the shooting.

The boy he remembers would not even have touched them without asking. The boy he remembers used to stop by his house and play with the dog, would carry out the trash to help his grandfather, was polite and respectful to his elders.

"He had this little sheep," he said, thinking back to a younger Andrew. "He raised it on a bottle."

He said his grandson liked school, that he went early to play at the playground. Unlike Mitchell, who was apparently teased, Andrew seemed to have no enemies, his grandfather said.

"As far as we know, he wasn't mad at anybody," Mr. Golden said.

Ms. Thetford said Andrew was an above-average student, often hyperactive, with "very supportive parents" who were interested in their son's schoolwork.

He misbehaved, but in little ways. He always did his homework.

"He was just one of those hyper children I would have to get on to," the teacher said, "but there were others a lot worse. A vocal reprimand was all he ever needed."

Students do not recall the two boys as fast friends.

As much as Jonesboro is puzzled by its tragedy, all the people here are a little tired of talking about it.

"Before we can start to heal, we got to quit scratching," Mr. Golden said. "It's like scratching at a sore."

Murder Trial Opens for First School Shooting Defendant

New York Times, June 3, 1998

DATELINE: Philadelphia, Miss., June 2

At the very beginning of the terrifying national string of school shootings is a 17-year-old boy who prosecutors say began a day of violence by stabbing his mother to death, because he believed she did not love him.

In a videotaped confession shown to stone-faced jurors on the first day of a murder trial here in this eastern Mississippi town, a sobbing Luke Woodham described how he put a pillow over his mother's face as she lay sleeping last Oct. 1, and stabbed her repeatedly with a butcher knife.

"She never loved me," he said in the taped confession, when asked why he killed 50-year-old Mary Woodham at their home in Pearl. As his image appeared on tape, the real-life Mr. Woodham buried his face in his hands at the defendant's table and cried.

After killing his mother, state prosecutors say, Mr. Woodham went on a shooting spree at Pearl High School just outside Jackson, killing two classmates and wounding seven others.

Those killings were the first in a troubling trend that would be played out in West Paducah, Ky., Jonesboro, Ark., and Springfield, Ore., as students, for as little apparent reason as petty grudges and bruised feelings, turned guns on schoolmates, teachers and their own parents.

Mr. Woodham, whose initial trial was moved from the Jackson area because of that community's anger and the publicity the case has drawn, is the first of the students charged in these rampages to go on trial.

But this trial will not even address the broader picture of school violence. Here, Mr. Woodham is on trial only in the murder of his mother.

A second trial is scheduled for next week in Hattiesburg, in southern Mississippi, to decide his fate in the Pearl High School shootings.

Today, as the jury of 12 women and 3 men looked on, a steady stream of witnesses described how they found Mrs. Woodham dead on her bed with the blood-soaked pillow on her head, her chest and arms punctured and slashed, apparently from trying to fight off her son.

Investigators wove a terrifying tale throughout the day of testimony as the jurors looked on, their faces showing no more emotion than the elderly bailiff, who worked on her needlepoint as the story unfolded.

Although investigators could not mention the school shootings, it was clear from their testimony that they found out about the killing of Mrs. Woodham only after Mr. Woodham had been arrested at the school after the shootings there and was about to be questioned in the police station.

Officer Ray Dampier testified that he noticed a bandage on the boy's hand.

"How did you cut your hand?" he said he asked Mr. Woodham.

"Killing my mom," Mr. Woodham answered, according to Officer Dampier's testimony.

Officer Dampier said Mr. Woodham did not seem troubled about anything that had happened to him that morning,

"He appeared to be very proud," he said.

Mr. Woodham's offhand comment about his mother sent investigators to the student's home in Pearl, where they found Mrs. Woodham.

Piece by piece, prosecutors introduced into evidence the bloody knife, a blood-soaked lace pillowcase, a bloodstained, slashed pillow and a baseball bat that investigators said was used on her face and body.

When investigators went into the house, they said, they found the knife and bat lying on Mr. Woodham's bed.

In confessions, both taped and written, he said he had "just stopped caring about anything" the night before his mother's death. He said his mother often stayed out late but would not let him stay out late, and that she said mean things to him.

"She said I was the reason my father left," said Mr. Woodham, between sobs, in the taped confession. Mrs. Woodham raised her son alone.

"She said I wouldn't amount to anything," he said in his confession. "She told me I was fat, stupid and lazy."

The morning of Oct. 1, "I woke up, I got the butcher knife and the pillow. I put the pillow over her head and I stabbed her," he said.

"She was always against me," he said.

He had joined a group of young people who considered themselves outsiders, a group that called itself "the Kroth" and had planned a takeover of the school, to be followed by a bizarre escape to Cuba, investigators have said.

One of those youths arrested and charged in the aftermath of the school shootings testified today, but the presiding state court judge would not allow reporters inside the courtroom for the youth's testimony.

Defense lawyers declined to make an opening statement and plan to wait until they begin their own case later this week. The trial is expected to last about a week, followed by the Hattiesburg trial.

The Pearl case is the most complicated of the recent school killings because of the number of students arrested.

Six other boys — one so young that he cannot be charged in state court — were arrested after the school shootings and were accused of plotting to kill other students.

Lawyers for Mr. Woodham have claimed that he was under the influence of the group's leader, Grant Boyette, 19. They are expected to argue that Mr. Boyette was the force behind Mrs. Woodham's slaying and that Mr. Woodham was not mentally stable at the time of the killings. In jury selection, prosecutors asked potential jurors if they would automatically consider someone insane if that person killed his mother.

But at least one of the investigators, Detective Aaron Richard Hirschfield, said he believed Mr. Woodham was not under the influence of anyone else as he walked into his mother's bedroom with the knife.

"Luke was in complete control of his actions," he said.

Arkansas Boys Who Killed Five Are Sentenced

New York Times, August 12, 1998

Just before a judge remanded 14-year-old Mitchell Johnson and 12-year-old Andrew Golden to a state juvenile detention center today for a school shooting spree that killed a teacher and four little girls, the older boy offered a courtroom filled with their relatives a child-like excuse.

He said he did not mean to do it.

"I thought we were going to shoot over their heads," said the trembling Mitchell, who pleaded guilty today in an adjudication hearing — the juvenile court equivalent of a trial — in the Craighead County Courthouse. "We didn't think anybody was going to get hurt."

Andrew Golden pleaded not guilty, but the judge convicted him in the shootings, in which the two boys used a false fire alarm at Westside Middle School to lure schoolmates outside and then fired repeatedly into the terrified mass of students and teachers with high-powered rifles.

Judge Ralph Wilson of Circuit Court ordered that the boys remain in the custody of the Division of Youth Services until their 21st birthdays.

Andrew was just 11 on March 24, the day of the shootings. His lawyer said his client was insane at the time of the incident and that he was not mentally competent to stand trial, though Judge Wilson did not allow him to plead so.

Judge Wilson, after a two-hour trial in which prosecutors quickly laid out an open-and-shut case this morning, found both boys to be "delinquent," the juvenile court equivalent of a guilty verdict.

Because state law prevents anyone under 14 from being punished as an adult, the judge remanded the boys to the Division of Youth Services. But the state has no holding center for adults who were sentenced as youths in juvenile court, so the two are expected be held in a juvenile detention center only until their 18th birthdays, and then released.

"The punishment will not fit the crime," Judge Wilson said. Families of the victims clutched each other and pressed tissues to crying eyes.

Gov. Mike Huckabee has said he will build or modify a prison to house the boys until they are 21.

And Judge Wilson ordered that the boys serve 90 days in jail if they are released before they turn 21. That means that Mitchell, if he does not commit any crimes in juvenile detention that could extend his sentence, could be out in four years. Andrew, who sat stone-faced throughout the hearing, could be out in six.

Relatives of the victims — nine other students and a teacher were wounded in the attack — had hoped the hearing would answer their questions about why the shootings occurred, or reveal what the boys were thinking. But Andrew, an award-winning marksman who stole guns from his grandfather for the shootings, made his plea but did not speak again, and Mitchell offered more of an apology than an explanation.

Although the police and ballistics experts have said that the boys methodically fired into the crowd — Shannon Wright, an English teacher, was hit twice by bullets from a 30.06 hunting rifle fired by Mitchell — the boy said he did not mean to shoot anyone.

"I am sorry," said Mitchell, who turned 14 today. "I understand that it may be impossible for some of you to forgive me. If I could go back and change what happened on March 24, 1998, I would in a minute. I have caused pain. I have asked God for forgiveness and that He will heal the lives of the people I have hurt."

For the relatives of the victims, the ruling was not nearly enough. They saw only two boys who, even now, refused to take responsibility for their actions.

In withering testimony, speaking directly to the two boys, Shannon Wright's husband, Mitchell Wright, asserted that the killings were intentional.

The older boy, Mitchell, was firing a rifle with a telescopic sight.

"You can't tell me it was random, son, not with the scope on that gun," Mr. Wright said, his face red, his eyes beginning to tear.

The bullets that left a sidewalk wet with blood took his best friend, Mr. Wright said, the mother of his 3-year-old son, Zane.

Mr. Wright said that the boy had been told that his mother was in heaven, but he still wonders why, when he wants to be rocked to sleep, she cannot come down and do it.

"Zane looks for his mother to come back," said Mr. Wright. "You have robbed a 3-year-old boy of his innocence. He told me, 'Don't worry about those two bad boys. If they break out of jail, I'll take care of you.'"

He talked about how his wife, who had taught Andrew, gave him extra time on one project.

Four other relatives of the shooting victims took the stand during the afternoon sentencing phase, including Lloyd Brooks, whose 11-year-old niece, Natalie Brooks, was killed in the ambush.

He pointed out that Mitchell had turned 14 today, but "we celebrated Natalie's birthday on May 26." Mr. Brooks, his voice shaking, added, "We brought flowers to her grave."

Juvenile hearings are typically closed to the public and the press in Arkansas, but the judge eased the restriction because of the intense interest in the case. About 100 family members and friends of the victims came to the courtroom, passing through a metal detector to reach the heavily guarded courtroom. State officials had said the boys had received several death threats.

Oddly, there were few people who came only for the spectacle. Most people here say they are sick of it, sick of the pain of it.

Andrew appeared to not be interested in the proceedings, as prosecutors built their case against him.

His lawyer, Val Price, said that the boy should have been allowed to claim insanity as a defense and that he did not even understand what was happening to him.

"My client today does not understand the nature of the proceedings," Mr. Price told the judge.

But teachers at the school, and people who knew the boy, said he did not seem to have any mental disorder, beyond a mild problem with his attention span.

The case prosecutors built was more of a synopsis, short and businesslike. The only real drama came when they showed the court two of the guns used in the shootings.

As one of the guns was cocked, loudly, some people in the courtroom caught their breath.

Mr. Price said, "The evidence put on by the state was overwhelming."

The boys had apparently planned the shootings for some time. Students at Westside said the incident was planned as revenge against Candace Porter, who had said she did not want to be Mitchell's girlfriend anymore — she was slightly wounded in the attack — and for the teasing the boys had received. But what made the boys respond so violently is a mystery.

Mr. Wright, like others here, asked the boys to someday "tell us why."

The Jonesboro crime, the deadliest in a series of school shootings that left people dead in Pearl, Miss., West Paducah, Ky., and Springfield, Ore., also killed middle school students Paige Ann Herring, Britthney Varner and Stephanie Johnson.

Prosecutors, without any objections from either of the public defenders representing the two boys, demonstrated how the boys, both of them dressed in camouflage, stole a van from Mitchell's house, loaded it with guns from Andrew's grandfather's house, and drove to a copse of trees that offered a clear field of fire into the schoolyard.

Andrew rang the bell, drawing the students outside, then went to join his friend in the trees.

"They fired numerous times into the gathering of students and teachers," said Mike Walden, the deputy prosecutor.

Then the boys fled toward the van, which they had loaded with camping gear, ammunition and junk food. But before they could reach it, police officers intercepted them and ordered them to throw down their guns and lie down. Mitchell did so at once, and then Andrew complied. At no time did they point their guns at the arresting officers.

Although several people here talked about finding peace after the verdict, the case is far from over. Andrew's lawyers said they would appeal the ruling, as did a lawyer for Mitchell's father, Scott Johnson.

Mr. Johnson said his son was mistreated while he was in the Craighead County juvenile facility. He was not fed well or treated properly by doctors or counselors, he said.

"I am not going to allow my son to stay in Arkansas," he said, but did not explain how he planned to accomplish that. "This isn't the place for a rabid animal, to say nothing of a 14-year-old boy."

Mr. Johnson, who said his son had been sexually abused as a little boy, said his son never explained the shootings. "He doesn't have an answer for why," he said.

Outside the courtroom, passersby barely paused at the bank of television cameras and microphones.

The Rev. Mike Martin, a pastor at Central Baptist Church, stood on a corner, his hands trembling.

"I'm just here to pray," he said, "for the boys, oh, the boys."

No one doubts the long-reaching impact of this crime on this city.

Lori Bounds, who has an 11-year-old son, was in the courtroom to see what happened. "A couple of nights ago my son asked for a BB gun for Christmas," she said. "And both me and my husband said, 'No, no.' Six months ago, we wouldn't have worried about it."

Living and Dying

Faulkner said once it was the only thing worth writing about.

Living with a Grief That Will Never Die

New York Times, March 22, 1999

Jim Larson is accustomed to the stares.

"People will see me and say, 'Is that him?'" Mr. Larson said. Is this the man, they wonder, who lost two women he loved to random killers, seven years apart, whose life was twice torn by men who enter others' lives only in bad dreams?

"I'm him," he said.

First it was his sister, Sonja Larson. She and a roommate were stabbed to death in 1990 by Danny Rolling, a serial killer who said demons spoke to him from inside his head.

Mr. Rolling killed and mutilated five college students in Gainesville, Fla., in ways that made his victims' families, and people across the country, shudder.

Mr. Larson remembers how he fell to the floor once, in his despair, and how his wife, Carla, hugged him, how she promised him that the evil that touched them was over and done. Mr. Rolling was sent to death row and the Larsons soon had a baby, Jessica, the symbol of their new beginning.

In 1997, Carla Larson was abducted in a supermarket parking lot by a man on vacation at Disney World. The police found her body in a shallow grave.

Mr. Larson, his hate used up, went dead inside. After his sister's death, he burned with rage. This time he just sleep-walked through a terse, private agony.

Sometime in March, his wife's killer, John Huggins, is to join Mr.

Rolling on Florida's death row, beginning a slow countdown to possible execution in the electric chair.

And that is Mr. Larson's celebrity, to have two high-profile murderers, in otherwise unrelated crimes, sentenced to die for killing women he loved. As a relative of the victims, he has the legal right to watch both men die.

Prison officials say they know of no other such triangle of misfortune, of anyone sandwiched by such cruel circumstance.

"It's like being a celebrity, but for nothing good," Mr. Larson said. "I'm labeled as this poor, sorry person. If I knew someone like me, I'd ask, 'What's this guy doing wrong?'"

UNRELENTING PAIN IN AN UNSAFE WORLD

Mr. Larson says he sometimes feels like he is trapped in a revolving door. Inside it, spinning with him, are the murders, all the sadness and horror of losing his sister and his wife. Outside is a safe and sane place that he has to get back to, but the doors just keep on turning.

It has left him with an emptiness and a dull and unrelenting pain, Mr. Larson said recently, as he sat in the neat living room of his house in a quiet, tree-lined suburb of Orlando, a home most people in middle-class America would see as safe. But they do not look at the world through Jim Larson's eyes.

"Sonja was safe in her bed when she died, and my wife was at a Publix supermarket at 12 noon, not in a nightclub, not in a 7-Eleven at 2 A.M.," said Mr. Larson, a trim, 38-year-old man whose narrow face has a sadness in it that shows through even when he smiles. "No one in my family had ever been to jail, because we just didn't have that kind of life. I felt we were good people. So, why? Why did it happen?

"I have friends who are Catholic, and I've heard them say that because they are close to God, bad things won't happen," he continued. "My sister never did anything wrong. My wife never did. I guess I just don't know what the plan is anymore."

DAUGHTER PROVIDES A REASON FOR LIVING

Mr. Larson is talking about finding reasons to go on living when a 2-year-old girl, with golden hair and laughing eyes, stomps into the room in fuzzy slippers. She crawls around the floor, then spots a stack of books. She wants a bedtime story.

And, because it happens every night, Mr. Larson finds his reason to keep on living in the face of his daughter, Jessica, and between the pages of Dr. Seuss. She prefers "Horton Hears a Who."

"Jessica," he said, "is the reason I'm still here."

Figuring that she is years away from understanding the crimes that took her mother and her aunt, he keeps on talking about them even as she pulls herself up into his arms.

It began in the summer of 1990, a summer of terror in the college city of Gainesville.

Sonja Larson, who wanted to be a teacher, had enrolled as a freshman at the University of Florida. One night in August, she went to a Wal-Mart with her roommate, Christina Powell, to buy some odds and ends.

Mr. Rolling, a drifter who claimed that he was possessed and that he followed the instructions of the demon "Ynnad" (his name, Danny, spelled backwards), saw the two young women and followed them home. He caught them in their beds, and stabbed them again and again.

"He confessed to killing five people," Mr. Larson said. "He cut their heads off, then played with them. He did the worst things you can possibly do to somebody and he's still alive. Why is that?"

Mr. Larson railed, at the time, about the sickness of it, the cruelty, and said he would have killed Mr. Rolling with his own hands. During the trial, he sat day after day in the courtroom as the defendant's nightmarish world took shape. One day, Mr. Larson said, he "just snapped."

"I ran back to my hotel in tears and rocked myself back and forth in a corner," he said.

BACK FROM THE BRINK AND BUILDING A LIFE

Mr. Larson said he was certain that his wife, Carla, saved him. She wrapped her arms around him, reminded him of the good things, of reasons to live, to be happy.

She had just graduated from the University of Florida as a construction engineer and they moved to Atlanta, then back to Florida, chasing work, building a life. She wanted a child, but he did not want to bring a child into any world where people like Danny Rolling stalked the innocents.

Finally, after counseling, Mr. Larson said he found some peace of mind.

Jessica was born. The Larsons bought a small house on a dead-end street in Orlando. They installed good locks and a home security system. They bought a guard dog, a Rottweiler.

The car Mrs. Larson drove was a big Ford Explorer, with air bags. He believed he had done everything he could to make them all safe.

"Carla always told me we would get through it," he said, "that she would always be there."

She was working for a construction contractor, building a new Disney resort, in the summer of 1997. On June 10, she left work to go to a Publix supermarket outside Orlando, to buy some fruit for lunch.

John Huggins, a landscaper who had been in and out of jail all his life, was on vacation with his wife and their five children. They were staying in a motel across the street from the supermarket.

In broad daylight, in a busy parking lot, he walked up to Mrs. Larson, punched her in the stomach and kidnapped her, driving away in her car.

He drove to a remote field and strangled her to death. Unlike Mr. Rolling, he had never killed before.

HUSBAND'S REACTION: PROFOUND DISBELIEF

Mrs. Larson was missing for two days. Some husbands might have held out hope, but Jim Larson knew his wife was dead.

"He seemed blank," said a friend and neighbor, Scott Peterson. "You could stare right through him."

When the police found her, half-covered in the sand, "he didn't feel one way or another," Mr. Peterson said.

The police were so puzzled by Mr. Larson's behavior that they gave him a lie detector test, to see if he was involved in her death.

Callers to an Orlando area radio talk show even accused Mr. Larson because he had seemed so blank during press interviews.

But what he was, was used up.

"He was in disbelief that this had happened to him twice," Mr. Peterson said. "He stopped eating and sleeping. He lost a lot of weight and walked around with dark circles under his eyes."

It was Mr. Huggins's wife who pointed the police to the killer. She told them that he had left her and the children in the motel at noon the day of the murder and came back that afternoon, sweating and jittery. Investigators found Mrs. Larson's engagement ring in the home of one of Mr. Huggins's relatives.

One of the things that haunts Mr. Larson most is this: Carla, because of what happened to Sonja Larson in Gainesville, knew how it would end when John Huggins took control of her. Her last moments would have been spent in a terrible understanding.

But while the death of his wife left Mr. Larson with a grief he may never get over, it also left him with a responsibility, for Jessica. He has gone back to counseling and, slowly, is pulling himself back from the despondency that threatened to take over his life.

He has a girlfriend, Brenda Benson, whose husband was killed when a tree fell on his Jeep. "We rely a lot on each other," she said.

FOR THE VICTIMS' KIN, NO HAPPY ENDING

Some people who have lost friends or relatives to murderers look to the execution of the killer as a place to dump some of their sadness. As a relative, Mr. Larson has a legal right to witness the executions of the two men if the State of Florida wins its legal battles to put them to death. But he is not certain that he needs to see it.

"I guess I would go to it," he said, to make sure it is over, to make certain some appeal or a smart lawyer does not set one or both of them free. "I don't really care anymore," he said. "It's not going to be even. Those two lives don't compare to Carla's life, or Sonja's life."

The men will be housed, prison officials said, "within spitting distance" of each other at the Florida State Prison in Starke. They could, conceivably, meet. They could, perhaps, discuss their crimes, discuss Carla Larson, discuss Mr. Larson's little sister, Sonja.

That prospect does not chill him. What happens on death row, he said tiredly, he cannot control.

But, it being an age when people can profit from even the most shameful acts, he does worry that they might write a book, he said, adding, "I don't want them making money off what they did."

For now, he does what other people do. He goes to work, cares for his daughter, finds happiness when he can. He just lives.

"Everyone has this tv movie mentality," Mr. Larson said, meaning that everyone in a television drama, no matter how sad, can be all smiles after the commercial. "It's not a happy ending," he added. "I don't feel good."

On Florida Bridge,
Troopers Are Also Suicide Counselors

New York Times, May 9, 1999

At the crest of the massive Sunshine Skyway Bridge, 200 feet above the jade-colored waters of Tampa Bay, Gary Schluter and James C. Covert of the State Highway Patrol have to persuade people poised on the edge of their own destruction to step back slowly, and live.

It happens again and again to these men and others who patrol the bridge on Florida's west coast. They regularly find a car pulled to the side of the span and see a woman or man sitting or standing on the concrete railing, watching one last sunset, working up the nerve.

Then, their nerves humming, the patrolmen try to convince complete strangers that lost loves, lost jobs or feelings of lost youth are not reason enough to step off into thin air.

"People look at that water and think it's very serene, an easy way to die," said Mr. Schluter, a 45-year-old corporal who, in two years, has been credited with saving four lives on the Sunshine Skyway.

"It's more like hitting concrete," said Mr. Schluter, who has seen the number of suicides, and attempts, climb steadily over the last few years. Like Mr. Covert, a 28-year-old trooper who talked down three people in four days in May 1998, Mr. Schluter has little or no formal training in suicide prevention, but they find themselves being increasingly called upon to save people who want to kill themselves at the bridge.

Though the Sunshine Skyway is no Golden Gate Bridge, where more than 1,200 people have killed themselves in the six decades since the bridge was built, a rising number of suicides here has officials concerned. At the urging of Gov. Jeb Bush, state transportation officials are expected to build a barrier — perhaps even a net to catch jumpers — and install telephones that would quickly connect counselors to people considering suicide at the Sunshine Skyway.

In 1996, six people jumped to their deaths from the bridge, and five people were persuaded not to jump, according to police reports. Eight people killed themselves there in 1997, but 11 others were saved after being talked down by state troopers, sheriff's deputies and counselors.

In 1998, Mr. Schluter said, 12 people jumped to their deaths from the bridge, and about the same number were persuaded to reconsider. In the first four months of 1999, five people died in suicides on the bridge, according to police reports, and at least four were saved, troopers said.

The bridge is more than four miles long, and the troopers have often been the only rescuers who make it in time to intervene. They must frantically get to know someone in a few tense minutes, understand why the person has given up on life and search that stranger's past for a reason, any reason, to go on living.

"If they have children, I try to get them to think about their children," said Mr. Covert, who has saved four people.

It is a drama that takes place almost in the clouds, so high that the sailboats that pass underneath look like toys in a bathtub, and most often it is just the two of them, the desperate stranger and a new best friend.

The bridge, as much a fixture on west Florida postcards as alligators and orange groves, is a tourist destination in itself. But it was born in tragedy.

On May 9, 1980, the freighter Summit Venture slammed into one of the pylons of the old bridge, also named the Sunshine Skyway, and knocked a part of its span into the bay. Eight vehicles, including a bus, fell into the water. Thirty-five people were killed.

The state closed that bridge and, over years, built a massive new Skyway, which opened in 1987 with majestic yellow cables that rise from its center span to towering concrete posts. The bridge is also a toll road costing $1.

The ones who jump usually do so before help arrives, leaving their cars and sometimes notes, apologizing, asking somebody to look after a house or feed a cat, the troopers said.

If the troopers get there in time, they must be gentle, though their own hearts are pounding so hard it almost hurts, because if their words are clumsy, if their movements are too forceful, they may crumple what hope the people hold. Here, so high, hope is the next-to-last thing they lose.

Once, when a man on the bridge said he was afraid of going to jail, Mr. Schluter took off his gunbelt and his shirt, to be less threatening.

It all unfolds with the troopers knowing that the despondent, unstable people could reach for them in desperation and, accidentally or not, drag them into the water. The railing is a thin concrete barrier about three and a half feet high.

"It's dangerous for us," Mr. Schluter said. So he tries, he said, to stay out of reach.

On New Year's Day, Mr. Schluter found a man sitting on the rail, his legs dangling over the bay.

"That's a long way down," Mr. Schluter told him as he walked carefully up to him. The man had tears running down his face.

"If you agree not to jump for 15 minutes," he added, "I will agree not to try and stop you for 15 minutes." So they just talked. He found out the man was in debt, that he was despondent over family problems.

They talked for about 40 minutes, calling each other by their first names. But the man seemed hurried by, of all things, backed-up traffic that had been caused by the drama on the span. It was as if he was sorry for causing others an inconvenience.

"He said, 'Gary, I'm really sorry but I really have to go,' and he started inching himself closer and closer," to the edge, Mr. Schluter said. Believing he was losing the man, he broke one of his own rules.

He motioned for another officer to inch up close behind his own back, close enough to grab onto him in case the man tried to take him over the wall, then he gently laid a hand on the man's leg. That simple touch, Mr. Schluter said, seemed to break through the bubble of the man's hopelessness.

"That's what I needed," he told Mr. Schluter.

He came down off the wall and meekly allowed himself to be handcuffed and taken to nearby St. Anthony's Hospital. Under the law, officers can take someone into custody and deliver the person to a mental hospital if he is a potential danger to himself. Most of the people who attempt suicide on the Sunshine Skyway are held for at least a while under the law, for evaluation.

Mr. Schluter and Mr. Covert do not know of a single person who attempted suicide again on the bridge, or elsewhere. Mr. Schluter gives his business card and beeper number to the people he talks down, in case.

Given a second chance at life, he said, most people use it. In a study of prevented suicides on the Golden Gate Bridge, researchers found that would-be jumpers rarely tried again.

The troopers do not think the people they talk down are just trying to get attention.

"I believe that everyone who goes up there has the intention of going through with it," Mr. Covert said. One was a woman who had been in an abusive relationship, and one had lost her job. Two others had lost jobs and lovers, and just gave up.

"They feel they've exhausted their options, and this is the last part of their lives they have control of," Mr. Covert said. "I tell them this is a permanent solution to a temporary problem."

Jumpers tend to die ugly, the troopers said. The fall, less than four seconds, ends in a bone-snapping, organ-rupturing trauma, but some jumpers do not lose consciousness, and drown in agony.

"We retrieve the bodies," Mr. Schluter said. "They are distorted, mangled."

He cannot imagine the hopelessness that sends them up that steep incline. Sometimes, Mr. Schluter said, people hand a toll booth operator their wallets and say, "I won't be needing this any more." Sometimes, he can prove them wrong.

Jazzy Final Sendoff for Chicken Man

New York Times, February 1, 1999

DATELINE: New Orleans, Jan. 31

People laughed as the dead man went by.

First, before the funeral procession had even started, his friends sprinkled a drop or two of gin on his wooden casket in the Charbonnet-Labat Funeral Home on St. Philip Street, because everyone who knew Chicken Man — even people who had known him all their lives did not know him by any other name — knew he always liked to sip a little gin.

Outside, mourners who never cried stood with tall, sweating cans of Budweiser in their fists, grinning even as pallbearers carried him from the chapel and slipped his casket into a black hearse drawn by two white horses. Freddie Thomas, who had known Chicken Man for years, lifted a black umbrella over his head and twirled it around and around, laughing, joking.

"He was a beautiful brother, man," he said, but before he could explain why he seemed so happy, a brass band washed away his words with "A Closer Walk with Thee."

At first, at least, it seemed like a funeral, but as the hearse and a processional of hundreds moved slowly toward the French Quarter, the swaying brass band suddenly riffed from its dirge into rich, hot Dixieland jazz, and the dignified march changed into a quick, sweaty strut. On Bourbon Street, a bone-pale stripper dressed in black underwear stood watching from a doorway, clapping, laughing out loud. On Dumaine Street, a man picked up a bottle and tapped it with a stick, keeping time. By chance, it was a gin bottle.

"I didn't even know the man," said 58-year-old Clementine Louding, who shimmied and skipped with the procession down North Rampart Street. "I came for the dance."

Chicken Man, whose real name was Fred Staten, was a self-taught voodoo priest who got his name because he used to bite the heads off live chickens in voodoo ceremonies, a shaman and a showman who took home stray dogs and people. He was one of the best-known faces in this city where being a little different has never been quite different enough, so he rated a funeral of a kind that is done only in New Orleans, where death has its own dance steps, and the grave is just a place to rest your feet.

It is called, simply, a jazz funeral, a true celebration of life that makes the wakes and eulogies of other cultures seem deadly dull in comparison. They have been going on here for as long as even the older New Orleanians can remember, usually reserved for jazz musicians, members of secret societies — like the Masons — or just anyone who is beloved enough to draw a crowd, said Gregg Stafford, a veteran trumpet player and leader of the Young Tuxedo Brass Band, who has marched in jazz funerals for three decades.

"It started with the jazz musicians, but in the 1980's other people started wanting them for their own people, lay people," Mr. Stafford said, using the term that jazz musicians and other entertainers use for anyone outside the city's culture of music and magic.

The jazz funerals have changed over the years, he said, from the early days when the bands inched along the narrow streets of the oldest parts of this city, breaking into their upbeat music only when the march neared its end. Today, the party starts much earlier, and people dance for miles, he said.

But it is natural, in this city where missing a day of work because of a hangover is considered a legitimate sick day, that people would want a party sooner rather than later, said Mr. Stafford, who sat in with the Treme Brass Band for the funeral on Saturday.

Chicken Man, who was 61 when he died of natural causes, "was voodoo in New Orleans," said Mr. Stafford and others who gathered to send him on to the hereafter. He took tourists on tours of the French Quarter, selling them candles labeled "Blessed by Chicken Man." He strolled the Quarter in a black top hat, carrying a long staff crowned with a plastic human hand and a monkey skull. Tourists loved him.

He was a survivor of the days "when voodoo really existed in the neighborhoods," Mr. Stafford said, when on almost every block there was an old woman with a kitchen filled with potions and petrified chicken's feet, who had learned this blend of African religions and Catholicism from Haitian ancestors.

"It doesn't exist that way now," he said. "It's a dying culture."

Chicken Man made his living making voodoo dolls and potions but died penniless, his friends said, because he gave almost all his meager proceeds away. He was almost laid to rest in obscurity, despite his popularity. His fame never translated into money, and in the past two years he had been less a presence, fading from the public's memory. People here knew he was dead but did not know that his body had been held for more than a month at the coroner's office, because there was no money to bury him.

Finally, a New Orleans businessman who had been out of the city when Chicken Man died came home from a lengthy trip and paid not only for the burial, but hired the brass band and horse-drawn hearse to send him out in style.

The businessman, Earl Barnhardt, was a struggling bar owner here in 1984, "about to go under," he said. As a last resort, he asked the tall, skinny Chicken Man to bless his bar.

"He made the sign of the cross on all four walls," Mr. Barnhardt said. "Overnight, we became the bar of choice for the Tulane college crowd."

Now, Mr. Barnhardt owns several businesses, and a few years ago he flew Chicken Man to a bar opening in Houston, to bless that one. "It's hard to buy a plane ticket for someone under the name of Chicken Man."

On Saturday, friends packed the tiny chapel.

As drums pounded, his mourners watched as two voodoo priestesses, Ava Kay Jones and Miriam Chamani, sang and danced. They blew smoke from a cigar on his casket, and then came the sprinkling of gin.

"I better give him a few more drops," Ms. Jones said. "I don't want him coming back to see me."

Then it was time to dance. Chicken Man's daughter, Anna Marie Gonzales, walked carrying his picture as the jazz funeral rambled through the French Quarter, led by anybody who wanted to march quicker, step higher. For the first block that was the man with the black umbrella, Freddie Thomas, who was still grinning.

"Because it's such a beautiful way to go out, man," said Mr. Thomas, a 43-year-old maintenance man.

The band played "This Little Light of Mine" and "Will the Circle Be Unbroken," but at a tempo that coaxed even strangers to step off the sidewalks and join in the dance. Puzzled tourists in Bermuda shorts thought it was just Mardi Gras come early, and stood waiting in vain for somebody to throw them beads. "Heeeeeyyyyyyy," yelled a drunken man, until he saw the hearse wheel into view on Bourbon, and then he took off his hat.

"A proper funeral," Mr. Barnhardt called it.

Later, when the procession was over and the punctuation to Chicken Man's life was finally properly stamped in the street history of New Orleans, a 67-year-old cabdriver named Elvorn Tate was asked if he knew him.

"Oh yeah, he was straight-up weird, but he was always smiling," Mr. Tate said. "They should put up a plaque to those guys like him, because they keep the people coming here. I saw him myself, just the other day."

When told Chicken Man had been dead more than a month, he did not correct himself. He just nodded.

About the Author

Rick Bragg, the Miami bureau chief and former southern correspondent for the *New York Times,* won the 1996 Pulitzer Prize in Feature Writing for his "elegantly written stories about contemporary America." He has also written for several magazines, the *St. Petersburg Times,* and the *Birmingham News,* and he is a two-time winner of the American Society of Newspaper Editors Distinguished Writing Award. His 1997 memoir, *All Over but the Shoutin',* was a *New York Times* best-seller and Notable Book of the Year and won several book awards.